INTO THE NEWSROOM

Into the Newsroom explores how journalists and the digital technologies with which they are entangled construct television news at the micro level of practice. It challenges orthodox readings of television news production to explore fundamental questions concerning the ways in which we understand how journalists and technologies combine with one another in unpredictable ways in order to create news. Hemmingway investigates the processes of regional BBC news production, by adapting ANT to an ethnographic study of a specific newsroom to reveal how news work is constructed by this contingent and complex interplay of digital media technologies and human actors.

The book provides a rigorous investigation of the everyday rituals that are performed in the television newsroom, and offers a unique suggestion that news is both a highly haphazard and yet technologically complicated process of deliberate construction involving the interweaving of reflexive professional journalists as well as developing, unpredictable technologies. Arguing specifically for a recognition and an exploration of technological agency, the book takes the reader on an exciting journey into the digital newsroom, using exclusive observation and interviews from those journalists working on the BBC's recent pilot project of local television news as part of its empirical evidence.

This book is an essential introduction both for those seeking to understand news processes at the level of everyday routines and practices, and for those students and scholars who are eager to adopt new and challenging ways to theorise news as practice.

Emma Hemmingway is a Senior Lecturer in Journalism at the Centre for Broadcasting and Journalism at Nottingham Trent University. She previously worked for the BBC over a period of 12 years within a variety of roles, which included TV reporter, producer and also news editor.

INTO THE NEWSROOM

Exploring the digital production of
regional television news

Emma Hemmingway

Routledge
Taylor & Francis Group

LONDON AND NEW YORK

First published 2008
by Routledge
2 Park Square, Milton Park, Abingdon, Oxon OX14 4RN

Simultaneously published in the USA and Canada
by Routledge
270 Madison Avenue, New York, NY 10016

Routledge is an imprint of the Taylor & Francis Group, an informa business

© 2008 Emma Hemmingway
Foreword © 2008 Robert Huffaker

Typeset in Perpetua by
Taylor & Francis Books
Printed and bound in Great Britain by
Antony Rowe Ltd, Chippenham, Wiltshire

British Library Cataloguing in Publication Data
A catalogue record for this book is available from the British Library

Library of Congress Cataloging in Publication Data
A catalog record for this book has been requested

ISBN 978-0-415-40467-9 (hbk)
ISBN 978-0-415-40468-6 (pbk)
ISBN 978-0-203-94067-9 (ebk)

CONTENTS

FOREWORD

Robert Huffaker

In the 1960s before reporting for CBS and Dallas's KRLD, I had covered small-town TV news with a black-and-white Polaroid camera. KRLD, like other metropolitan stations, then used 16-millimetre black-and-white motion-picture film. Early videotape machines were so huge that a crane had lowered KRLD's first one through a hole cut in the roof.

Until 22 November 1963, we covered on-the-spot TV news with 16-millimetre film – neither live nor videotaped. Our hand-held Bell & Howells shot silent film, and unwieldy Auricons shot film with an optical sound track alongside the strip of pictures. Our 65-year-old George 'Sandy' Sanderson had been shooting movie film since he'd cranked the cameras by hand.

Before that wrenching November day, we had reserved live mobile television principally for broadcasting Dallas Cowboy games and other public events. On that Friday, Dallas-Fort Worth stations had pooled their mobile TV vans to broadcast John F. Kennedy's Fort Worth breakfast speech, arrival at Dallas Love Field and luncheon address. Wes Wise and I broadcasts JFK's motorcade live on radio only. But when the assassin fired, we repositioned our mobile TV vans to broadcast live vigils at the hospital and police headquarters nationwide. Over the next days, US networks assumed the sad duty of broadcasting the tragedy from Washington, while we continued from Dallas.

Television news has kept improving its on-the-spot broadcasts ever since, and today's 24-hour news has evolved from what we began in 1963. Technology has taken us from grainy black-and-white images produced by barely-mobile equipment to live two-way broadcasts around the globe by digital, portable equipment with audio and video of quality we did not dream of.

Before communication satellites, ham radio operators helped me relay radio news by single sideband. I unscrewed telephone handsets, alligator-clipped them to tape recorders, and thereby sent CBS News better audio than the handset would produce alone. Broadcasting the Oswald shooting live on CBS, I knew that Nelson Benton and I were both on the air at once, with no way of seeing or hearing each other. And I knew that Nelson was quick enough to sense our dilemma too. We knew our technical capabilities, we knew each other and we interacted with colleagues from Dallas to New York.

Emma Hemmingway's new book aptly demonstrates that broadcast reporting, especially with today's rapid mergers of digital electronics with cybernetics, requires a deeper understanding of both the evolving technology and of the reporters, producers and technicians who cooperate to bring news and analysis to the world. By charting the complexity of these relationships *Into the Newsroom* makes an important and compelling contribution to the development of our understanding of news technologies and of their significance in the reporting of all news, whether it is the most local of events, or the assassination of a president.

Bob Huffaker
Author, *When the News Went Live: Dallas 1963*
Reporter CBS News

PREFACE

Although those who concern themselves with details are regarded as folk of limited intelligence, it seems to me that this part is essential, because it is the foundation, and it is impossible to erect any building or establish any method without understanding its principles. It is not enough to have a liking for architecture. One must also know about stonecutting.

(Maurice de Saxe, 1756, p.5)

In one way, this is a book about stonecutting. How so, you may ask? Isn't this a book about television news, as its rather grand title suggests? What does a television newsroom buzzing with the activities of journalists and producers, crowded with digital cameras, computers, untidy desks and half-drunk coffee cups have to do with the rather old-fashioned craft of cutting stone? The two worlds are divided not only by more than two centuries, but also by a million cultural and social differences; how could the one possibly be of relevance to the other?

The answer lies in how we come to an understanding of these different worlds, existing as they do in separate times, harbouring within them separate cultural values, made up of very different people and even more different machines; the sharp tool that hones a building's first foundation stone, or the PD150 camera that fits neatly into the crook of the video-journalist's shoulder. It is in the way in which we try to make sense of these worlds, stumbling across both as outsiders, members of neither group, unrehearsed in the rituals or routines of either community and ignorant of their separate languages. As observers we are strangers to both of these cultures, which is in fact what makes the worlds strangely similar.

You are interested in news – in the meanings of news – in how news relates to society – in what news can offer us as citizens – in how news technologies are developing to assist us in getting faster, better news in our uncertain, globalised world. Already your interests have swept you way above and beyond the small provincial newsroom with its tattered chairs, outdated computers and dark dreary edit suites and you're hurtling ahead into the more fascinating, brighter world of news corporations, capitalism and global conflict. This is the lofty height from where news should be explored! This is where news matters! This is where news and society come crashing in on one another and make meaningful, often dangerous, relationships in our overly complicated lives.

Let us return to our humble stonecutter for just one moment. If he shared your views, he'd be standing at the top of the Empire State Building by now, certainly not wandering aimlessly around in the basement examining the lift shafts. And from such an exalted position what precisely could he see? What do you see? What can you glean of the world of news if you concentrate only on the grandiose claims society makes for it, or that it makes for society? How have those claims been constructed? Where do they come from, what gives them validity, what makes them stick? What of the grand phenomenon of digital, 24-hour, global news? How does it actually work? Who makes it work? What technologies and humans come together in their many, varied ways to construct the world, instantaneously, in order for you to make claims about news and culture, news and politics, news and society, or news and citizens? If you don't know how it works, in what minute, complicated, painstaking, contingent and maddening way it works, how then can you fly off into the brighter world of context, politics, social meanings and messages, with any confidence that you'll stay airborne?

The point may be effortlessly simple, but the task is inordinately challenging. There are so many people who scale the heights of the tallest cultural edifices to look down on the social world of millions of minute, visible but unintelligible bits and pieces. How many people get down in the dirt and explore the hidden engineering systems, the hydraulics, the dark lift shafts and the steel girders that keep such grand social theories precariously aloft? As the French philosopher and sociologist Bruno Latour potently argues, this painstaking and sometimes tedious work is necessary if we are to gain a better understanding of the cultures we enter into as researchers.

> One must remain as myopic as an ant in order to carefully misconstrue what 'social' usually means. One must travel on foot and stick to the decision not to accept any ride from any faster vehicle. Yes, we should follow the suggestion that interactions are overflowed, by many ingredients already in place that come from other times, other spaces and other agents; yes, we should accept the idea of moving away to some other sites in order to find the sources of those many ingredients. But as soon as we get out of some interaction, we should ignore the giant

signs 'towards Context' or 'to Structure'; we should take a right angle, leave the freeways, and choose instead to walk through a tiny path not much wider than a donkey's trail.

(Latour, 2005, p.171)

This book will demand that the same detailed and often frustratingly slow journey be taken through the world of television production. It will provide the reader with a way to observe and explore a digital television newsroom. It will show the reader examples of the latest developments of television's digital technologies and attempt to reveal how both humans and machines adapt to these developments in unpredictable, often surprising, ways. It will introduce the reader to a new language with which to make sense of this mysterious and seemingly unintelligible world mixed up of humans and machines. It will attempt to persuade the reader that to fully understand news processes one must wander through the shadowy basements and explore the darker corners of the newsroom. One must also venture along the unlit corridors, or accompany those humans and technologies that leave the comfort of the newsroom to construct news in other places, and observe how each intricate constellation of people and machines connects with the next, and the next, and the next, until a more complete picture of the complex network of news production slowly comes into focus.

This level of focus, and likewise this depth of field, cannot come from standing on high and gazing down through the haze. It comes from being as close as one can – as detailed and as intricate as possible – as thorough and as exhaustive in the observations made and as relentless in the questions asked.

Far from such work being that of a foolish man, as the opening quote from de Saxe might suggest, this is a rare and difficult challenge that provides the researcher, the student or the social scientist with the opportunity to see the world around them as infinitely more complex, problematic and strange. But it also provides the greatest opportunity to see that new world with a clear vision, to fully understand its hidden rituals and its unspoken languages and to discover in its grounded details its wider significance.

ACKNOWLEDGEMENTS

This book simply would not exist without the enthusiastic and sustained support of the BBC employees in both the Nottingham and Birmingham newsrooms that I have observed and interviewed during the past three years. I would like to thank each one of them for their patience, their intelligent insights and their adroit understanding of the television news production process in which they are involved. I only hope I have managed to faithfully narrate their stories within these pages. The driving force of this book has always been to create a space wherein the construction of news facts can be identified and explored to allow others as detailed a glimpse as possible of their complicated and magical world. If I have succeeded, my gratitude is to them for their ability to share the commitment they have to their work with those of us who are trying to understand the peculiar and complex structure of their newsrooms and news routines. Any failings they perceive are entirely my own.

I have been extremely fortunate in several friends and colleagues who have taken the time to inspire and assist me in the composition of this book. It has been an honour for me to work with them. Without the tireless and detailed support of Professor Joost Van-Loon, whose brilliant mind and detailed eye has watched over this work, and whose true and remarkable friendship has kept me buoyant in the deepest waters of its journey, this book would never have been completed. I am deeply indebted to him for both his intelligence and his humility.

I have had the pleasure to work with and discuss the theoretical and empirical content of the book with a number of scholars. I would like to thank Dr Christopher Farrands for his rigorous interest in upholding both the structural and theoretical validity of this work. Without his guidance I would still be floundering somewhere in the shallows of my ideas. I would also like to express my sincere gratitude to Professor Stuart Allen who offered me invaluable advice after reading and discussing earlier drafts of this book. I have also been assisted enormously by being able to discuss my ideas about the media and Actor Network

Theory (ANT) with Professor Nick Couldry whose own ANT work I greatly admire. Nick has always offered me his unswerving support as I have attempted to develop my own theories of news production within an ANT framework for which I am both humbled and grateful. I am also indebted to Professor Roy Boyne who has assisted me in clarifying my own ideas with regard to the treatment of the human subject within ANT, which has become the central focus of Chapter 8 of this book. Others who have assisted me in developing my ideas with regard to the study of media processes are Professor Simon Cottle, Dr David Woods and Dr John Farnsworth. I would like to thank each of them for their insights.

I have had the opportunity to write the majority of this book away from my usual daily lecturing and teaching commitments and I would like to thank all the staff at the Centre for Broadcasting and Journalism at Nottingham Trent University for their flexibility and individual hard work that has enabled me to have the time and space for this project.

A number of personal friends have also helped to make this journey not only bearable, but also illuminating and enjoyable. My dear friend Matthew Menhennet has read earlier drafts of my work and listened to my ongoing theoretical ramblings and I am greatly indebted to him. I would also like to thank my close friend Patrick Collins for his sustained interest and unswerving support for this endeavour, and in particular for introducing me to the amazing Bob Huffaker, without whose analysis of the reporting of the assassination of President Kennedy and the subsequent murder of Lee Harvey Oswald on live television, this book would not have such historical resonance. I am so grateful to Bob and to his fellow reporters for their compelling testimony of those early days of television reporting and of the complex relationship of humans and technologies in their coverage of those momentous events. I would also like to thank Bob for his personal endorsement of my book, which I consider to be a great honour.

The composition of this book has been an exhausting but exhilarating journey that has brought me into contact with a whole host of truly gifted and wonderful people. For me, that has been its greatest reward. I owe so much to my loving parents who have continually supported both my journalistic and my academic endeavours and without whom I would not have had the courage to pursue such separate goals. And my final, deepest debt of gratitude goes to my husband John, for his unrivalled patience, love and humour, which always keep me afloat and navigating the right course.

1

INTRODUCTION

Before we begin our journey through the practical world of television news production, acquainting ourselves with the daily routines, tasks, practices and technologies that together constitute this complex yet haphazard milieu, I want to spend a few minutes telling some 'technology stories'. These three particular stories that are situated in different places in the world, that occur at different times in our history, and which all involve different technologies, have one remarkable thing in common. And it is this common thread that holds these stories together that we also need to recognise and understand if our own journey is to make any sense to us.

Our first story involves a young Hungarian known as Endre Friedmann, but perhaps better known today as Robert Capa. Capa is regarded as one of the most famous war photographers of the twentieth century. He photographed five different wars: the Spanish Civil War, the Second Sino-Japanese War, World War II across Europe, the 1948 Arab–Israeli War and the First Indo-China War. He is probably best remembered for his relentless documentation of World War II in London, North Africa, Italy, the Battle of Normandy on Omaha Beach and the liberation of Paris.

Capa first found photography work in Berlin in the very early 1930s but as he was a Jew he quickly moved from Germany to France to escape from the rise of Nazism. At that time, he adopted the name Robert Capa as he felt it would be more recognisable and familiar and that it sounded American. In 1936 his name became known for a particular photograph that he took on the Cordoba Front of a Loyalist militiaman who had been shot and was in the process of falling to his death. But it was to be his coverage of World War II, and in particular the 1944 D-Day landings, that was to bring him worldwide fame. And it is the story of these photographs that concerns us as we begin our exploration of the crucial role that technologies play in the construction of news facts.

On 6 June 1944, Capa swam ashore with the first allied assault wave on Omaha Beach. He was armed with two Contax 11 cameras mounted with 50-millimetre lenses and several rolls of spare film. Stumbling ashore under heavy enemy fire, Capa managed to take 108 pictures, or four rolls, of what should have become some of the most significant photographs in history. Much of the new close-up action style of war coverage was attributed to the advances in photographic technology. News photographers at the front lines were all using small, portable 35-millimetre cameras, such as the Leica, which could take up to 36 photographs before being reloaded. But it was what happened to the photographs in the darkroom developing process that has played such a key role in their acquiring an unforeseen notoriety.

Capa sent the photographs back to *Life* magazine to be developed and published. A 15-year-old laboratory assistant called Dennis Banks then made a crucial mistake in the darkroom and set the dryer at too high a level. All but 11 frames of the pictures were melted and ruined. *Life* magazine printed 10 of the remaining 11 frames in its June 1944 issue with captions that described the footage as 'slightly out of focus', explaining that Capa's hands were shaking in the excitement of the moment. The shakiness of the footage was in reality caused by the negatives being damaged in the drying process. Capa himself used this phrase as the title of his autobiographical account of the war, *Slightly out of Focus*.

This story tells us two things. First, it shows how the relationship between news gatherers and their available technologies is absolutely crucial to the construction of news facts. If it wasn't for the development of the small, portable cameras, Capa could never have got close enough to his subjects to photograph them effectively. But it also shows us how these technologies are unpredictable, and that our relationships with them can be haphazard and even beyond out control. These relationships are not constant or reliable; they do not act within set parameters that we may predict. As this story shows, our whole visual understanding and appreciation of the D-Day landings, one of the most famous moments in modern European history, is determined by a single error that occurs within an ad hoc relationship between a 15-year-old laboratory assistant, a photographic heater and a hundred negatives.

Nearly 20 years later, across the Atlantic Ocean, our second story also involves the coverage of a monumental historic event, the assassination of President John F. Kennedy in November 1963. To tell this story we can turn to the testimony of those newsmen who were directly involved in reporting this devastating event and who've since written about their experiences in a gripping book entitled *When The News Went Live, Dallas 1963*.

Bob Huffaker, Bill Mercer, George Phenix and Wes Wise were all young newsmen who never expected to find themselves at the centre of what was to become one of the biggest news stories of all time. They were responsible for covering the president's assassination and its subsequent aftermath, including television's first 'live' murder.

As Dan Rather, the former CBS news reporter and managing editor, outlines in the book, these four men were on the ground covering what they had imagined would be nothing more than a short presidential visit to the city.

> From the Presidential motorcade to Parkland Hospital, from Lee Harvey Oswald's shooting to the trial and lonesome death of Jack Ruby, they were there, on the inside. The view they were afforded of these events was unique; the tales they have to tell, one-of-a-kind.
>
> (Dan Rather, in Foreword to *When the News Went Live*,
> Huffaker *et al.*, 2004)

Their individual testimonies of this unpredictable yet momentous occasion quickly reveal how crucial were the roles that the available technologies played in the construction of the events. The story of the assassination of a president and the murder of a suspected assassin is on one level the story of the individual relationships forged between men and their machines, relationships that develop in arbitrary and often surprising ways. All four of these young journalists were reliant upon the often unwieldy and cumbersome technologies of their day.

> We wrote our own copy. There were no news readers among us. Eddie demanded versatility and all of us were prepared to report and write as well as shoot film and operate audio equipment. Video – as opposed to our 16 mm news film – was the purview of our engineering and production people. There were no tape cassettes or cartridges in those days, and both video and audio were recorded on reel-to-reel devices. Videotape machines weren't yet portable. The size of deep freezers, they were either installed in a studio or mounted in a van, using reels of tape two inches wide.
>
> (Huffaker *et al.*, 2004, p.36)

The authors argue that this particular news story, with its sudden demands on journalists to be able to broadcast live from a location, without any prior warning or preparation, signified a turning point in the history of the use of news technologies. This was the day when television news reporting 'grew up'. As their stories reveal, this new-found maturity was only achievable by means of the various associations that evolved during that specific day between journalists and their particular technologies.

> When I arrived on the morning of Saturday November 23rd, the press room was overrun with out-of-town reporters and cluttered with camera

equipment, film canisters, extension cords, audiotape recorders, food wrappers and Styrofoam cups. I made the rounds of our mobile van out at the Commerce Street curb and talked to the operators and floor directors running our inside cameras. We stationed one camera in the basement to glimpse Oswald being taken through the jail office. The other remained on the crowded third floor, where reporters were jostling for position in the narrow hallway between the elevators and Captain Fritz's homicide office. I hooked up with Dan Rather's CBS reporter Nelson Benton, a former World War II bomber pilot who proved to be a good friend as he and I took turns with the third-floor camera's mike.

(Huffaker *et al.*, 2004, p.39)

Huffaker's account of the coverage of Jack Ruby's spur-of-the-moment shooting of the suspected assassin, Lee Harvey Oswald, is in essence a story of a group of men struggling with inadequate technologies, and the intrepid but wildly contingent strategies they adopt as they attempt to develop a relationship with this machinery to report live to the world.

Seconds after the shot, I knew that from up in our vans, Nelson couldn't possibly figure things out on the monitors. I couldn't distinguish one torso from another in the fracas as I fought to keep my footing. Twice I said, 'Oswald has been shot.' Then to avoid covering up anything Nelson might be saying, I stopped talking, hoping that Nelson had heard me. He hadn't.

With tapes rolling in both Dallas and New York, Nelson had begun his broadcast a split second after Ruby pulled the trigger. Not having heard the gunshot, he said, 'This is the basement of Dallas City Hall, and there's a scuffle down there.' As Nelson continued to talk, I was trying to stay out of our camera's field of view, and I fell silent so that I wouldn't conflict with Nelson's reporting. Neither of us could hear the other, and Nelson was reaching for words as he found it impossible to see what was happening on the black-and-white monitors. He began trying to reach me, but I couldn't hear as he said on the air, 'We're going to try to bring in Bob Huffaker of KRLD. Bob, can you hear us down there? Can you give us an account of what happened?' I couldn't hear anything except the din in the basement. Jim English was glued to his camera and unable to tell me anything, and Bob Hankal had disappeared, headset and all. People were stepping on my mike cord and my feet, pushing and elbowing, wrestling and shouting.

(Huffaker *et al.*, 2004, p.56)

This historic moment certainly illustrates the burgeoning power of television news. But more significantly, it also reveals the developing knowledge that journalists were beginning to acquire of a network of human and nonhuman actors, which together, and in constant but continually changing associations with one another, are responsible for the construction of news facts.

These men would probably not have described their work in such terms. They certainly wouldn't have had the time or luxury to analyse these sponta- neous and often short-lived constellations of technologies and people within which they found themselves operating. But there is an important realisation in their recollections not just of the central role of technologies, but of how highly contingent and random are the relationships they developed with them in their attempt to produce their news reports. Taking a short section describing the moment that Oswald's murder is broadcast live, we can begin to see just how many seemingly unrelated factors had to come together in order for this groundbreaking broadcast to be successful.

> Fort Worth's WBAP-TV was feeding NBC correspondent Tom Pettit's broadcasts from their engine-challenged van, which a wrecker had deposited at the curb. Pettit's guys in New York had switched to him when he said, 'Let me have it. I want it.' Their NBC cameraman had to take a wide establishing shot then rack his lens turret on the air for a tight shot of the shooting, while our Jim English had the optical advantage with our camera's giant zoom lens. Jim zoomed out and framed the struggle as detectives dragged both Ruby and Oswald toward the jail office. Jim had a headset, but I had no way of commu- nicating with anyone. Bob Hankal, our floor director, also with a headset, had been stationed left of the lens, but I lost sight of him as the brawl tossed me hard to the right.
>
> We'd just broadcast television's first murder. I had missed Oswald's middle name, and Nelson had called the place the Houston County Jail once, but I had managed to stand up and hang onto the mike.
>
> (Huffaker *et al.*, 2004, p.60)

While CBS's Bob Huffaker and Nelson Benton, along with NBC's Tom Pettit, were reporting live from the scene on national TV, their colleagues were con- tinuing to depend upon the success of the lengthy film-developing process before they could air their 16-millimetre black-and-white footage. As we saw with Capa's earlier material this process was highly unpredictable and prone to both human and technological error. While Huffaker was reporting the Oswald shooting live, his KRLD reporter George Phenix was also capturing it with his big Auricon optical-sound-on-film camera:

We put the film in the developing process, and Eddie Barker called the FBI. I paced and smoked and waited for the film to be developed. The night before, I had loaded the film wrong and ruined an exclusive interview that CBS reporter Nelson Benton had grabbed with Police Chief Curry. Anxiously I waited as Dean Angel threaded the film through the projector. 'Please God let there be at least some sort of image on the film.' I knew if anyone could pull the film through the long line of developing tanks intact it would be Dean. He was calm under pressure. More than once, he had saved my hide by getting an image despite poor photography. The film finally came out of the soup and there Jack Ruby was, standing just off my right shoulder. He stepped in front of my camera and – bang. I walked out of the screening room, shaken. I would see my film only one more time.

(Phenix, in Huffaker *et al.*, 2004, p.88)

Thus one of the world's most momentous and devastating events is captured on film and processed for the waiting world, only by means of the specific relationship between a young journalist, a roll of film, a set of developing tanks and a fortunate individual who just happened to be calm under pressure. As our first story of Capa's D-Day footage revealed, if any of the individual components in this story had been changed, or had in association with the others performed in a slightly different way, the entire course of television history as we now know it would have been significantly altered.

They're giving us an up-close portrait of a dramatic time. While they were breaking the news, they were also breaking new ground. There was no precedent for television news broadcasting for four days straight without commercial interruption. There was no precedent for the drama of broadcasting a violent murder on a Sunday morning coast to coast. These were young men who were thrust into a devastating local story that had international significance. They realised – in the moment – that this was the story of a lifetime. Unlike other Americans they had no time to mourn the president's passing; rather they had a job to do and they did it well.

(Jeff West, director 1993–2004 The Sixth Floor Museum
at Dealey Plaza, in Huffaker *et al.*, 2004, p.96)

Our final story is a long way from the experiences of young journalists and photographers attempting to capture the most significant moments in recent history. Instead it is the story of a local television reporter, a lorry carrying pots of coloured paint, a roll of film and the attempt to fill the airtime of regional morning and lunchtime television bulletins. Yet this too is a similar story, out-lining the complex relationships between journalists and their technological partners in the production of news.

This particular story takes place in Nottingham, England in 1987, more than 20 years after the assassination of President Kennedy. On that particular morn-ing a television reporter arrived at the BBC's Nottingham newsroom at 7.30am. His job was to provide news material for the half-hourly morning and the 12.30pm lunchtime bulletins. While the half-hourly morning bulletins were being broadcast a colourful accident occurred right outside the building.

An articulated lorry pulled up sharply at a set of traffic lights and as it did so more than seventy pots of coloured paint were suddenly catapulted off the back of it onto the road, where they promptly exploded, showering the road with tons of various coloured paints. The traffic congestion and chaos that ensued brought Nottingham city centre to a complete standstill as the road flowed with dozens of multicoloured paint rivers.

For a local television station this was a great picture-story that fortuitously had happened on their very doorstep. A cameraman was immediately sent out-side to the scene, but this was still in the days of film cameras as opposed to video cameras. By 8.00am the scene had been captured on film, but there was no technical facility in the Nottingham newsroom to convert the film to video for broadcast so the pictures were effectively unusable.

A local dispatch rider had to be organised, who collected the film reel from the Nottingham newsroom and delivered it by motorbike to engineers at the BBC's larger news centre in Birmingham where the film could then be pro-cessed and transferred to videotape for broadcast. This process took around four-and-a-half hours. Once the film had been developed and transferred to video format, the Nottingham reporter then had to pay for a video-line booking from Birmingham to the Nottingham newsroom in order to get the material transferred back. The entire production process took more than five hours to complete. The morning bulletins and the lunchtime bulletin had of course been transmitted hours earlier without the required pictures, and the original footage could then not be transmitted until the main programme at 6.30pm that eve-ning. By that time the road was cleaned and traffic was travelling normally throughout the city. The news story had in effect well and truly disappeared!

This local story illustrates how events that may at first seem to be easily accessed for news purposes are still crucially entangled with whatever available technologies we may have at our immediate disposal. In this example the filming of the material was not the problem. But the subsequent development of that material for broadcast made its proximate location to the Nottingham news-room irrelevant. So a story that happened as close as possible to the hub of Nottingham's news production facilities became as distant and unreachable as if it had occurred fifty miles away, simply because of the technological inadequacies of that particular newsroom infrastructure.

Here we have three separate stories occurring at different times in history involving three different journalistic endeavours to produce news footage. Yet there is a common thread that runs through each and that links the individual testimonies. That thread is the recognition of the contingent, unpredictable, but crucial relationships that are made between journalists and those technological machines or apparatuses that are equal constituents in any news-production process.

Having said this, where does it leave us? Isn't it clear to anyone who has an interest in the production of television news that it involves complex technologies whose operations we may not completely understand? That is certainly the case. But we need to concentrate our efforts on understanding not just the role that technologies play, but more importantly, the *associations* that we discover between human and technological actors. It is the relationships, the alliances and the linkages that we will discover between these seemingly disparate constituents that help us to gain a fuller understanding of news processes.

A camera does not act in isolation. A journalist never works alone. A satellite truck cannot produce news independently. Yet how do these three actors, the camera, the human and the truck, come together? How do they relate to one another in order to create a live broadcast? With these types of questions we are being asked to map the associations between these different components. If we return to our three stories, in all of them we have seen glimpses of these associations between the different elements that may constitute the specific news event. But our stories alone cannot give us the tools with which to begin to unpick these relationships, to chart them in detail and to articulate what we find. In order to get that close to the production processes we're exploring, to track all of these associations and linkages, we need a new language and a new set of tools to help us in our detailed, stone-cutter like excavations. That new language is *Actor Network Theory (ANT)*.

> There is nothing more difficult to convey than reality in all its ordinariness. Flaubert was fond of saying that it takes a lot of hard work to portray mediocrity. Sociologists run into this problem all the time: How can we make the ordinary extraordinary and evoke ordinariness in such a way that people will see just how extraordinary it is?
>
> (Bourdieu, 1998, p.21)

It is this same ordinariness to which Bourdieu refers that we will now begin to explore using ANT, a theoretical framework that originates within the field of Science and Technology Studies (STS). Actor Network Theory can assist us greatly as we attempt to get down among the foundations and hidden corners of the newsroom to reveal the detailed processes of television news production in the digital age. By so doing we will be better equipped to chart the complicated and ever-changing associations that are made and unmade between journalists and technologies, alliances that we have only touched upon during these three 'technology stories'.

As Latour playfully points out, ANT is a highly appropriate name for this type of study. As ANT explorers we must journey along the smallest, most winding and sometimes intricate paths of our chosen environment. We must pay particular and detailed attention to all of the associations, the links and the traces we can find between the elements we may come across. It is in these continual associations with one another, in the relations they develop, sustain or destroy, that the meaning of our world will become clear to us.

> Just follow the trails myopically. Ant you have accepted to be, ANT you will remain! If you stick obstinately enough to the decision of producing a continuous trail instead of a discontinuous one, then another mountain range begins to emerge. It is a landscape which runs through, crosses out and totally short cuts the former loci of 'local interaction' and of 'global context' It is not that there is no hierarchy, no ups and downs, no rifts, no deep canyons, no high spots. It is simply that if you wish to go from one site to another, then you have to pay the full cost of relation, connection, displacement, and information. No lifts, accelerations, or short cuts are allowed.
>
> (Latour, 2005, p.176)

This book will take us on a similar journey. We will identify, explore and develop an understanding of regional and local news production, by adopting this alternative theoretical focus to the reading of news. The purpose of using ANT is to examine the detailed construction of news facts *as they happen*. We will mention some of the more established methods of reading and defining news in our next chapter. And we will show that in place of grandiose, global and often hopelessly all-encompassing theories of news production, it is the internal routines, self-reflexive practices, technological arrangements and the unstable, constantly changing practical constraints that actually govern news production, just as our three technology stories reveal.

> What counts is the possibility for the enquirer to register that kind of 'networky' shape wherever possible, instead of having to cut off data in two heaps: one local, one global. To tell an actor-network story is to be able to capture those many connections without bungling them from

the start by some a priori decisions over what is the true size of an interaction or of some social aggregate ... ANT is first of all an abstract *projection* principle for deploying *any* shape, not some concrete arbitrary decision about *which* shape should be on the map.

(Latour, 2005, p.178)

So with any preconceived assumptions about how and why we should study news production assiduously discarded, and without thinking in advance about what we might discover once we begin our enquiries, I now invite you all to enter the world of news production with a different purpose. We will simply try to adopt the most exact method to reveal and make sense of what we discover, as we discover it, always paying the closest attention not just to the individual actors we come across, but more importantly to their fluid and problematic associations with one another.

2

ACTOR NETWORK THEORY

As soon as we let the actors clean up, so to speak, their own mess, some order can be retrieved which is quite different from the inquirer's own attempts at limiting controversies in advance.

(Latour, 2005, p.161)

Walking into the BBC television newsroom in Nottingham there is an atmosphere of quiet organisation. The room is spacious, seemingly half empty, with groups of desks arranged around a large central space in which people may occasionally gather together to discuss something, or through which they simply travel to other areas of the newsroom. There are two distinct groups of desks: one on the right-hand side towards the long windows at the edge of the room, the other placed more centrally towards the left. Deliberately divided from one another these two areas represent the separate but interrelated zones of regional BBC news production. On the right of the room is what is known as the 'news-gathering' zone. Here news is sought, identified and tracked down. The more central group of desks represents the 'output' zone. Here the news is written, produced and transmitted. These separate zones constantly struggle for control of logistics, staff and resources. And in the quiet central space between these zones many of the major decisions regarding the production of television news are made (Hemmingway, 2005).

Journalists, planners, directors and camera operators all sporadically inhabit this central area. Within its invisible boundaries story ideas are discussed, logistical arrangements finalised, meetings conducted, technical complexities explored and resolved. At other times journalists and producers may be seen hurrying across the space from one department to the other as the deadline of a news bulletin creeps ever closer. If one simply stands in the space to observe and listen, half-formed snippets of unfinished conversations can be heard carried on the air. It may sometimes be possible to follow a direct instruction uttered and a subsequent action performed as two producers finalise the running order of a lunchtime bulletin. Alternatively, one might witness the construction of a digital headline sequence by a director and reporter huddled together in front of an output monitor. Or perhaps a glimpse of what looks like a routine edit performed by a video-journalist at the adjoining workstation may help shed some light on this seemingly unobtrusive and elliptical process of news making?

Within the small space between these two desks instructions are communicated, actions are taken and tasks completed. The individualised use and the manipulation of both the space and time within a newsroom by both humans and machines alike characterises this collective arena wherein the production of news is organised and managed by both humans and technologies working to produce daily news programmes.

To the untrained eye the myriad of daily processes will seem mystifying, obfuscating and extremely difficult to interpret. Even those individuals who are used to working within the newsroom are often not able to fully articulate their daily actions, reflect upon the continual decisions they make, or understand the ways in which they are intertwined with the technologies that they use. For those of us who may peer upon such a scene not knowing what it is we are witnessing, and equally for those actors enmeshed within its fluid boundaries, a new language needs to be found and a narrative written to make sense of what we shall refer to as the 'mess of method' that is news work. Without such a narrative, these daily processes that are often almost impossible to even observe, let alone detect, go unnoticed, and therefore unexplained. But if we find a way to let these daily tasks and routines speak for themselves, we will come closer to knowing what is happening inside the newsroom.

It is the purpose of this book to develop such a narrative, to produce a new way to make these actions and routines understandable in all their minute and ever-changing detail so as to provide a way for the reader to understand how the human and technological actors that inhabit this mysterious space work together to produce regional television news.

We may ask why such a book is necessary. There are several books already published that have attempted to take the reader into hundreds of other newsrooms so as to analyse the news production process and show how news is produced. The practice of news work is not therefore unexplored. There is a whole tradition of excellent, in-depth research into the various different news processes, both in this country and abroad, so why will our journey be any different or our findings any more significant?

Within such a long-standing and popular tradition of exploring, observing and reading media, there has been a tendency to overlook what could be referred to as the chalk face of news production, or what we may refer to as the 'news episteme', and to concentrate instead on a wider conceptual field, so that media as a phenomenon simply become representations of the social, the political or the cultural. The daily tasks and activities of a newsroom are not in and by themselves judged worthy of sustained enquiry. They often become subsumed by wider debates regarding politics, economics or cultural mores and concerns. As Van-Loon has cogently argued, drawing on Inglis's earlier presumption that media theory is simply a branch of political theory, the analyses of media are by and large derived from an assumption that media are merely empty vessels that deliver content. Thus most media analyses have focused on either the political economy of media production, the semiotics of media texts or the socio-psychological effects of media consumption (Van-Loon, 2007). Empirical studies of media have thus tended to fix their gaze upon the way in which media industries are managed and operate, or have explored audience consumption of media, or paid closer attention to media texts. All of this work has its own value and many of these studies have enabled us to glean far greater understanding of media organisations, media content and media consumption. Far less work has been carried out into the actual 'processes of mediation', which is, after all, what is meant by 'media' (Van-Loon, 2007).

In this book we will aim to cultivate a more critical appreciation of such processes of mediation, in particular to explore the connectivity between the various human and technological actors within a specific newsroom that together and in continually evolving and changing constellations construct news facts. During this exploration, we will have to discard some of the more traditional ways of thinking about both the human subject and the technologies with which they are bound up, and adopt a more radical approach to perceiving the relationships between humans and machines. The human will no longer be conceived of as an integral and unchanging entity, but more as an actor within a network of other actors, both human and nonhuman, who by themselves may be of little consequence, but in complex associations with one another have the capacity either to adapt to changing conditions by translating situations and manipulating others into action, or to become translated by the associative actions of other actors within the same network. The human and the machine are thus enfolded together and the routines of news making can be recognised as technologically embedded, determined by the interconnectedness of a multiplicity of agency, wherein the human subject may not be any more or less significant than the machine.

Perhaps this re-evaluation of the human subject as merely another actor within a network may seem too revolutionary, even far fetched. But by using Actor Network Theory (ANT) to explore the minutiae of daily television news production, preconceived views of the anthropocentric and privileged status of the human subject must be put aside. An ANT account requires a reconsideration of the divisions commonly held between the social and technical, the human and nonhuman, and an acceptance that the alternative being offered has some validity (Neyland, 2006). It requires conceptual hard work. It may even demand, at least at this early stage, a philosophical leap of faith.

Actor Network Theory, which developed in the quite separate field of Science and Technology Studies (STS), will help us to analyse news production at the specific level of news practice. While it might seem injurious to critique the developments of the media-studies tradition, before jumping ship to borrow theoretical frameworks from an entirely separate field, we will reveal why such a cross-disciplinary focus is necessary if the media and communications field is to be developed more critically beyond a priori, abstracted, or political readings of news that often fail to acknowledge production and technological processes as the primary ontology of news.

We will not spend valuable time providing an over view of all of the theoretical viewpoints within the media-studies tradition. The territory is immediately altered from whichever perspective one begins, and very soon muddied once clarity is attempted. There have been a number of bold attempts to make sense of this conflicted and uncertain territory (Boyd-Barrett & Newbold, 1995; Stevenson, 2002; Cottle, 2003). It is interesting to note that in Cottle's work there is a similar recognition that the processes of news practice are under-analysed.

> In between the theoretical foci on marketplace determinations and play of cultural discourses, there still exists a relatively unexplored and under-theorized 'middle-ground' of organisational structures and workplace practices ... The ethnographic approach often proves invaluable as a corrective to speculative and abstract theory and the generalising claim to which this can give rise. Too often the complex and multi-dimensional nature of media production is short-circuited by those holding a priori theoretical commitments, or rigid political views and expectations.
>
> (Cottle, 2003, p.4)

14

The crucial difference here is one of emphasis. Practice is still ultimately the handmaiden of the more significant political or grander theoretical argument; rarely does it venture upon the cultural field on its own and for its own sake. The particular still only resonates, and is considered worthy of exploration, by its ability to contribute or crucially to represent the wider social or political sphere.

We need to move away from deploying a dualism of 'strategic intentions' versus 'practical applications' to analyse what news is, how it comes into being and why it has evolved in such a way. Far from being only a consequence of externally imposed forms of power (mediated by management, rules and procedures, professional cultures, hegemonic ideologies or threats), we need to begin to understand the routines of news making as technologically embedded, but not indifferent to meaning (Van-Loon, 2007).

In other words, unless we begin to dismantle the epistemological straightjacket within which the analyses of media have been hitherto confined, and adopt a new methodology for discovering the ontology of media production, as well as a new language to describe the fluid and heterogeneous nature of news production and content, we will continue to neglect this undiscovered terrain.

On the face of it, this different approach may seem remarkably simple. Surely it is far easier to watch journalists as they work and to describe their actions as accurately as we can, than it is to try to detect political or cultural significance in these everyday routines? Isn't it far easier to describe what we see around us, than it is to try to explain these observations as part of a bigger picture with cultural, social or political meanings that resonate far beyond our original newsroom? Calling to mind our stone-cutter once again, isn't it a simpler task to inspect the brass hinges on the opening doors of the building, than it is to figure out why the entire edifice was constructed in a particular style and what kind of message this sends out to the rest of the world?

You might think so, but you'd be mistaken. The mistake is dividing the world around you into small and big pictures; the micro and the macro; the observations that you make and the meanings that you then take from what you have seen; the description of a scene and the explanation you then construct from the description that you have made. We will attempt to eradicate this critical but misplaced division between these two sites; the humble description that must then give way to the grander explanation. Instead we will present a world where the micro reveals in and of itself the macro; where the description is at one and the same time the fullest explanation; and where the tiny detail unlocks the farthest horizon. To do that we need an effective and unusual tool kit. And it is with this in mind that we turn, perhaps surprisingly, to the field of science and technology; to ANT.

Actor Network Theory is a method for describing what we see around us, but to see it in the clearest, most accurate detail, embracing the widest panorama with the sharpest focus, and representing that as a faithful text, so that others can also see that the picture we present is not really simple at all. And it becomes even more difficult when everything we see is forever moving and changing shape, where nothing stays still or remains constant, where the scene is haphazard and unpredictable at all times.

Far from the world of media and communication studies, ANT was developed by the French philosopher, Bruno Latour, and Steve Woolgar, a British sociologist, who spent two years at the Salk Institute for Biological Studies in San Diego, California, observing the minute processes of scientific experimentation. These observations included the scientists' note taking and discussions, animal experimentations and culture sampling, the transcription of results and writing-up of successive research papers, and the observation of endless arguments and counter-arguments between various scientific researchers. Though they were not scientists, Latour and Woolgar wanted to look behind the existing, official accounts of scientific method, which they believed were all too clean and reassuring, to try to understand the often ragged ways in which they believed knowledge is produced in research (Law, 2004).

Latour and Woolgar's initial aim was to find a way to make the highly scientific routines that they observed *descriptable,* to render the world of the scientific laboratory understandable to an outsider. They used a number of established ethnographic research methods including observation, participation, interviews, absorption, textual and product analysis as well as performing actual scientific experiments themselves. All these practices allowed them to map the activities they observed and to establish crucial connections between these practices that in turn began to establish a network of practice. The emphasis here was on ways to unveil a mysterious, often invisible, world.

But what made ANT such a radical departure from what were at the time already well-established ethnographic research methods, namely observation and participation and in-depth interviewing of those involved in the processes being observed? Indeed all of these skills had been used for many years in the field of anthropology, and were not in themselves particularly new or revolutionary ways to read cultural processes. The difference lies in Latour's determination to recognise the construction of networks of *both* human and nonhuman actors, paying as much attention to the behaviour of technologies, machines, scripts and tools as to the human actors who use them. Before this time, technological development had already been conceptualised in a similar way in that it had been considered to be part of a wider social web, but within that web there still existed defined subjects and objects in the form of humans and machines (Hughes, 1983).[1] Thus to recognise how ANT signals such a bold departure from previous scientific methods of analysis, we need briefly to engage with wider issues of philosophy and epistemology.

In his intriguing essay 'In the shadow of the deconstructed metanarratives: Baudrillard, Latour and the end of realist epistemology' Steven Ward places Latour in a strongly Nietzschean context, so determined is Latour to deconstruct traditional epistemological boundaries.

> When Nietzsche argued that God was dead, he was not simply making a statement about the secularisation of occidental culture. God and religion certainly were dead for Nietzsche, but so too was 'everything that in rapid succession, [had] tried to take its place, eg; the ideal, consciousness, reason, the certainty of progress, the happiness of the masses, culture etc.' (Blanchot, 1986, p.121). For Nietzsche, truth is not a fixed state that can be apprehended and spoken by a pure rationality, but socio-political, rhetorical and hence, variable (1983, p.68). . . . The Nietzschean and Durkheimian legacies and problems are important starting points for understanding the post-epistemological positions of both Baudrillard and Latour.
>
> (Ward, 1994, p.75)

This is not necessarily revolutionary in itself. There had been a growing preoccupation for some time before Latour with the discovery of more liberating ways with which to understand scientific knowledge.

> In the words of Bruno Latour (1988c, p.156) 'denying rationality does not mean that the sky is going to fall on our heads, because the sky is supported by many other firmer pillars.' These other pillars are social or associational in origin. They have a facticity beyond the reaches of ideational or textual deconstruction alone. From this position, knowledge, truth and reality do exist, but not as purely ideationally or philosophically distinguishable entities. Truth and reality are the cries of a strong coalition and a practically successful social construction.
>
> (Ward, 1994, p.74)

Latour's unique intervention in the study of scientific knowledge occurs not just with the eradication of the traditional subject/object paradigms, but with the substitution of a context-specific, heterogeneous and unpredictable network of human and nonhuman actors. Latour argues that actors do not have a momentum of their own at the outset that allows them merely to pass through a neutral social medium (Latour, 1987). Rather they are subject to contingency as they are passed from actor to actor and are thus continually shaped and reshaped (Bijker & Law, 1992). Actor Network Theory thus seeks to replace the traditional subject/object distinctions with specifically empirical observation and analysis of both human and nonhuman actors in a series of fluid and unpredictable relations with one another.

> I have attempted to substitute another pair — that of humans and nonhumans — for the subject–object dichotomy ... an objective nature facing a culture is something entirely different from an articulation of humans and nonhumans. If nonhumans are to be assembled into a collective, it will be the same collective, and within the same institutions, as the humans whose fate the scientists have brought nonhumans to share.
>
> (Latour, 1999, p.295)

For Latour and Woolgar, the world of practice includes a whole range of instruments, machines, technologies, objects and people. All of these connect with one another to build scientific knowledge in a process that the authors stress is active. In addition, they argue that particular and different realities are constructed by particular practices, or what they refer to as *translations* within the network.[2]

This is a fundamental point that necessitates further discussion as it is of direct significance to a thorough understanding of ANT and also to the choice of the research environments and the methodological rationale for this particular book.

In order to pursue what is known in ANT as the notion of *specificity*, both a conceptual and a methodological issue that is explored by Latour in various guises throughout his work, it is helpful to mention the historian and sociologist, Thomas Kuhn, and introduce his notion of the *paradigm*. Kuhn writes in *The Structure of Scientific Revolutions*:

> ... each paradigm will be shown to satisfy more or less the criteria that it dictates for itself and to fall short of a few of those dictated by its opponent ... no paradigm ever solves all the problems it defines.
>
> (Kuhn, 1962, p.348)

A paradigm is a commonly-held belief in a theory and its principles, and Kuhn argues that as the principles of reality are not fully known, this incomplete knowledge must always leave puzzles. Kuhn's work was seen by many sociologists as presenting a profound challenge to the perspective on science customary within their discipline. Such sociologists concluded, after reading Kuhn, that there were probably no universal criteria for judging knowledge and that the criteria that scientists appeared to use were extremely flexible and depended for their interpretation on prior personal and social commitments.

18

A particular characteristic of Kuhn's argument is the recognition of the determining effect of specific locations, technologies or even groupings of scientists in certain settings. For Kuhn the production of scientific knowledge is certainly social, but he also argues that the environment within which that pursuit of knowledge takes place is a determinant in the outcome of that pursuit. Central to Kuhn's argument regarding the social contingency of scientific work and findings is this notion of *specificity*. Kuhn and Hughes both assert that technologies develop in more than one way and that different groups of technologies may alter the same paradigm shift differently (Kuhn, 1962; Hughes, 1983). In his exploration of the discovery of oxygen gas for example, Kuhn asserts that if there had been different constellations of actors or technologies, the development and the discovery of the gas would have been radically different, thus emphasising that the social contingency of scientific discovery resides as much in the *specificity* of location or actor groupings. The point may be straightforward, but its ramifications on both the conceptual and methodological level are significant.[3]

The issue of specificity, introduced by Kuhn and further developed by Latour, is highly relevant to the research carried out for this book. The exploration of ANT as a method for reading news work will demonstrate the continued significance of actor specificity at different locations within the news network and reveal how a minute alteration in an actor's location, or timeframe, or social position can have a significant determining effect on the outcome of a network translation.[4]

The concept of specificity is also of importance to the book's methodological rationale, in particular with regard to the choice of a single, regional BBC newsroom that has been used as the environment within which to conduct most of the research for this study of news production. The focus of the study is thus not on the randomness or arbitrariness of a varied sample, characteristic of many of the more traditional media studies, but on a single case. In this way the research seeks to maximise the contextual validity of the empirical work. The objective of this book is not to offer empirical generalisations, but to provide a synthesis between theoretical propositions and particular empirically-observable and practically-relevant processes. The book will argue, just as it will demonstrate on the empirical level of observing practice, that the specific choice of newsroom, and the certain constellations of actors within that newsroom and the implications of that choice are just as fundamental to any findings as they are in Latour's laboratory, or to Kuhn's individual paradigm shift.

This book does not attempt to read *media*; alternatively, it will demonstrate how to read *certain media practices*. Had a separate newsroom at a separate time been selected, the specific conclusions drawn may well have been significantly different, even as the theoretical framework remains constant. We see an excellent example of this in Chapter 6 where we venture out from the newsroom in

Nottingham to explore the world of video journalism situated in the Birmingham newsroom and the adjoining local radio stations within the West Midlands
where the BBC local television project is piloted. The specific locations are thus
radically altered, and also more widely dispersed, but as we discover, we are
still situated within the news network, and as such the same theoretical tools
apply so that we are able to read the processes occurring in these various parts
of the network in just as much detail and with just as much accuracy as we can
from within the slightly more enclosed world of the Nottingham newsroom.
The network to which we are referring is vast; its many linkages, nodes and
vessels through which all human and nonhuman actors travel are made up of
thousands of other, related constituent actors. Yet to read each point of the
network accurately, we must just remain faithful to the specifics. Actor Network
Theory allows us to do this by providing us with particular tools with which we
can chart each actor's exact position in any part and at any particular time in the
network. This will become clearer in each of the following chapters as we learn
how to use ANT to chart these individual actors in the news network.

Thus to read media without addressing the specificity of the news environments they observe, is to misread the contingency of news practice. As we'll see
in each of the following chapters, the specificity of actor positions has a significant determining effect on the outcome of actor and network behaviour.
Thus the specificity of the newsroom, the time of the study, the duration of the
ethnographic work, must all determine the findings and will therefore be discussed in detail in each of the empirical chapters.[5]

Before we can begin to do this, we need to return to our exploration of the
main principles of ANT. To summarise, the most fundamental point is that the
different objects, statements, actors and techniques that are found in the scientific laboratory exist only because of their *connections* and *alliances* with one
another. There is no originating or 'master subject' at work here. There can be
no a priori (previous) presumptions. There is only a network of actors, where each
piece of machinery, each pipette, person, object or piece of paper is an actor.
There is no distinction to be made between the human and the nonhuman.

> An actor is any element that bends space around itself, makes other
> elements dependent upon itself and translates their will into a language
> of its own.
>
> (Callon & Latour, 1981, p.286)

Latour's scientific laboratory is a world that to most of us, had we wandered
into it unawares, as does the fictional researcher in Latour and Woolgar's
Laboratory Life, would seem completely alien. It is a world that seems to deliberately shroud itself, through both its practices, and how those practices are

perceived by the outside world, as elliptical and highly secret. Actor Network Theory seeks to find a way around the laboratory so as to discover that the scientific processes are not as confusing as first imagined. And by doing so it seeks to continually challenge 'common-sense' beliefs about our relation to a reality that is assumed to be both external to and independent of our own actions and perceptions. It seeks to demonstrate how these beliefs only limit our method of understanding and of defining any reality.

Despite its rather unhelpful name, ANT is not a theory, it is a method. It is a means of describing what actors do and how their actions are inscribed both by themselves, and by other actors so as to create *translations* within the network that continually becomes more or less stable depending on the successful convergence of such translations.[6] The subject/object paradigm is eradicated in the very process of action and description. And the description, the accounting for the actions taking place, what has been referred to as the 'anthropological reason' is as much a part of the process as the actors being described (Van-Loon, 2002). That is to say, method is constituted merely as another actor.

A logical first step in understanding ANT as a method is to examine Latour's definitions of both an actor and of reality. Rejecting traditionally accepted subject/object paradigms, Latour simply states:

> There is no other way to define an actor but through its actions, and there is no other way to define an action but by asking what other actors are modified, transformed, perturbed or created by the character that is the focus of attention.
>
> (Latour, 1999, p.122)

The definition of an actor is thus located only in the process of action, and that process of action is itself redefined by the movement, interference or resistance of other actors in that process. The notion of *resistance* is a highly-significant concept for ANT. Once again Latour echoes Nietzsche whose vision of a single force or principle leads him to argue that there is absolutely no other kind of causality than the movement of domination between one will and another (Nietzsche, 1968, p.347). For this reason will must be rigorously detached from abstract psychological categories such as desiring or demanding, which place a conscious idea *before* the expenditure of force. There is no such thing as willing, Nietzsche declares: there is only willing something. For Nietzsche, the entire movement of life is produced by the conflict between the will to the accumulation of force and that which resists incorporation into a stronger will (Spinks, 2003, p.138).

Similarly, Latour argues that an actor is defined only by the series of *trials* that it experiences, and the *resistances* provided by the actor to overcome these. Yet it must not be assumed that these trials are in some way designed, or already in existence. It is only in the exchange of the actor with the event that it resists, that the two are defined. Resistance is thus what defines reality (Latour, 1988a).

Some difficulties that beset ANT as a method can be found in this stubborn insistence to define actors only by their ability to withstand trials of force. This in turn signifies a weakness of ANT to address more complex issues of human strategy, power and intentionality, insisting instead on a total eradication of difference between human and nonhuman actors, defining each only by their ability to resist force in whatever event they encounter.

The empirical evidence provided in Chapter 8 highlights certain restrictions that befall ANT in its insistence on making no distinction between human and nonhuman actors and its reluctance to define power as anything but resistance to trials within the network. But before these are explored, let's return to our discussion of ANT as a methodology, and in particular to Latour's specific interpretation of the work of Louis Pasteur, which will help us understand how and why humans and nonhumans are treated as equal actors within the network.

Analysing Pasteur's scientific experimentation, which led to the pasteurisation of the Western world, Latour argues that neither Pasteur, nor the fermentation process, nor the yeast itself, is defined a priori; rather they are all dependent on the experiment in which

> Pasteur and the ferment mutually exchange and enhance their properties.
> (Latour, 1999, p.124)

The reality of an actor is therefore only constituted by the trajectory that links it with all other actors that have both constituted it, or have been constituted by its trajectory.

> There is no reason to believe that an experiment is a zero sum game. On the contrary, each of the difficulties posed by Pasteur's paper suggests that an experiment is an event. No event can be accounted for by a list of elements that entered the situation before its conclusion, before Pasteur launched his experiment, before the yeast started to trigger the fermentation, before the meeting of the academy.
> (Latour, 1999, p.126)

Similarly, in *Laboratory Life*, Latour and Woolgar argue that

> Many aspects of science described by sociologists depend on the routinely occurring minutiae of scientific activity.
> (Latour & Woolgar, 1979, p.152)

The contention is that unless the nonscientist is provided with a method by which to understand how scientific facts are constructed the so-called mysteries of 'Science', with a capital S will always claim an undeserved mythical position within society (Latour, 1999). Latour's aim is to dispel this myth by exposing the working practices of science, untangling them from the traditional, epistemological acceptance of the status of science as the production of a particular form of highly specialised knowledge. Latour argues that this knowledge resembles very little of what scientists actually do, and that before any event or claim becomes part of 'Science', it has already undergone a complex series of modifications, alterations, translations and even accidents or omissions. Latour's starting point is simply to 'follow the actors'.

> The fact that we do not know in advance what the world is made up of is not a reason for refusing to make a start, because other story tellers seem to know and are constantly defining the actors that surround them ... what they want, what causes them, and the ways in which they can be weakened or linked together ... the analyst does not need to know more than they ... the only task of the analyst is to follow the transformations that the actors convened in the stories are undergoing.
>
> (Latour, 1988, p.10)

To 'follow the story' is to map the network translations. Through translation, actors emerge and are stabilised, or redefined, sequences of events, of causes and effects, come into being and black boxes are made or destroyed.[7] A fundamental concept to ANT, *translation* achieves the ongoing creation of an actor network. Numerous actors within an organisation may be involved in a different process of translation, each with its own unique characteristics and outcomes. To clarify this it is useful to focus on a single actor, from whose specific vantage point we can then recognise the process of translation.[8] Translation is also linked to an actor's specific ability to resist other actors' behaviour. If resistance is successful the original actor remains unchanged by its coming into contact with another actor, but translation may still occur on a separate part of the network that has played an earlier role in constituting the original trial. If, however, resistance is unsuccessful, translation occurs within the single actor. While this may initially seem somewhat confusing, once we begin to map this in action, the process readily reveals itself.

We have defined actors all of whom are translated and redefined by the resistance to trials within the network, but Latour further clarifies this constellation of forces by introducing the term 'actants'. Actants are divided into three categories: humans and animals, technologies and gods.[9]

There has been much discussion within the fields of STS and ANT regarding the consistency of the specific definitions of actors and actants as there seems to be some confusion in Latour's writings as to what exactly constitutes an actor and an actant at various stages of his analyses. At this stage of our enquiry it is enough to define an actant simply as any element in the network that acquires strength in association with others.

The processes through which actors and actants undergo translation, and the stages that characterise those translations, occupy both *Laboratory Life* and *Science in Action*. It is not necessary to provide a précis of these, but it is important to introduce significant aspects of these translations that will inform our own study of news processes. One such term that Latour returns to time and again, and that performs a major role in the analysis of news work, is the notion of the *black box*. Latour introduces this as

> ... something to which cyber-technicians refer whenever a piece of machinery or a set of commands is too complex. In its place they draw a little black box about which they need to know nothing, but its input and output.
>
> (Latour, 1987, pp.2–3)

This term is not original to Latour, but first appears in the writings of Layton and Whitley. Yet Latour further clarifies it to denote a part of an individual network that has become temporarily closed, or impervious to dispute. A black box has managed to resist all trials thus far, and is therefore unable to be translated by any activity within the network at that specific point. Latour often uses the term in a similarly pejorative sense to Layton, to indicate how science brackets off from analysis that which is deemed to be too complex to understand in terms of the mechanics of practice. He argues that the closure of such black boxes is therefore interpreted at an epistemological level as remarkably different from the reasons for the closure in practice. It is as if Science is afraid to reveal its humble workings, lest it loses its exalted position in the minds of the nonscientist.

> We will enter facts and machines while they are in the making; we will carry with us no preconceptions of what constitutes knowledge; we will watch the closure of black boxes, and be careful to distinguish between two contradictory explanations of this closure, one uttered when it is finished, the other while it is being attempted. This will constitute our first rule of method and make our voyage possible.
>
> (Latour, 1987, p.13)

It is primarily this first definition of the black box, that of an uncontested and stable actor within the network, that has resisted all significant trials to date, and is not fully understood by other actors within the network, that will preoccupy the study of news in the following chapter. However, we will also argue that it is precisely this inability to decipher the mainly technological actors within the news network – and the majority of the black boxes in this network are technical, nonhuman actors – that has resulted in previous readings of news that have failed properly to consider technological microprocesses as associative factors in the content of final news products or that have produced false theoretical debates about technological determinism.[10]

It is also imperative at this stage that a working definition be established for the *network* to which ANT refers. This is especially important as the news production network has some similarities with Latour's laboratory cited in *Science in Action*. Yet there are also significant differences that occur at both the methodological and the conceptual level, and these are analysed in turn as they are revealed.

> The word network indicates that resources are concentrated in a few places – the knots and the nodes – which are connected with one another – the kinks and the mesh – these connections transform the scattered resources into a net that may seem to extend everywhere.
>
> (Latour, 1987, p.180)

ANT as a method for analysing news work

> There is an Ariadne's thread that would allow us to pass with continuity from the local to the global, from the human to the nonhuman. It is the thread of networks of practices, and instruments, of documents and translations.
>
> (Latour, 1993, p.121)

As I have mentioned, traditional studies of media have for the most part concerned themselves with the media as a series of semiotic texts, or as various structures of production. While these studies may not agree on their primary theoretical focus, they have in the main tended not to engage with rigorous analyses of media as practice. To take just one example, as Latour was venturing into the Salk laboratory in order to gather his data for *Laboratory Life*, Stuart Hall was arguing that mass media form the main ideological institution of contemporary capitalism (Hall, 1977). Hall's agenda, based on an obvious critique of capitalism, defined media as operating through the production of hegemonic codes that cement the social together (Stevenson, 2002). Political readings that argue that media's primary motivation is to 'effect' society, tend also to afford to the journalists themselves relatively little autonomy or decision-making faculties in the production of news.

But using ANT as a tool to examine human and nonhuman actors in the news-production network the polarities of society and subject, internal and external on which such political studies crucially depend, can begin to be discarded, and in so doing the human actor and his or her agency fundamental to the practice of news work may also be identified more clearly. Once the network is recognised, there can no longer be an authorial subject or a relational object, there can only be actors.

> We want to demonstrate the idiosyncratic, local, heterogeneous, con-textual and multifaceted character of scientific practices.
>
> (Latour & Woolgar, 1979, p.153)

This quote also comes some way to illustrating how ANT can inform our readings of the process of news production once we replace the word *scientific* with *news*, and *laboratory* with *newsroom*. The use of ANT can begin to reveal the study of the news process as a network of actors all negotiating with and for and against one another within a complex network. This network is certainly similar to Latour's scientific laboratory in that the construction of news facts, just like the construction of scientific facts, is realised by means of a series of translations within the network. Latour argues that facts constructed in a scientific labora-tory are not somehow *extrinsic* to that laboratory. They do not exist in some external place waiting to be plucked down from the sky by lucky scientific geniuses. The same is true of news facts. The news product does not therefore suddenly appear after the news process is in some way completed. Rather the news product is at one and the same time an inextricable part of the process; it takes on an active capacity within the network becoming yet another actor. We shall begin to see how this happens once we enter the newsroom in the following chapters.

There are, of course, some major differences between the laboratory and the newsroom, both at the practical and conceptual level. To begin with, in the Salk laboratory, scientists are constructing new facts from various amalgams of pro-ducts and processes. In the BBC East Midlands television newsroom, it would *seem* that the final news product is constructed in order to illustrate an already recognised ordinary and everyday 'reality' – that is the events that are happen-ing beyond the newsroom in an external world. This would initially seem to refute Latour's most central tenet that there is no established notion of a reality out there or extrinsic to the process of construction. For isn't the entire process of news production seeking to convey events that are extrinsic, self-contained and independent of the news machinery?

That is certainly what the majority of media studies have argued. By keeping the world outside quite separate from the world inside the newsroom and by constituting media production as an endless struggle towards verisimilitude at one extreme or political manipulation at the other, the machinery of news production has almost gone unnoticed, while the deliberately separated product has been exhaustively analysed. Yet by using ANT to speak up for the nonhuman actors in the news network, and to dismiss the notion that journalists act as unaware political automata, the hitherto separated external and internal worlds of news production can be systematically dismantled.

Far from there being a distinguishable reality beyond the newsroom that journalists attempt to portray, there is suddenly only a network that extends from the machinery of the newsroom, through its personnel, its news technologies, skills and working practices, beyond the newsroom and out into the messy world beyond. The news network incorporates all of the traditionally defined internal and external realities, and dismantles the concept of internal and external substituting these for a network of translations, practices and actors that in and by itself constitutes the 'reality' of news. News production should not be viewed as shaped and conditioned by a series of external forces; rather it should be recognised as a nonreducible, semi-autonomous constellation of forces that are not merely phenomena of a more generic societal-structural logic, but whose socio-logic operates on interpersonal levels within a whole range of network actions.

Putting to one side for a moment the specific difficulties that have been mentioned that may arise when using ANT to analyse human motivation and strategy, the network of news production is still characterised by practical differences that are not found in Latour and Woolgar's scientific laboratory. The most significant is that much of the news work that will be analysed is highly implicit and cannot be analysed effectively by the use of observational techniques alone. It is the very invisibility of some of the news processes that will be analysed that has perhaps led other media scholars to disregard the importance of practice. In short, they may simply not have recognised processes as they were occurring. By using ANT, and holding fast to the mechanics of its own procedures, and not simply relying on observation alone, we can begin to reveal those hidden processes and to shed much needed, brighter light on the world of news production.

> A very specific interest in laboratory life concerns the way in which the daily activities of working scientists lead to the construction of facts. How are the facts constructed in a laboratory?
>
> (Latour & Woolgar, 1979, p.40)

How are they constructed in a newsroom? For as Latour argues with regard to the laboratory, it is not only that facts are not constructed extrinsically, but that they are only constructed by means of a myriad of translations of actors and technologies intrinsic to that network in that *specific* location. Therefore within the newsroom, the facts, the journalists and the commissioning editors, are only as significant as the technologies they use, the machines that they operate, or the digital-editing system through which they transmit the final event.

> It is not simply that phenomena depend upon certain material instru-
> mentation; rather phenomena are thoroughly constructed by the material
> setting of the laboratory.
>
> (Latour & Woolgar, 1979, p.64)

And so it is with the newsroom. There are no external hypotheses to be tested. News work is itself a method. It is a culturally inherited and implicit method, shared by members of the network, but not necessarily explicitly articulated. And a further tension exists between these socialised modes of working, and other sporadic and singular actions taken by human actors that may occur within the network at arbitrary points.[11]

So how do we begin to go about using ANT to read news production? Let's look at the evidence that we will have at our disposal. We'll be let loose in a BBC regional television newsroom for a period of three years, as well as observing a nine-month research study of the BBC's local television pilot project in BBC newsrooms across the West Midlands. Returning to the notion of specificity, it's important to point out that all the newsrooms are fully digitised and were, at the time that the research was carried out, conducting a rapid video journalism implementation policy. Any other BBC regional newsroom would have yielded different findings; some are only partially digitised, and many have not yet introduced the practice of single-authored video journalism to the same degree as BBC Nottingham or Birmingham.

The decision to concentrate on regional television news, as opposed to national television news is also deliberate. As Cottle notes (1993) in a regional newsroom the tension between the determining methods of filling the obliga-tory half-hour news 'chasm' and the contingency of news work is brought into starker relief. Returning to the notion of invisible or elliptical news processes, it is also important to reveal that it was in this particular BBC newsroom in Nottingham that has the East Midlands area as its geographical and editorial patch that I worked for a period of twelve years as a television reporter and producer.

The ethnographic work can thus be divided into two major projects. The first incorporates a three-year period observing news practice in the BBC Nottingham newsroom, going out on the road with reporters and satellite trucks, as well as analysing news production in the adjoining video journalism satellite bureaux in the editorial area. Each of the following empirical chapters is devoted to an in-depth analysis of one area of news production – the media hub in Chapter 3, Personal Digital Production (PDP) in Chapters 4, 5 and 6, and 'live' reporting in Chapter 7, all of which are interconnected and converge in the final empirical chapter where the human actors are analysed. The second project consists of a nine-month study of the BBC's own pilot project into what is referred to as *local television news;* that is news that will be provided for a particular town or a smaller geographical area similar to that serviced by a BBC local radio station. Similar observations and interviews were conducted during this period, and the study, which is explored in Chapter 6, is mainly preoccupied with charting the development of digital video journalism, beyond the newsroom to engage the general population in making their own films for broadcast on digital platforms such as broadband and satellite television.

We shall discover how each of these detailed ethnographic explorations into the world of news has permitted the exposure of temporary fragmentations of the network so that each constituent part can then be analysed. This has certainly involved self-reflexivity on behalf of those individuals interviewed. The purpose has been to reveal the implicit nature of news work to those actors working in it, just as much as to those of us studying it from beyond the newsroom. The book intends to encourage these actors to reveal the nature of the network to themselves, just as much as to the readers. Only then can the embedded method of news construction be properly drawn out.

In each of the following chapters an individual actor and its particular resistances and translations of the network are revealed. In the final empirical chapter an attempt is made to follow the human actors within the network and to map the extensive nature of the translations that occur in a single day's news production. I have used a ten-hour shift incorporating the production of a lunchtime bulletin and the main evening news programme, including observation of live reporting and interviews with planners, journalists, directors, technicians and producers involved in the programme production process. Within this case study all the actors previously studied in Chapters 4, 5, 6 and 7 are also further analysed so as to reveal the continued fluidity of their positions within the network. These empirical chapters will also reveal how the technological apparatus at journalists' disposal is enfolded with the human actors and together influences network translation. While it has obviously not been possible to find a voice for the technological agents within the network, by asking actors to articulate how technological constraints or possibilities determine actions, the necessary technological agents can be represented.

Weaknesses of Actor Network Theory as a method for reading news processes

It's imperative that as part of a full exploration of ANT as a justifiable methodology for reading news work, significant weaknesses are highlighted at an early stage. To do so we need to return to the early development of ANT as a method for reading scientific processes, before exploring how similar frustrations may also arise in our own attempts to read news work.

Initial rejections of ANT as a valid approach to reading scientific work primarily focused on its delegation of power to nonhuman actors, and what was seen as its adherence to a monolithic and unrealistic sociological constructivism (Collins & Yearley, 1992; Sokal & Bricmont, 1977). These attacks, which became known within the STS field as the 'Science Wars', centred around the idea that the traditionally accepted split between nature and society could not simply be jettisoned or ignored as Latour and Woolgar were demanding. It was thus with the central philosophical tenets of ANT that these authors took most umbrage, continuing to espouse essentialist paradigms and schisms as ontological givens. Referring to Latour and Woolgar as 'prosaic, radical symmetrists', Collins and Yearley condemned their application of ANT on both the philosophical and the methodological level. In a scathing attack on Latour's scientific work, they refused to contemplate any divergence from the tradition of an unproblematic division between society and nature, and the attempt to question this epistemological position was hotly refuted as philosophically untenable and methodologically flawed.

> The absence of methodological control over fantasy allows Latour to develop his concept of 'delegation' unhindered by traditional problems. Using imaginative licence to the full, he is able to tell convincing stories about the way in which we delegate power to technological artefacts. The lack of control over method allows control to be given to things ... the reflexivity and actor-network theory approaches both exclude explanation in the descriptive languages they provide.
>
> (Collins & Yearley, 1992, p.307)

Yet there was to be no epistemological middle ground reached between the two divergent theoretical approaches as Callon and Latour's forceful response to Collins and Yearley made evident. In their contribution to this philosophical and methodological crusade teasingly entitled *Don't Throw the Baby out with the Bath School*, both authors called upon Collins and Yearley to entertain the possibility of a different ontological status for science and society, accusing them of an epistemological hegemony that was methodologically weak.

Why is this reading by Collins and Yearley so inevitable? Because they
cannot imagine any other yardstick for evaluating empirical studies than
the one defined above, and they cannot entertain, even for a moment
another ontological status for society and for things. All the shifts in
vocabulary like actant instead of actor, actor network instead of social
relations, translation instead of interaction, negotiation instead of discovery, immutable mobiles and inscriptions instead of proof and data,
delegation instead of social roles, are derided because they are hybrid
terms that blur the distinction between the really social and human-
centred terms and the really natural and object-centred repertoires.
But who provided them with this real distribution between the social
and the natural worlds? The scientists whose hegemony in defining the
world Collins and Yearley so bravely fight.

(Callon & Latour, 1992, p.343)

The war was thus fiercely waged between those who accepted the epistemological order of a clearly separated society and nature, and the hierarchies of
power between humans and nonhumans that this necessitates, and those whose
aim was to replace this with an associational network of actors and to disentangle them from defined and stable hierarchies of size, power or agency.

We never wished to accept the essential source of their [scientists']
power; that is the very distribution between what is natural and what is
social and the fixed allocation of ontological status that goes with it.
We have never been interested in giving a social explanation of anything, but we want to explain society, of which the things, facts, artefacts, are major components. If our explanations are prosaic in the eyes
of Collins and Yearley, it is OK with us, since we have always wanted
to render our texts unsuitable for the social explanation genre. Our
general symmetry principle is thus not to alternate between natural
realism and social realism but to obtain nature and society as twin
results of another activity, one that it more interesting to us. We call it
network building, or collective things, or quasi objects or trails of
force.

(Callon & Latour, 1992, p.343)

After the debates of the so-called 'Science Wars' subsided, more recent criticisms of ANT have tended to focus upon its insistence on the symmetry
between human and nonhuman actors within a network, and its stubborn refusal
to acknowledge the human subject as discernibly different from its nonhuman
counterparts. These concerns may vary in their primary focus, but social and

cultural theorists such as Couldry, Boyne and Law all observe the limitations of ANT to address the complex interplay of subjectivity and power between human actors within networks, and have attempted in their separate ways to widen the theoretical field so as to achieve a more refined and perhaps more adequate exploration of the role of human actors in the network. It is worth pausing for a moment to explore their concerns with ANT and to consider their own contribution to its development.

Couldry's attempt to relate ANT to media practice begins with a refreshing awareness that media studies have been hampered by the preoccupation of media as causally effecting society, with little time spent on the exploration of news practices. Couldry asserts that

> An advantage of starting with practice – what types of things do people do/say/think that are orientated to media – is that there is no intrinsic plausibility in the idea that what people do (across a range of practices and locations) should add up to a functioning whole.
>
> (Couldry, 2006, p.4)

Yet, Couldry's definition of practice differs somewhat from my own. For Couldry ANT is useful in helping to unravel a complex network of what he refers to as media practice, and to reveal how such practices are received and then taken up by the audience and by society at large. Thus practice is defined by means of an external, fragmented audience that consumes media, and the mechanics of news production to which we will refer, is not necessarily included within this definition of practice. His argument does maintain that because of such fragmentation, traditional, ideological readings that argue that media is able to create a unified effect, cannot be easily sustained, but his work does not choose to focus on the use of ANT as a tool with which to venture into the newsroom where the actual practice of news work is taking place.

Though Couldry relates ANT to a primarily sociological reading of media, rather than using it to explore media practices, his criticism of ANT as a methodological tool is important. He states that while ANT has a significant role to play in an attempt to provide a new paradigm that theorises media as practice, rather than as a text or an organisational structure, its failure to grapple with issues of human agency in networks is a fundamental flaw. Quoting the sociologist Roger Silverstone, Couldry argues that

> . . . a network sets agents in *positions* relative to other agents and things (relative, that is, to other 'actants' as ANT calls them in a term that is deliberately ambiguous between humans and non humans). Those positions limit the possibilities of action in certain ways, but they do

not tell us about the *dynamics* of action. Specifically, the existence of networks does not explain, or even address, agents' interpretations of those networks and their resulting possibilities of action (and it is only human agents that interpret the world, even if, as Woolgar argued, objects and technologies have inscribed within them particular codes and instructions for actions).

(Couldry, 2006, p.108)

He concludes that ANT's most serious flaw is its insistence on the description of human and nonhuman actors only through network action, and that these actions do not demonstrate differentiated levels of power that human and non-human actors may possess.

For all its intellectual radicalism, ANT comes charged with a heavy load of political conservatism that is, I would argue, directly linked to its professed disinterest in human agency. Power differentials between human actors matter in a way that 'power differentials' (if that is the right term) between non-humans do not: they have social consequences which are linked to how these differences are interpreted and how they affect various agents' ability to have their interpretations of the world stick. ANT has much to contribute to understanding the 'how' of such asymmetries, but it is strangely silent when it comes to assessing whether and why they matter. Its deconstruction of the human subject is here disabling ...

(Couldry, 2006, p.112)[12]

Boyne's exploration of ANT also concerns the presentation of the human subject, and while it is not appropriate to elaborate on this at this stage, it is significant to note that Boyne asserts that while Latour rejects the classical metaphysical certainty of the subject, he still relies on the idea of a subject to establish his arguments. Boyne argues that Latour's repudiation of the subject is a careful one.

The human subject is conceived to be an actor on account of his or her acquisition of material forces: Only thus can one 'grow'.

(Boyne, 2002, p.27)

Boyne's argument is that Latour does not reject the notion of a human subject, but he does present it as, at one and the same time, hybrid and unstable, yet also in some senses safely compartmentalised. Human consciousness, with its myriad of psychological and emotional traits, never preoccupies his explorations of working practices.[13]

As was mentioned at the beginning of the chapter, Law's particular criticism of ANT once again focuses upon the human subject, but this time in relation to Latour's definition of power within networks, and how such a definition precludes any exploration of human motive or strategy.

In an intriguing essay, *The Powers of Association*, Latour delineates a paradox. When an actor has power, nothing happens, but when an actor *exerts* power, it is *others* who perform the action. Latour's argument, which is reminiscent of Foucault, is that power is not something that one can merely possess.

> The sociologist should, accordingly, seek to analyse the way in which people are associated together, and should, in particular, pay attention to the material and extrasomatic resources (including inscriptions) that offer ways of linking people that may last longer than any given interaction.
>
> (Latour, 1986, p.264)

Power is therefore a method of translation between actors within the network, and can only be obtained by the enrolment of successive actors. Law develops this idea arguing that Latour's model of translation fails to deal with the exploration of any motivational strategies other than a somewhat Nietszchean idea of pure forces at work within the network, as mentioned earlier in the chapter. For Law, there are also a series of calculative strategies at work within a network, all of which indicate a sense of power being stored and of power being redistributed.

> My hypotheses thus suggest that we might try to characterise actors in two dimensions – on the one hand as a series of putative strategies with power storage and power discretion effects, and on the other hand as a series of materials which, in some measure reflect those strategies, but also as a series of relational effects: the two are connected in part simply because this is the way things are: on the one hand we live in and are constituted by a set of relations which are organised in a range of different ways and have a series of different effects; and on the other hand, we are embodied in a range of materials.
>
> (Law, 1991, p.174)

Turning now to the news network, the study of human actors within the news production process aptly demonstrates that far from Latour's insistence on power as simply the translation of actors, human actors certainly do display intentionality, formulate strategies and harbour individual motives. In Chapter 8 several of these strategies are explored in detail so as to reveal the motivational and manipulative techniques that human actors, in a highly self-reflexive way, often adopt in order to strengthen their own positions or to gain recognition by other actors within the network. This analysis will therefore involve a further critique of Latour's reluctance to recognise power as anything other than simple force or resistance, which could impede the successful adoption of ANT as a method for analysing a more complex organisational network, such as a newsroom. Yet a possible development of ANT will also be explored; a translation of its own methodology if you like, so as to move from beyond this apparent methodological weakness to recognise and fully explore human intention without threatening the validity of ANT as a method.

Conclusion

It would be helpful to summarise what we have learned about ANT and its ability to help us read news processes at the level of everyday practices. As has been illustrated, the recurring epistemological problem with an ethnographic approach to studying any cultural situation is that it is highly dependent on the ability to observe.[14] Many aspects of the news production network are invisible to the untrained eye. Large parts of the network are also invisible to individual actors working within it. It is a network made up of constituent and interlocking nodes, but not all of these are visible to all actors at all times. Indeed, as we shall soon discover, it is the very invisibility of the network to specific actors at specific times that is fundamental to the overall success of the production process.

This poses a serious problem for the researcher or student of news. He or she cannot be omnipresent within the network, and even if this were possible, many actions would still be invisible, as so much of the news method is itself embedded and implicit. Therefore it is a significant advantage for this type of study that the ethnographer is in some way an initiated member or ex-member of the network. Certainly my own autobiographical reflexivity as an initiated actor, as an ex-journalist, occupying different positions within the network has enhanced my ability to unveil the 'mysterious' process of news construction. But this is not the whole story.

The following chapters will soon reveal how it is the mechanics and strategies of ANT as a particular method, its ability to read actors in certain timeframes and occupying very specific positions that allows the researcher more access and more 'visibility' than simply standing by and observing one group of actors at a time. Actor Network Theory permits the researcher to be able to observe actions occurring at more than one place as it is the *connections* between the actors and the network translations these create that are being so studiously mapped. This also raises important issues of *reflexivity,* either on the part of the researcher, acutely aware of his or her position as an observer within the newsroom, or on the part of the human actors being observed, the journalists, directors, planners, technicians and producers themselves. These issues will be explored as and when we come across them in our journey through the news-production process.

For it is the sustained marginalisation of human agency that occurs in so many traditional media studies that has hampered a full understanding of news production at the level of practice. Contrary to what many media theorists have argued, journalists are self-aware. They do not simply act. They reflect not only upon their own actions, but also upon the actions of others in the network. And unlike Latour's laboratory, where the actions of scientists are for the most part visible, scientific findings are textually inscribed and those findings discussed openly between scientists, the newsroom network is characterised by invisible nodes within it, unobserved by certain actors but through which they may still be translated. This is also one of the most fundamental challenges facing the ANT researcher when they choose to 'follow the actors'. To research the news production network, as an actor within that network, the researcher has to learn how to follow the story. We return here to the hypothesis made earlier in the chapter that there should be no artificial division made between the *process* of news construction and the news *product* in some finalised form. In the following chapters we will begin to demonstrate how the exploration of news production is just as much preoccupied with following the news story itself, as it is with following the actors. The story is just one more actor that undergoes a series of translations during its construction. The following chapters show us how it is not feasible to discern a beginning and an end to the construction process. As with every other actor within the network, the news story is also forever in flux, metamorphosing as it undergoes continual translation.

As we have argued, human actors in the network display a highly self-reflexive and often critical awareness and far from being satisfied with Latour's insistence that only actions define the actor, there is more at stake here and the anthropological reasoning that the observer brings to the 'object' of study is also confused and disorientated. The power of observation is therefore replaced by the entry into a contingent network as an actor. That network is forever in flux, and is constantly being translated and retranslated by both human and nonhuman actors within it. Not only that, but the human actors are themselves self-reflexive, they are equally observing and developing the network that we, the observers, are attempting to study.

Having criticised Latour earlier for his somewhat reductionist definition of power, it is worth returning to it as he develops the idea within a wider social context, arguing that society too can only be constructed as a result of collective action, rather than being a constant and ostensible reality about which we then try to search for explanations.

> If society is made before our eyes then it cannot explain our behaviour
> but is rather shaped by our collective action. It is no more a cause of
> the latter than power itself.
>
> (Latour, 1986, p.270)

Latour thus rejects an 'ostensive' definition of the social, in favour of a 'performative' definition.

> Society is not the referent of an ostensive definition discovered by
> social scientists despite the ignorance of their informants. Rather it is
> performed through everyone's efforts to define it.
>
> (Latour, 1986, p.273)

Thus it is with the newsroom and the construction of news facts. Rather than positing an ostensive reading onto news work, it is now time to seek out the performative definition of news in the making, by entering the network as a researcher, and in so doing bidding farewell to the traditional, safe, anthropological reason of the observer. As Latour discovers

> social scientists raise the same questions as any other actors and find
> different practical ways of enforcing their definition of what society is
> about.
>
> (Latour, 1986, p.273)

As researchers, we are actors let loose in the network. The purity of research as a method imposed from outside on an already formed, stable and consistent reality is no longer sustainable. Nor is it enough to merely observe, to conduct interviews or to textually record findings or articulations. The observer needs to be a reflexive part of the network and to recognise its ever-changing and elliptical characteristics. As Law argues

> We're not in the business of epistemology – we are no longer trying to
> find good ways of narrating and describing something that was already
> there. Instead, or in addition, we're in the business of ontology. We are
> making our objects of study.
>
> (Law, 1994)

But having recognised this process of reflexivity, the researcher must not then box him or herself into an endless self-referential debate regarding the credibility of knowledge claims stemming from reflexive observation. They must take an extra step. They must tell a meaningful story that brings alive the world of which they are now part. This is more than grappling with the methodological headache caused by the researcher changing a situation by entering into it. There is no 'entering into it'. The 'it' is not formed, is not stable and does not remain consistent. It is mutable and performative, and includes a plethora of actors including the researcher and including the method.

Actor Network Theory is a method, but it too is not immutable to translation, as we shall see in Chapter 8 where certain tenets of ANT are themselves developed as we explore the issues of human intentionality and power. As we have already seen, ANT has undergone translation by its migration from the scientific laboratory to the newsroom. It is not a theory that can be used merely to decipher or to provide a stable narrative of a separate process from which it has no involvement and upon which it has no translating influence. It is itself an actor. But by using it as a method through which the network may be observed, it is possible, for example, to rethink the nature of technologies and to recognise the relative autonomy and power of agency of nonhuman actors, and of what were considered to be established systems. This should encourage both social scientists and media theorists to develop their analysis of the social beyond traditional subject/object paradigms and to recognise that systems are not made by subjects but are instead temporarily held together in fluctuating networks by both human and nonhuman actors.

Previous media studies, be they political, semiotic, phenomenological or ethnographic in their approach, have for the most part tended to conclude that news is in some way instrumental in informing society, shaping society, or manipulating society in one form or another. Let us then explore an alternative view. We will soon discover that unless news production is analysed and rendered 'descriptable' at the micro level of process, the implicit 'magic' of journalistic practice and technique will always be insufficiently translated into political or ideological readings on an organisational, political or economic level. The organisational, the political and economical readings certainly have their relevance, but they do not come close to showing us how the news fact is actually constructed, or to explaining exactly what happens inside the newsroom.

It is now time to find out, and to faithfully relate what we discover by using ANT as a meticulous tool kit, and our own eyes and ears as a means of discovery. Just as our stone-cutter would do, it is time to divert our eyes from the vast social panorama shining out before us, and to accustom them to the dimmer recesses of the newsroom, so that we can begin to tell a different story of how news facts are *actually* constructed, not by simply and silently appearing over that glimmering horizon towards which we hopefully gaze, but hammered and bullied into shape in the more complex, detailed, haphazard and ever-changing entanglement of humans and machines.

3

ENTERING THE NETWORK

The media hub and its status as a black box

In the following six chapters we will journey into the news network to observe and experience the complicated world of news practice, using Actor Network Theory (ANT) as our exploratory tool. As the analysis of ANT in the previous chapter hinted, we should not be expecting to stumble across astonishing or hitherto unknown discoveries, but to open our eyes instead to the ordinary, mundane and everyday routines that occur all around us. You may ask how this journey can be worthwhile. How will it lead us anywhere new or show us anything we might consider significant, noteworthy or illuminating? How can such a tedious journey, rooted as it is in the dull soil of the everyday, reveal anything remarkable or miraculous? This is where we must take that leap of faith mentioned at the beginning of the book and take our eyes off those vast media landscapes of the global, the economic or the political, to turn the handle of a smaller door into what may seem at first to be the more limited world of regional news production. Once we adjust our eyes, and begin to properly observe and to understand this world, getting to grips with the complex entanglements of all the humans, machines, objects, routines, constructions and performances that define news work, we will find our vision will become more clearly focused, more illuminating and, crucially, more helpful to us when it's time to leave that newsroom to travel through those grander landscapes once again.

The BBC Regional Newsroom in Nottingham

We will begin our journey by trying to visualise the newsroom into which we are taking the first tentative steps, but this simple and descriptive account is only provided while you are adjusting your eyes to the light. Once we're ready we will then begin to enter into the world of humans and technologies, by using some of the more rudimentary tools that ANT provides, namely the concept of the *actor*, as we discussed in the previous chapter, *actor translations* and the *black box* status of certain actors.[1]

The BBC television newsroom in Nottingham is an open plan, but specifically demarcated, space, wherein two separate departments that are denoted by two separate collections of desks oversee the *newsgathering* and the subsequent *production* of news. Subdivisions comprising single individuals, or entirely separate units, are located within the newsgathering department. These make up the planning department, known by those working in the newsroom as *futures,* made up of one senior planning journalist, a second senior planning journalist and a third planning journalist. There are also *four specialist television correspondents,* and a *resources* subdepartment, which comprises all the technical resources available to the newsroom, from satellite trucks to camera crews, studio lights and mobile editing facilities. Newsgathering also includes the *personal digital production (PDP) operators* or *video journalists.* These are individual reporters, camera operators, videotape (VT) editors or technicians who all have their own digital cameras and have been specially trained to film and edit their own material.[2]

Situated on the other side of the room, opposite the newsgathering department is the production department, normally referred to by those working in the newsroom as *output.* Here the news is written, produced and transmitted. This department comprises all of the production staff on shift in the newsroom. These would normally be a *general production journalist*, a *senior production journalist (SPJ)* responsible for the production of the shorter bulletins and the 11-minute lunchtime bulletin, a *lunchtime presenter,* a *weather presenter,* and two *main programme presenters*, as well as the main *output producer* who is responsible for the production of the evening programme, which is 28.40 minutes in duration. The output producer occupies the most senior position as he or she is responsible for all the daily editorial decisions regarding the evening programme. The output producer is answerable to the station manager, the *Head of Regional and Local Programmes (HRLP)*, who is the BBC's chief management figure for each particular region. The HRLP is responsible not only for all of the television output, but also for the output of the region's radio stations and online services. Each of the radio stations also provides a dedicated internet service, which is located on the BBC *Where I Live* sites. This is managed within the individual radio station by separate online editors but is also managed indirectly by the HRLP.[3]

The newsgathering and output departments are crucially interdependent, and individual journalists, producers and technicians working within each have a shared tradition of knowledge, based upon experience and inherited work regimes. Thus there is communal recognition of accepted output between departments, and as Cottle (1993a) also recognises in his study of independent regional news, both departments work towards a shared understanding of the specific news form. This could initially lead one to assume that, putting the methodological intricacies of ANT aside, journalists, at least, are routinely, or even organisationally, conditioned to produce expected news formats and content.

Yet, as we've already mentioned, such studies of the manufacture of news that have attempted to address the mechanics of news organisation (Tuchmann, 1978; Tunstall, 1971; Fischmann, 1980; Schlesinger, 1978; Soloski, 1989) and that reach similar conclusions based around evidence of organisational or corporate bias, have still tended to neglect the subtle complexities of what we will call the *internal news episteme*. It is to this that we refer when describing specific routines, or certain protocols recognised within the newsroom. A tradition of working practice is certainly commonly observed, but even the separate news departments, although they are similarly structured and may share both staff and resources, often adopt distinctive, unpredictable or even idiosyncratic approaches to individual stages of news production. It is these varied and often contingent practices, crucially characteristic of the *internal news episteme,* that using ANT we can begin to explore in more detail.[4]

The regional television newsroom is responsible for the transmission of separate news bulletins throughout the day. The early-morning journalist known as a *broadcast journalist (BJ)* produces and presents breakfast bulletins of four minutes' duration every half-hour from 6.30am until 9.00am. These have been written by the *overnight journalist (OJ)* and mainly edited the previous evening. The lunchtime bulletin, which is 11 minutes long, is transmitted at 1.30pm after the BBC's national lunchtime news that runs from 1.00–1.30pm. The main evening programme, which is known as *East Midlands Today*, is transmitted at 6.30pm and is 28.40 minutes in duration. All the regional programmes are transmitted immediately after the BBC's national news and are deliberately linked to the main national news programme with the national presenters handing over to the BBC's regional news teams, or within a national news programme such as *BBC Breakfast News*, from which the regional newsroom opts out for its four-minute half-hourly bulletin transmissions.

The regional television newsroom in Nottingham is also shared by BBC radio Nottingham and both are responsible for providing the BBC's national radio and television newsrooms with material should they request it. The BBC in Nottingham used to operate as a *bi-media newsroom,* which meant that a television journalist working for *East Midlands Today* would be expected to provide material for the local radio bulletins by recording interviews and voice pieces while out on location filming his or her television package. This practice has been almost completely disbanded during the last two years, due to the implementation of PDP and the increase in the use of video journalists (Van-Loon & Hemmingway, 2005). But journalists within the two newsrooms, situated as they are in the same room, still work very closely together, often collaborating on stories at both the planning and the reporting stages.

Although the main local radio station is radio Nottingham, the Nottingham newsroom also services what is known as a local radio cluster. The cluster for

BBC East Midlands comprises five local radio stations, managed separately by local radio managers, but also managed at the regional level by the HRLP. The HRLP thus has managerial responsibility for the regional TV station at Nottingham, as well as all the local radio stations in the East Midlands geographical area.[5]

In the East Midlands the radio stations are radio Nottingham, radio Derby, radio Lincolnshire, radio Northamptonshire and radio Leicester. Each radio station has an individual radio editor and is staffed by a team of local radio reporters. However, each station still relies on the newsgathering department of TV East Midlands based in the Nottingham newsroom to supply them with news that may be being covered in their own geographical area by TV reporters, even though formal bi-media practice has been more-or-less eradicated. Until about a year ago the radio editors would be in regular contact with a senior TV journalist, known as the *news organiser*, to find out what news was being covered, and what material they could expect to receive. Since the embedding of PDP, the news organiser position has been disbanded.[6]

Situated within the newsgathering department there are also two journalists who work for the BBC's national *News 24* channel. These are a presenter/reporter and a producer. The posts are financed by the national News 24 service and the journalists are responsible to that channel. They work closely with the regional television journalists and constantly communicate the news stories being covered in the region to the national news organisers who are situated in the national newsroom at Television Centre in London. *News 24* often chooses to cover the same news stories as the regional newsroom, but uses its own dedicated reporter and producer team to gather and report the news.[7]

Servicing the two main newsgathering and output departments in the TV newsroom is what is known by all staff as the *media hub*. To use some ANT terminology for just a moment, within the newsroom this is one of the network's primary technological agents, and can be described as an important *obligatory point of passage*, which is defined by Latour (1987) as a specific point on a network through which a significant number of other actors must pass. It therefore denotes a position of strength. In ANT terms, it forges together a system of alliances and enrols actors within the network by their inclusion within these alliances. This is our first definition of a *black box*, a key ANT concept with which this chapter will be mainly preoccupied.

> It is not simply a question of allies but of their acting as a unified whole. With automatism, a large number of elements is made to act as one ... when many elements are made to act as one, this is what I will now call a black box.
>
> (Latour, 1987, p.131)

But before we begin to drift inexorably into the confusing theoretical terri-tories of ANT, let's briefly return to our initial discussions of ANT and its relationship to media studies, which we explored in the preceding chapter. It's important that we understand why, as we begin to delve more deeply into the processes of regional news, we are grasping the particular tools of ANT in our quest to find a clearer vantage point from which we can view this tangled world of humans and technologies.

Actor Network Theory and the silent world of objects

As has been mentioned, this is not the first study that seeks to exercise the theoretical concepts of ANT within the field of media analysis. Both Nick Couldry, and John Farnsworth and Terry Austrin's work is of relevance here and a brief exploration of their findings will assist us in our understanding of how ANT can make a significant contribution to reading media. The most direct and obvious input ANT makes can immediately be located in an analysis of the term 'media'. As Farnsworth and Austrin argue in their adept ANT analysis of medi-ated poker playing, an actor network restores the term 'media studies' to its fullest sense. As Latour (2005) emphasises, ANT is the study of how actors or mediators *mediate;* how they join, negotiate and translate from one network to another. They argue that what distinguishes ANT from other approaches to media studies is that it emphasises that *all* social activity requires mediation, and that *all* forms of objects and technologies are potentially mediatory depending on the networks in which they are engaged. Social worlds, Latour (2005) argues, are only possible because of such interrelationships. This view is in contrast to more conventional distinctions of mass communication institutions and practices (Williams, 1975; Marvin, 1988; Boddy, 2004; Farnsworth & Austrin, 2006).

The authors develop the idea of fully mediated ever-changing social worlds to explore internet poker playing, which is, of course, both mediated and also occurs simultaneously in many different sites. This leads them to make very interesting discoveries about what have thus far been considered to be unpro-blematic categories or formations of the social or the cultural – including media studies itself.

> In the process, as we have suggested, activities such as mediated poker problematise what is meant by 'media' or 'media technologies' since the components, repertoires, actants and networks which assemble media worlds can be readily reconstituted to assemble other worlds. To track these, ANT emphasises the method of following: following, in

particular, how new, unanticipated worlds are put together, stabilised or re-constellated. It also points to metatheoretical questions about the way the disciplinary formations of media and cultural studies, themselves assemblages of other disciplines, might be reconstituted. Indeed, ANT can be said to problematise the enterprise of media studies by questioning how 'media' are delimited in the first place and how, precisely, they are related to social formations. Latour raises similar questions with regard to ANT and sociology. Disciplines, in short, are themselves unstable formations.

(Farnsworth & Austrin, 2006, Paper for Media and
Social Change Conference, CRESC, September 2006)

Another important contribution Farnsworth and Austrin make in developing a theoretical justification for using ANT to read media is with regard to the methodological problem of reading media routines simultaneously in more than one location. They draw heavily on Nick Couldry's own ANT ethnographic analysis to argue that it is by recognising mediated processes as occurring within a network that incorporates many different sites, that a full analysis of media can be achieved.

Couldry develops a 'passing ethnography', a version of multi-sited ethnography, an approach grounded in recent ethnographic discussion about ways to trace cultural formations across and within various sites of activity. Kalocsai (2000) follows Marcus' (2000) seminal thinking to suggest that 'ethnography moves out of a single site and into multiple sites in order to 'examine the circulation of cultural meanings, objects, and identities in diffuse time-space' (Marcus 1998: 79).' This, broadly speaking, is the approach taken up by Couldry in relation to media ethnography. This opens up the possibility of identifying similar mediated cultural practices in very different locales: a method well-suited to new internet, mobile and digital domains (Couldry forthcoming).

(Farnsworth & Austrin, 2006, Paper for Media and
Social Change Conference, CRESC, September 2006)

The authors realise they need a theoretical approach that can capture and articulate a fully mediated, but ever-changing social world, and that can also incorporate the multilocations of media to which Couldry alludes, to illuminate the elliptical and secret nature of internet poker. They discover, as we shall do, that ANT provides the most satisfactory approach because it keeps track of constantly reworked boundaries of institutional forms, cross-media linkages, genres, participation and spectatorship. The authors argue that these in turn persistently open up questions about how new media and socio-technical worlds are constituted, just as our own journey will do.

We will use ANT to capture, not the world of mediated poker, as do Austrin and Farnsworth, but the complicated, socio-technical behaviour of regional news production, and our network exploration is not so much concerned with the interlinkages of the social at the political or institutional level, nor at the level of the spectator or audience where Farnsworth, Austrin and Couldry all focus their analyses. Our network is constituted by thousands of interactions and interlinkages that occur between humans, machines, objects and technologies during the daily construction of news. Of course, if we follow the logic of an ANT analysis, we must accept that there is no boundary to our network. It will and must incorporate both the micro and macro; the tiny tasks of an individual edit, as well as the political ramifications of a story for a regional audience; the pushing of a single button in the television gallery, together with the corporate weight of the BBC as an institutional machine. These are all within our network, and must be accounted for, if we are to understand how the news process that we seek to explain is fully socialised, fully mediated and fully integrated. But we must start from somewhere. So we will start by entering into the technical and multi-sited world of news itself, and we'll spend considerable energy exploring this construction process, before we lift our gazes from the newsroom to grasp the further contingencies of our network as it travels beyond these specific sites of production.

Our first problem, once we enter the newsroom, will be with all the objects we discover. We'll find that it's crowded with machines and technologies that cannot speak for themselves. If we are to explore the relationships these have with our human actors who we can interview, observe and more clearly understand, how will we find a voice for them? How can we do them justice, if they cannot account for themselves? This is a problem with which our ANT fieldwork must continually engage. Latour himself discovered that cultural analyses had too often been reliant on researchers' abilities to understand their subjects of study as if they literally needed to be on the same wavelength. How could they possibly hope to do that once confronted with a world of objects?

> Once built the wall of bricks does not utter a word – even though the group of workmen goes on talking and graffiti may proliferate on its surface. Once they have been filled in, the printed questionnaires remain in the archives forever unconnected with human intentions until they are made alive again by some historian. Objects, by the very nature of their connections with humans, quickly shift from being mediators to being intermediaries, counting for one or nothing, no

matter how internally complicated they might be. This is why specific tricks have to be invented to make them talk, that is to offer descriptions of themselves, to produce scripts of what they are making others — humans and non-humans do.

(Latour, 2005, p.78)

The majority of studies of news technologies tend to neglect the role of these objects, or they are only considered significant once they have entered into specific relationships with humans. This need not necessarily be a problem per se, and there are some very insightful studies of our relationship with media technologies. Brian Winston's seminal work, *Media Technology and Society; A History: From the Telegraph to the Internet*, strives to develop technological analysis away from rather simplistic and alarmist deterministic accounts prevalent during the 1970s and 1980s. His adroit historical account does recognise both the social and cultural as significant driving forces in the development of technology, and he manages to provide a highly elucidating and exhaustive study of the development of media technologies throughout the twentieth century.

This book has been a history of electrical and electronic systems of communications. I have used this account to mount a case against the concept of technological determinism, arguing instead that social, political, economic and cultural factors are the prime determinants of technological change. In passing, as it were, I have also disputed the concept of an Information Revolution, taking particular issue with the rhetorical hyperbole it has engendered. Instead I have suggested that change is accomplished slowly. My case has been grounded in the pattern of actual development which has led to the creation and diffusion of these various telecommunications technologies over the better part of the last two centuries. ... I have tried to show how social forces both push and hinder these developments, forcing a social 'fit' upon them in the process. This 'fit' is essentially achieved by suppressing the disruptive power of the technology to impact radically on pre-existing social formations. I formulate this as a 'law' of the suppression of radical potential.

(Winston, 1998, p.342)

We should question the final statement of this quote. For as soon as we begin to use an ANT analysis, and learn those 'tricks' that will enable our objects and technologies to begin to account for themselves, we'll soon discover that the disruptive power of technology, to which Winston refers, is not quite so easily placated, and that, without straying back into the purely deterministic camp, we will recognise that such technologies possess agency, just like our human actors, and are able to manipulate the networks within which they are situated. Once we use ANT, we start to realise that it is not only the human subject that can act, and our world of objects widens out before us, revealing to us its own agency in its complex associations with human and nonhuman actors within the network, as it slowly starts to account for itself.

It is this sustained refusal to accept that technologies possess agency that also hinders Raymond Williams's famous analysis of media. There is no space here to present an in-depth discussion of Williams's significant contribution to the study of media, and others have already provided far more comprehensive accounts of his work (Stevenson, 2002; Boyd-Barrett & Newbold, 1995; Van-Loon, 2007). We touch on it only to illustrate that the vast majority of highly regarded, seminal studies of media technologies have tended to avoid a full analysis of the object, and concentrated instead only on the object's relationship with the human subject. Williams certainly argues against readings of technology that are simply deterministic, as well as readings that see technology merely as symptomatic of change of some other kind, providing instead what he refers to as a new interpretation, which does at least retain the analysis of technology as central to his argument.

> In technological determinism, research and development have been assumed as self-generating. The new technologies are invented as it were, in an independent sphere, and then create new societies or new human conditions. The view of symptomatic technology, similarly, assumes that research and development are self-generating, but in a more marginal way ... Each view can then be seen to depend on the isolation of technology. It is either a self-acting force which creates new ways of life, or it is a self-acting force which provides materials for new ways of life.
>
> (Williams, 1975, p.14)

He insists that his new interpretation manages to steer a tricky course between both deterministic and what he calls symptomatic readings of technology.

> The technology would be seen, that is to say, as being looked for and developed with certain purposes and practices already in mind. At the same time the interpretation would differ from symptomatic technology in that these purposes and practices would be seen as direct: as known social needs, purposes and practices to which the technology is not marginal but central.
>
> (Williams, 1975, p.15)

As Van-Loon argues the most significant contribution Williams makes to theorising media technology is his insistence on the central importance of technology use for the way in which particular media become intertwined with distinctive social and cultural forms. Yet he does not manage to engage with the notion that technologies could possess agency, even though as Van-Loon adeptly points out, his analysis seems at times to be unwittingly pointing towards this conclusion.

> He does acknowledge that there are technological limitations to the way in which technologies can respond to needs. Yet, the very recognition of such limitations did not spur him on to take a closer look at the nature of technological agency. However, if technology can set limitations by itself, it is undeniably an actor ... Williams remained a rationalist and was not willing to make a more radical leap of faith to accept non-human agency ... simply because for Williams, social needs are the main driving force of history.
>
> (Van-Loon, 2007)

There are a handful of more recent news studies that do at least recognise the need for developing the empirical study of news technologies and which come much closer to recognising technological agency, even if they don't refer to it directly. Simon Cottle and Mark Ashton's illuminating analysis of the changing nature of the BBC newsroom in Bristol pays particular attention to the detailed socialisation of news technologies.

> Though there is no doubting the remarkable advances in recent news technologies nor their facilitating impact on processes of news generation and dissemination, when analysed in relation to a particular news operation, its corporate context of change and their professional incorporation into working practices we find – not surprisingly – that things are far from *technologically determined* ... Today it is easy to mistake technology for an independent causal force determining both the pace and form of change, rather than as a 'creature of our own making' – a creature that is, which inhabits, was born out of, remains dependent on, and is 'socialised' and put to work within determinant social environments.
>
> (Cottle & Ashton, 1999, p.23)

Drawing on Hardt, Cottle calls for a more thorough investigation into the development and internalisation of news technologies, which he argues is significantly under-researched.

Newsrooms like factory floors, have been a laboratory for technological innovation and a battleground of economic and social interests for over 100 years. ... They are evidence of the impact of technological change on the lives of news workers as an historical problem of understanding the internalisation of technology in the practice of journalism.

(Hardt, 1990, p.355; in Cottle & Ashton, 1999, p.24)

The article provides interesting insights into the way in which the Bristol newsroom has been redesigned in order to facilitate bi-media and multiskilled working practices, which Cottle indicates have been adopted as a direct result of the acquisition of new digital technologies. Yet the analysis is focused primarily on the role of BBC managers and the changing working conditions for journalists and we need to ask why Cottle, with a specific interest in what he refers to as the cultural shaping of technology, still prefers to concentrate on the way in which humans have adopted and adapted technologies, rather than on the way that the technologies themselves have become embedded, and how this embedding has altered the news network within which they are situated. To illustrate how we might begin to respond to the central question of technological agency, which is of crucial significance to our use of ANT to read news, we will now turn to an analysis of the media hub and its network status as a black box.

The media hub and black box status

Technologies belong to the human world in a modality other than that of instrumentality, efficiency or materiality.

(Latour, 2002, p.247)

As Figure 3.1 illustrates, the media hub consists of a matrix of connected digital interfaces, or computer hard drives, which are then connected to the entire technological infrastructure of the newsroom. This includes the desktop computers in the newsroom, the adjoining three editing suites, the main studio downstairs from where the programme is presented, and the gallery situated next to the studio, from where the programme is transmitted. The interface of the media hub can also talk to all the BBC national television and radio newsrooms, all other regional BBC TV newsrooms situated in adjoining editorial areas such as Birmingham, Leeds, Northampton and Norwich, and all BBC local radio stations within the local radio cluster.

The hub is our automated play out server and what we use to store all of our clips and all of our rushes. Everything goes onto the hub – well, is supposed to go onto the hub. The way that the hub is connected to

Figure 3.1 The media hub in the BBC Nottingham newsroom.

everything is via three VT machines. We also have VHS, SVHS, Hi8, Satellite Freeview – so we have all of these different sources within the hub set up. The way the hub is structured is a server based system, so effectively it's split into profiles – the A pro and B pro – and we take things in on these – A and B are just two separate sections of the server – each of those are split into 4 – so we have A, 1,2,3,4 and B, 1,2,3,4, and this means we have 4 ports which can access this information on the A section. If you think of it like a filing cabinet, you have 4 files in the A drawer and 4 files in the B drawer, so that other people can access the information. We then have T pro – which is T literally because it's the Transmission Profile, TX Profile allows us to play the clips out. This hub is connected to every single one of our edit suites, so our edit suites can dub things, they can use clips or rushes that we have on the profile and they can take them into the edit suite, cut their story and then dub their story onto the T pro for transmission.

(Vicky, media-hub operator, BBC Nottingham)

All the recorded digital material has to be 'fed' into the hub so that it can be digitised before it can then be viewed on any workstation in the newsroom. Like Latour's *obligatory point of passage*, the hub represents both a technological facilitator, but also an effective gatekeeper. The dissemination of the digitised material is achieved by the fact that the hub is directly linked to the newsroom's two digital communication, and video-editing and play-out systems, which are known as the *Electronic News Production System, or ENPS* and *Omnibus.* The entire technological infrastructure is known collectively as the *programme production system* of the newsroom.

> The idea of the programme production system is that when people come back from stories they take the media they have and put it on a server and then everyone can get to it; radio can get it for clips, headlines and promo shots, without disturbing the journalist who is editing the story. Ideally it would make better sense if the stories were edited within the server so once they go onto the server they just sit there and everyone who wants to use it can just use it. But when this was installed things were not quite at that level, so we have a system where the pictures are put onto a server and copied again into an edit system and it slows down the process. It's then edited within the edit suite with voice and music and then dubbed back onto the transmission profile on Columbus in the media hub.
>
> (Mark, director, BBC Nottingham)

Described by the Head of BBC News, Richard Sambrook, as the 'spine of the BBC's daily news production across 12 radio and TV networks and the internet', the Electronic News Production System (ENPS), developed by the Associated Press, is the BBC's networked, desktop information service, enabling newsrooms across the country to communicate with one another, to view each other's material and to access news running orders. Described in rather glowing terms by the Associated Press itself, ENPS is said to be responsible for thousands of words of text and hundreds of hours of audio and video pouring in and out of the BBC every day.

The Electronic News Production System has more than 12,000 users across the BBC as a whole and all staff can utilise the system for email communication between newsrooms, for the dissemination of information and ideas, as well as for the creation of programme running orders and the writing of news scripts and links. As we've seen, in the Nottingham newsroom, ENPS is directly linked to the Omnibus and Columbus editing and play-out system, a technical detail peculiar to the Nottingham newsroom, but which has significant implications, as will become evident.

The Omnibus and Columbus system automates the input of video and audio media, provides communal browse and editing facilities online, as well as permitting access to archive material by means of a series of connected servers. The automated play-out facility is known as Columbus. There are two Columbus servers, one in the media hub itself and one in the gallery. Both of these are directly linked to one another and, crucially, to ENPS. Columbus cannot transmit any recorded material to air unless it first recognises that material within the ENPS system where it has been logged.

> The hub is linked to ENPS. So the only reason the hub will ever make sense is if you store things in the correct format, because at the end of the day, it feeds from the information that you give it and that's all that it can do. The way that the transmission works is there's what you call Columbus, and it actually reads what we put in ENPS, so every single clip you want to play out, if it's coming from this server, you have to have the clip name on ENPS matching identically with the clip name you have in the TX Pro.
>
> (Vicky, media-hub operator, BBC Nottingham)[8]

One of the first significant factors of the ENPS and Omnibus systems is that both are designed to facilitate the instantaneous dissemination and retrieval of news material, from almost anywhere in the world. These systems represent some of the most advanced digital technology for immediate worldwide access to, and retrieval of, recorded news material. They also make up a worldwide technological network extending far beyond the network of any individual newsroom, with digital tendrils stretching across thousands of miles, transporting video images and sounds from across the globe.

Yet, our analysis soon reveals that far from being used for instantaneous worldwide media retrieval, the programme-production system in the Nottingham newsroom has a specifically localised and therefore in some aspects a severely limited position within the interior network of the newsroom. The evidence suggests that the media hub certainly enjoys a black box status within the network, as it has managed to forge enough resolute alliances to ensure that its position is relatively stable, but its function does not extend far beyond the parameters of this network, and its inherent technological capabilities are thus significantly under-utilised.

Our research will further demonstrate that far from enjoying the technological freedom that worldwide media retrieval and instantaneous communication can afford, certain actors on the network actually consider the programme production system to be a hindrance to the production of even their own local news. Some actors on the network even attempt to avoid this *obligatory point of passage* altogether, with differing degrees of success. From exploring certain actor positions it is evident that the media hub is generally accepted as a black box, but that its use is limited to the permutations of the specific network of the newsroom and that its inherent technological capacity is therefore also bound by the parameters of its specific black box status within that specific network. This will become evident as our analysis develops.

One of the most commonly observed rituals, which also emphasises the hub's black box status, occurs in the daily practice of 'feeding' the hub. All reporters returning to the newsroom after filming must first of all hand over their material to the media-hub operator so that it can be played into the hub. Significantly, the reporter is unable to do this task autonomously but has to rely upon the technical expertise of the operator. The reporter is thus forced to surrender ownership of the material, for as long as it takes for the video and audio to be played into the system in real time, before subsequently gaining renewed access to it via the communal server, Omnibus. This the reporter does by asking the media-hub operator for a port, from which they can then view their material and select what sections of the rushes (the unedited material) they want to include in the edited piece. At this point the reporter has also effec-tively relinquished editorial control of the material, as it is now available to any other actor on the network. These actors can access it simply by asking the media-hub operator for a port on which it can be viewed and edited at any workstation.[9]

> There are so many departments now that need to access that material. We try our hardest to get everything onto here [the hub]. It doesn't matter that it's in real time that it goes on, because as soon as I load it onto a profile, everybody else, at exactly the same time, on the other three available profiles, can start watching it in real time as well. So an edit suite can be taking it in real time and at the same time graphics is searching for the right picture and edit two is taking headlines for lunch, whereas before if you just took a tape and went into an edit suite you couldn't get that access. But that still happens. People don't like putting their tape onto the hub because of the digital pass.
>
> (Lynne, media-hub operator, BBC Nottingham)

The 'digital pass' referred to in the quote refers to the actual process of feeding the video material from the camera into the media-hub server, to then literally be 'passed' around from one workstation to another, all of which access it via the central server. The journalist's reluctance to surrender the material is based upon both a concern over the time lost by the process for the selection and basic editing of shots at the workstation, as well as a perception that the material should be edited offline in an editing suite first and only then be fed into the server once it has been completed.[10]

The tapes have to be put into the server in real time. So if you've shot 45 minutes of material, it will take 45 minutes to load into the profile. What then slows the so-called immediacy of news is that when you go into an offline edit suite to edit, the editor also needs to take the pictures and interviews in real time. It might be great for people to be able to access your material once it's on the hub, but it's extremely vexing when you look at the actual amount of time you need to collate the pictures to cut a report. It's easier to try to bypass the hub and just go in and edit with your own tape.

(Quentin, reporter, BBC Nottingham)[11]

This illustrates a tension between an individual actor whose primary objective is to retain autonomy while performing a single task, and the demands of a decentralised, communal network. The resistance to network translation by certain actors, whose position necessitates at least perceived autonomy, is most clearly observed when PDP technology enters the network, analysed in the following chapter. But it also occurs at various other stages throughout the network, and the widespread resentment towards the media hub among reporters manifests itself in this specific way.

Let's take a specific example to illustrate what we mean here. On one particular day, the lunchtime presenter, who was situated at a workstation in the newsroom, was observed attempting to edit a headline sequence for the lunchtime bulletin. Having been asked whether or not she could access the material she needed, she confessed that though she should have informed the media-hub operator of her actions, there just wasn't sufficient time to follow this procedure.

All the stories are on the hub – if they're on A or B pro, but you need to be given a port by going to the hub to ask, but I'm being a bit cheeky – this is the transmission profile so I can't actually lock it, but what I intend to do is look at what's on it and then play it and then edit it – so yes, I am effectively editing it – to make a headline. It's just one of the duties that has now fallen to the presenter and yet again, we haven't got the luxury to tie up edit suites for headlines – so heads and promos have to be done on here.

(Carol, lunchtime presenter, BBC Nottingham)

What is significant is that the presenter is only able to bypass the protocol of the network because of her enhanced understanding of the technology. Had she not known that the transmission profile could be used for editing short sequences without being locked off, she would have had to approach the hub for assistance. The example illustrates that the varying levels of technological awareness among journalists are also directly proportionate to the level of individual human agency they can enjoy, and thus their success at bypassing the media hub altogether. It also brings into sharp focus the tension that exists between technological agency and human agency.

This tension between an actor's autonomy and their subsequent network translation is evident in most of the related production activities within the network, which we will discuss as we come across it throughout our journey. It is also highly significant when we attempt to refute the findings of studies that purport to recognise evidence of preconceived ideologies or bias common to *all* newsroom personnel. For it is only through the recognition that at the level of *practice,* certain actors do exert autonomy and bypass or translate the network to achieve their own personal objectives, while others are translated by stronger actors or alliances of actors within it, that such readings are exposed as highly problematic and in some cases simply inaccurate. The *news episteme,* analysed here at this microcosmic level, certainly involves evidence of a corporate routinisation of tasks and duties, but it also illustrates variability in the performance of these duties by individual actors and, significantly, that this variability manifests itself at times as a challenge to the existing network, and at other times as a surrendering to the translation process within the network.

Black boxing within a network creates the notion of stability. The performance of routines that the black box necessitates in order to retain control over its sets of alliances, and the translation of other actors into which it comes in contact, serve as deliberate ways to exteriorise and extend its significance throughout the network. Yet the actual contents of the box itself remain opaque. The media hub is a technological actor whose function is certainly understood by all other actors, but whose actual mechanisms are shrouded in mystery. As Latour argues, nonhuman actors, in particular technologies, possess an ontological stability by the nature of their being physically durable; yet as they are also socialised within networks, they are at one and the same time malleable, exemplified already by the variety of responses to the media hub's function and significance so far. This point will be discussed in more detail later in the chapter.

> Nonhumans stabilize social negotiations. Nonhumans are at once pliable and durable; they can be shaped very quickly but once shaped, last for longer than the interactions that fabricated them. The involvement of nonhumans resolves the contradiction between durability and negotiability. It becomes possible to follow, or to black box interactions, to recombine highly complicated tasks, to nest sub programmes into one another.
>
> (Latour, 1987, p.211)

While the media hub enjoys its black box status, due in part to the technical complexities of its subprogrammes, as well as its ability to perform a central facilitating or prohibitive role in the dissemination of material, the actual operators of the hub do not occupy senior positions within the BBC. Most are production assistants or facilities assistants, roles that are considered to be fairly mundane within the newsroom hierarchy. Yet they coordinate all the material, allocate ports and profiles to reporters and producers, and maintain an ostensive authority over the network by means of the direct facilitation of that material.

> This job really is the centre of the newsroom – the programme wouldn't happen without it. The presenters could sit there and talk for twenty-five minutes but they wouldn't get any pictures. Edit suites are also always on back up – a piece can be played out from an edit suite because it is not unheard of that one of these will crash. So whatever the edit suites cut they will keep so they can play it out, but it's really the hub where it all happens.
>
> (Vicky, media-hub operator, BBC Nottingham)

It is the recognition of the technological shortcomings of the media hub, and the programme-production system in its entirety, and the accompanying frustration that this generates among staff, that most threatens the status of the hub as a black box. All the operators express varying levels of consternation with the daily use of the hub as both a server and a programme transmitter. Among these opinions it is interesting to note how the responses to the technology are often overtly anthropomorphic.

> Basically it's like getting three computers that are shoved together that are storing your video, that's all they are, they're just computers, and they're pretty dumb and stupid.
>
> (Tony, media-hub operator, BBC Nottingham)

> We have had occasion where both the Columbus dub and the Columbus transmission – Columbus transmission is obviously the programme that is transmitting, Columbus dub is the programme that is used to dub stuff, have tried to grab the same port at the same time, and that's when we have had black holes on air – because two into one don't go. And it doesn't say; 'After you, no after you', it just sits there and says, 'I've got a problem and I don't know what to do!' If you're on the phone you won't see the dub going through – or you won't see that someone is dubbing into the wrong clip. The edit suite person should

notice – sometimes they don't. It has happened. It is a system that maximises human error, it doesn't minimise it.

(Mark, media-hub operator, BBC Nottingham)

Successfully performing all of its varied functions is what causes most anxiety among media-hub operators. The hub is continuously carrying out more than one duty, equipped as it is with such multifarious technological capability. Yet there is only one operator at any given time, and almost every other actor in the network is unable to describe how the hub works, and certainly not able to operate it. Even among operators, there is often confusion as to how to carry out certain tasks, and sometimes claims of disbelief that the hub 'is acting strangely again'. As these operators are not senior figures, their own status within the newsroom is inextricably bound up with the status of the hub as a black box. In a sense the operators can be viewed as mere extensions of the hub; their function is to further enhance the position that the hub holds; so in ANT terms, they are *folded* into the nonhuman actors with whom they are combined (Latour, 1999, p.211).

Yet before we simply afford to the hub a position of absolute technological supremacy in the wake of its own operators, we need to analyse in more detail the complaints voiced by operators and other actors alike. As we have seen, the most widespread criticism is that the Columbus and Omnibus systems are linked with ENPS. So if any script details from ENPS are inserted incorrectly into the play-out system, the system simply does not function.

If the information is wrong, it defaults – it maximises the error – so if you don't put times in for the Aston,[12] it will come up at the beginning of the item, all together, rather than not come up at all. If the Astons are too close together – it kind of gets muddled up and it will put whatever you last left on the preview bank on the mixer to air – which is normally a studio shot – so you'll get a presenter flash up in the middle of an item – it has a whole list of things which are very unfriendly and not very helpful.

(Mark, director, BBC Nottingham)

Thus a valorisation of enhanced technological instrumentalism begins to give way to a general perception that the media hub often impedes the successful production of news, in that it slows down the process of editing, and that its slavish reliance on absolute technical accuracy can also hinder programme transmission.

The reporter would be on ENPS typing in the Aston names and the time of the Astons, so nobody else is double checking those, so if they get the times wrong, Columbus plays them out automatically. If the reporter gets the template completely wrong, nobody knows that until it goes out. The director is far too busy to notice tiny little details like that. They wouldn't know the timings anyway. If the editor dubs the wrong thing, it may look right to the hub person, but they won't know if it started half way through because they might think it should start like that; sometimes things have been transmitted as they have still been dubbing so you have no idea what's at the end of it.

(Tony, media-hub operator, BBC Nottingham)

As the majority of the human actors within the network, including those ostensibly responsible for making the main editorial decisions, such as the output programme producers, do not have any understanding of how the hub operates, this level of technical ignorance causes ongoing tensions between the hub operators and other actors in the network, both inside the Nottingham newsroom as well as in adjoining newsrooms in the cluster with which the hub communicates. It is also significant to note that all of the human actors within the network also refer to this digital matrix as the 'media hub' – the language further emphasising the mystification process that is at work here in an attempt to define the digital technologies that are both shrouded in mystery yet also accepted as integral actors within the network.

People sometimes forget that there is a process to the things that go on here and they just think they can take this or that – and you think, well you booked the line from 6.00pm until 6.15pm and you've actually booked it at three minutes past six and they don't seem to realise that there are a number of different things happening here – really small things – like you might be clipping something up and you're trying to remember what you're doing, and someone has just told you something and wandered off and your phone starts ringing, and you're speaking to someone, and you know, you think, 'For God's sake, just hang on – just give me 30 seconds!'

(Vicky, media-hub operator, BBC Nottingham)

Mapping actor positions: the sociogram, technogram and chronogram

Although the hub performs a number of simultaneous tasks throughout the day, these are usually all specifically local. For example, on one particular morning a series of specific tasks was performed during a two-hour period. Let's take a brief look at what these were. Recorded audio and video was fed to the hub from the adjoining PDP bureaux in Derby. An interview was played out to a local radio station. BBC TV in Leeds, who shares an editorial area with a part of the *East Midlands Today* geographical patch, made a line booking in order to obtain a cut news piece from Nottingham. Nottingham then booked a line to the BBC's political studio known as *Millbank* in London, in order to obtain filmed material of a local MP speaking in the House of Commons. Two reporters returned to the newsroom and fed their analogue rushes into the hub to be digitised. *News 24* in London requested a cut story from the previous evening's *East Midlands Today*, and a PDP operator returned with footage that was fed into the hub and digitised.

We can immediately see from this example how the hub's technological capacity to beam footage or to receive material from the far corners of the globe, is continually sacrificed to the daily trawl and catch of the geographically and editorially local. Thus the hub's socialisation within the specific network of the Nottingham newsroom severely curtails the exercise of its wider technological capabilities. This is a very important point and one which will inform most of our exploration of all of our human and nonhuman actors within the news network. Latour argues that it is this precise relationship between an actor's *technical* ontology and its *social* positioning that enables us to recognise its significance in any network.

> If you take any black box and make a freeze frame of it, you may consider the system of alliances it knits together in two different ways; first, by looking at who it is designed to enrol; second, by considering what it is tied to so as to make the enrolment inescapable. We may on the one hand, draw its sociogram, and on the other, its technogram. Each piece of information you obtain on one system, is also information on the other.
>
> (Latour, 1987, p.139)

So let's consider a freeze frame at this particular point. We could argue that the hub's *technogram,* what is meant by its inherent technological capability, is subordinate to its *sociogram,* which is its social position, and therefore its function within the network in the newsroom is under-utilised. This tells us that the hub's status as a black box is not just determined by its technological capabilities, but by this more mundane function within the newsroom. That function is itself determined by the hub's social position within the network, and how many actors the hub is able to enrol in that specific position.

But if we consider a couple more freeze frames in our attempt to explain why the hub enjoys black box status the picture becomes a little muddier. These two randomly selected quotes represent remarkably conflicting views of the hub.

It's actually just following a really simple, logical process, it's not doing anything fancy or anything complicated, I can understand why people hate it because it is hideously logical- – it's what people have with every computer problem, there is always a sense of user non-friendliness, that's the aim that everyone puts into their software packages – they want them to be user friendly, but there is always something that makes it not user friendly and this one is that it can be a bit vicious, but its logical side, I love.

(Vicky, media-hub operator, BBC Nottingham)

It does have limitations – if your item is very late – it's difficult then to insert it once the previous item is cued up. You can play it out from an edit suite – you can move it down the running order and then back again – there are little tricks that you can do, which are a pain. It's you basically working around the system, not the system helping you. It wasn't really designed for news – it was designed for MTV playing out music videos, which you're going to know about in advance. To use it for a live news programme, and any decent news programme ought to be a dynamic event, the idea of trying to automate is very odd really – because to automate you have to know what you're doing ahead of time.

(Mark, director, BBC Nottingham)

If we take a freeze frame of the hub using the information from the first quote, and track both the sociogram and technogram, the result is crucially different from that which the earlier analysis revealed. Here, the operator is extolling the logical infrastructure of the hub with regard to how it communicates with ENPS – its technogram – and explaining that the hub is only considered to be unhelpful because of other actors' inability to comprehend this logic – which we could define as its sociogram. The technogram of the hub in this instance is considered to be unfairly maligned as a direct result of its social positioning within a network of other actors who, it's inferred, may be technically ignorant.[13]

Following exactly the same process, in the final quote the status of the hub as a black box is once again called into serious question. Here the technogram – that is the hub's inflexibility to react to sudden changes of information it receives, is pitched directly against its sociogram – that is its position as the transmitter of a dynamic live news event. The tension between the technogram and sociogram here results in the hub being perceived as occupying a dubious position on the network, based upon its weakened technogram, a weakness that creates a doubt in other actors that it can effectively sustain or even justify its sociogram.

Now let's take this analysis one step further. For in this example it is imperative that we also include the chronogrammatic axis, which we will use to refer to an actor's temporal position within the network. The director makes a specific reference to the inadequacy of the news production system being able to react 'ahead of time' – essential for what he considers news to be, which is a 'dynamic live event'. Thus the freeze frame we construct must also include the added weakness of the actor's chronogram; that is its inability to deliver live news as a result of both its technogrammatic and sociogrammatic formulation; being used ostensibly as a digital delivery system for a live event, yet lacking the technical capability to live up to the expectation of that social position.[14]

This somewhat complex methodology that the freeze-frame examples reveal is not simply an exercise in identifying various perspectives. What is being illustrated here is a significant characteristic of the black box itself.

> The black box moves in space and becomes durable in time only through the actions of many people; if there is no one to take it up, it stops and falls apart however many people may have taken it up for however long before.
>
> (Latour, 1987, p.137)

Therefore it is the *negotiability* of the status of the black box that is a crucial component of the network. Nonhuman, technological actors may retain their durability for longer periods than human actors, but they are still malleable. They are pliable as a direct result of their being socialised within networks. And as we have seen with the hub, this socialisation is itself in constant flux. We could have chosen three other examples, and mapped three entirely different sets of sociograms, technograms and chronograms within the network. The exercise does initially tell us that varied perspectives are an important component when human actors and nonhuman actors are folded into one another. But it tells us something more significant. It reveals how any position within a network, however stable it may ostensibly seem, is still open to translation by other actors. The media hub retains its status only by its ability to forge alliances that so far have not yet fallen apart. Its status is not only dependent upon its technological ontology, but on the altering tension between its technogram, sociogram and its chronogram.

> The black box is between these two systems of alliances, that is, it is the obligatory passage point and that, when it is successful, it con-centrates in itself the largest number of hardest associations, especially if it has been turned into an automaton. This is why we call such black boxes 'hard facts'– or 'highly sophisticated machines', or 'powerful

theories' or 'indisputable evidence'. All this alludes to strength and power and rightly points out the disproportionate number of associations gathered in these black boxes, so disproportionate indeed that they are what keep the allies in place. However this disproportion often leads us to forget that they hold things and people tightly together only as long as other strategies are successful.

(Latour, 1987, p.139)

Thus the ontology of the media hub is defined by both its technical capability and its social place. Only through the complex negotiation of these two elements, and being bound to a number of actors who crucially cease to question its status, can the hub retain that black box status. As the quote suggests, and as the empirical research illustrates, this is being continually challenged by other human and nonhuman actors. The hub has retained its position thus far, only through the constant marshalling of and resistance to those trials. And its ability to achieve this so as to retain stability is only possible by its exact social positioning on the network.

The media hub and other proximate actors

To define the hub's intricate social and technical positioning more fully we now need to explore the immediate environs of the media hub and to chart the relationship between the operator of the hub and the other most proximate actors. Located on an adjoining desk, in front of the hub, is the *camera diary assistant* (CDA). Responsible for booking camera crews, the satellite truck, and the lines that are used to feed material in and out of the building, the CDA works in almost constant and close contact with the media-hub operator. The CDA is also responsible for arranging the copying, or dubbing of material for use by other stations, although the hub actually performs the dubbing procedure. There is thus an intricate overlap of roles and responsibilities between the media-hub operator and the CDA.

> The hub has to do the dubs, but they're channelled through me because while we are doing the dubs, we might not be able to take stories in from elsewhere. It was just wall to wall – we still only have one line in and one line out – although we have four different machines over there – you have to have something to dub something off and onto so it still ties stuff up. You have to fit in dubs where you can. People think because of the hub, things have gone away from us, but it's actually causing more problems elsewhere.
>
> (Lynne, CDA, BBC Nottingham)

62

The hub's technological capabilities ensure that it successfully performs all the necessary technical tasks, but the logistical arrangements that need to be finalised in order to carry out those tasks fall to another actor in the network. The CDA, and until recently the news organiser (whose position underwent radical translation with the implementation of PDP and was finally disbanded), are located near to the hub so that they can facilitate this logistical support. Yet there is widespread confusion among other actors as to who actually does what, and evident frustration among the CDAs who feel that their workload has substantially increased since the hub became the focal point of all media dissemination.

> Now we do much more with the radio stations because you have all the PDP operators based in Derby and Lincoln and Leicester, and they all want to send headline shots and it's got to all go through me. The times that they've tried to phone the hub and the hub can't take it and they say, 'Well you need it for the programme!' And the hub operator asks them if they've booked their line. And they haven't booked it through me. And of course Leeds is forever using Lincoln, because they have a VJ in Lincoln and they use the equipment that we put in there but we both can't use it at the same time – so there's another problem – so although people think the job has got easier, it's actually just caused more problems.
>
> (Lynne, CDA, BBC Nottingham)

As has been already discussed, such frustrations with the amount of work that the hub is perceived to have created on other points of the network would seem to seriously threaten its status. These frustrations are articulated specifically at the level of practice; they focus specifically on the hub's inability to assist actors in carrying out daily routines quickly and effectively. They illustrate the tension between a desired autonomy of certain actors within the network, and the centralisation of individual tasks. How then does the black box status of the hub manage to hold?[15]

Echoing the earlier example of the presenter who had managed to navigate her way around the technological infrastructure of the hub, and by doing so had gained partial autonomy from the network, the black box status is retained by the hub through the uneasy alliance of its positioning – its sociogram, technogram and chronogram. That alliance is most strongly forged by the fact that other actors are ignorant as to the actual workings of the hub. It is no surprise that although the CDA voices frustration over the position she occupies vis-à-vis the hub, there is no way she could swap roles with the hub operator. Significantly the same is true of the hub operator, who has no ability to perform the tasks of the CDA.

63

Her job [the CDA] is organising the crews and going through the filming today – and who is going where when, and who needs a break when, and I don't know anything about people's break times and the limitations on that, or how long it takes to drive from there to there, or how long you're supposed to give someone to drive. I don't deal with that. I know how to make a booking because I had to make one once – but I don't do her side and she couldn't do this side of it. She can load clips and look at them and review what's on the system and if I am snowed under and I have a telephone call – the media hub has two telephones and yesterday things got really busy and I was constantly sat on this phone and because I was on this phone, people kept phoning me on that phone up there, and so she can load clips up in that situation and have a look, but she wouldn't know how to do anything else on the technical side of things.

(Vicky, media-hub operator, BBC Nottingham)

The significance of this quote is that these two actors remain fairly ignorant of the other actor roles that are not available to them. This ineptitude to perform the tasks of an actor occupying another network position serves in this instance to further protect the status of the hub as the network's most significant black box, as we have seen how it stabilises its social position through the alliance with its technological capability. Not even the hub operator can aspire to this position, and other actors who may be frustrated by a series of network complications that the operation of the hub creates, are still unable to pose a serious challenge to it as their alliances with other actors are too few, and therefore not as strongly forged, and thus their individual knowledge of the entirety of the network remains limited.

An actor grows with the number of relations he or she can put, as we say, in black boxes. A black box contains that which no longer needs to be reconsidered, those things whose contents have become a matter of indifference. The more elements one can place in black boxes – modes of thought – habits, forces and objects – the broader the construction one can raise.

(Callon & Latour, 1981, p.284)

Significantly, the programme producers, who are those actors who are directly responsible for editorial decisions regarding news content, share this acute indifference as to the mechanics of the hub and the entire production system. This causes associated tensions with other actors such as the hub operators and directors whose knowledge of the system far exceeds those who are ostensibly 'in charge' of the final news product.[16]

64

It's not helped because producers haven't really understood the system – every system has its limits – if you work within the limits of any system its probably going to be ok but if you don't know what the limits are the chances are it's not going to work. So you do get producers who think they can just leave it all until they're reading the link and then decide whether we can go to the item – you can't do that at the drop of a hat – and you have to be thinking one step ahead when you're directing, so you don't leave a big hole in the programme.

(Mark, director, BBC Nottingham)

A direct link is being forged here between human agency and technological proficiency. To return to Latour's methodology, according to the direct quote, the producer's sociogram, that is his/her position as the editorial controller of the news product, is seen to be limited, if not even directly challenged by his/her technogram; that is, his/her ignorance of the technologies with which she/he is linked. But this is more than a reading of human ineffectiveness in the wake of developed technology, which might encourage one to draw technologically deterministic conclusions. We have already discussed the technology's own fluid positioning, and how black box status is retained only through the delicate manipulation and *assembling* of other actors.

What we have here is an example of one of those *assemblages;* the producer who is folded into the technology but whose lack of technical understanding fixes his/her social position within the network, and once again will guarantee that the black box status will be retained. What is less clear at this stage, but will become clear as we explore more of these nested positions actors hold within the network in the following chapters, is how far the *news product* is determined by the interplay between these heterogeneous and ever-changing network positions.

It is as if we might call technology the moment when social assemblages gain stability by aligning actors and observers. Society and technology are not two ontologically distinct entities but more like phases of the same essential action.

(Latour, 1991, p.129)

Conclusion

What we've seen in this chapter is how the media hub's black box status is achieved and retained through the constant realignment of other actors, and that this realignment is itself effected only by the delicate tension that exists between each individual actor's sociogram, chronogram and technogram. These *systems of alliances* as Latour describes them are never constantly fixed. They can be read differently at every point within the network, where an actor comes into contact with other actors. They are also responsible for every effect that the actor makes at that point. If an actor can find a position in which their own internal systems of alliances are more resistant than that of the network at that specific point, they may achieve translation of that network. If an actor cannot force translation of the network, they are translated by it. We will explore a translation process in detail in the following chapter when we analyse the rise of video journalism or what is known as PDP.

The media hub has managed to forge enough strongly intermeshed alliances that it translates most actors that come into contact with it, and as we have seen those translations are, for the most part, unchallenged. They may be questioned, but they do not present themselves as serious forms of resistance that might alter the status of the black box. This tells us something significant about the socialisation of both human and nonhuman actors within the network, and highlights the artificiality of the distinction between human and nonhuman. It also shows us very clearly that nonhuman actors do possess agency. All actors embody the process of the network within their own selves. They are defined by the network process. Michel Callon has referred to this specific *interiorisation* of the network by agents in his quite different exploration of ANT as a method for explaining the behaviour of economists and stockbrokers.

> If agents can calculate their decisions, it is because they are entangled
> in a web of relations and connection; they do not have to open up their
> world because they contain their world. Agents are actor worlds.
>
> (Callon, 1998, p.185)

This is true of the actors within the news network. Rather than reading news processes as being located in the conflicting worlds of the artificially constructed newsroom, and the *reality* that exists somehow, 'out-there', we can now more accurately define the process by the interiority of the network within the newsroom, and the further interiorisation of that network by the different actors positioned within it. It is within this assemblage of actors, all with their own socialised alliances, and varying degrees of resistances to one another, that we can more accurately locate the ostensive *reality*. It is then possible to begin to redefine our notions of external and internal worlds as separated from one another, and to create instead, a social and material network where the external and internal paradigm is replaced by the constant presentation and re-presentation of that which is 'hidden' by that which is immediately present.

If new realities 'out-there' and new knowledge of those realities 'in here' are to be created, then practices that can cope with a hinterland of pre-existing social and material realities also have to be built up and sustained. I call this enactment of this hinterland and its bundle of ramifying relations, a method assemblage. These may be understood as enactments of relations that make some things (representations, objects, apprehensions) present, 'in-there', whilst making others absent 'out-there'. The 'out-there' comes in two forms – as manifest absence (for instance as what is represented), or more problematically, as a hinterland of indefinite, necessary, but hidden otherness.

(Law, 2004, p.13)

This rather complex quote defines the network as a presentation of that which is immediately visible, present and 'in-there' as well as containing within that presentation, that which has been folded into it from what was once considered to be 'external' and 'out there'. The network is both internal and external, being and absent. A specific example of this assemblage to which Law refers is the process by which the media hub folds into itself the presentation of an external reality by playing-in the recorded material and digitising the pictures. Once this process is initiated it is impossible to make meaningful distinctions between the external and internal; the very architecture of the machine prohibits such distinctions by its technical capability to begin to alter the recorded material, before the digitisation process is complete; a capability deemed by other actors to be one of the hub's most impressive technical features, as this quote, that has already been used in a different context earlier in the chapter, also reveals.

As soon as I load it onto a profile, everybody else, at exactly the same time, on the other three available profiles, can start watching it in real time as well. So an edit suite can be taking it in real time and at the same time graphics is searching for the right picture and edit two is taking headlines for lunch, whereas before if you just took a tape and went into an edit suite, there was only one person who could access it.

(Vicky, media-hub operator, BBC Nottingham)

An exploration of the position and the significance of the media hub within the newsroom neatly illustrates Law's notion of a 'method assemblage'. We have seen how the hub literally mixes up what may be defined as 'out-there' or absent from the news process, and that which is present, visibly defined by the various processes that occur at any given time. Those processes are determined by the hub's technical capability to perform a number of tasks at any one time.

Some actors understand certain processes, while others do not. Some of these processes are visible to other actors, while others are hidden. The hub represents the method assemblage to which Law refers – a conundrum wherein the polarised paradigms of internal and external, absent and present, are replaced by a heterogeneous representation of both absence and presence, as well as that hinterland of indefinite, hidden otherness.

The hub's black box status is further defined by its ability to process both forms of externalised 'reality' – the first by simply representing the external by way of producing recorded pictures, and the second by creating a folding of the absent into the present through the dissemination of this material gathered from beyond the network, but located and defined only by the technical capability of the hub within the network. This reading of the hub thus resists the usual alternation between the technological and the social, the internal and the external, the absent and the present. The hub integrates these polarities into an assemblage of the social and the technical, wholly unified only at the specific position that they are located within the network at that exact time. Actor Network Theory thus begins to permit us to redefine the news process, and to dismantle hitherto fixed epistemological positions.

> The main difficulty of integrating technology into social theory is the lack of a narrative resource. We know how to describe human relations, we know how to describe mechanisms, we often try to alternate between context and content to talk about the influence of technology on society or vice-versa, but we are not yet expert at weaving together the two resources into an integrated whole.
>
> (Latour, 1991, p.130)

The weaving together of an object's social, technical and temporal context in order to define its network configuration, and the eradication of established definitions of inside and outside, absent and present, will be developed more fully in the following chapter. By exploring the status of the media hub as a black box, we have only just begun to describe the news network, to map out the complex configuration of actors, the positions that they occupy, and the social and technical contexts that make these positions stable or unstable. We are beginning to explain the process of news, intricately bound at the level of practice with both human and nonhuman actors, and the relationships they forge with one another. And in this meticulous and detailed description we can begin to offer alternative explanations concerning the content of news.

But at this early stage, we need to ask whether description, even at the most detailed level of practice, can possibly open the door to explanation. Surely we should accept that the research process by which this empirical evidence is gathered must then be extrapolated upon before we can make any meaningful conclusions? Doesn't the data simply *represent* or *indicate* a number of grander epistemological positions?

In answering these questions, we need to return to Latour, so that we can recognise how this artificial but widely accepted distinction between description and explanation, once again threatens to limit our understanding of how inter-woven is the news product with the mechanics of news practice, and how a description of that process can and does provide a more than adequate under-standing of the product.

> The description of socio-technical networks is often opposed to their explanation, which is supposed to come afterwards. Critics of the sociol-ogy of science and technology often suggest that even the most meticulous description of a case study would not suffice to give an explanation of its development. This kind of criticism borrows from epistemology the difference between the empirical and the theoretical, between 'how' and 'why', between stamp collecting – a contemptible occupation – and the search for causality – the only activity worthy of attention . . . Yet nothing proves that this kind of distinction is necessary. If we dis-play a socio-technical network – defining trajectories by actants' asso-ciations and substitution, defining actants by all the trajectories in which they enter, by following translations, and finally, by varying the observers point of view – we have no need to look for additional causes. The explanation emerges once the description is saturated.
>
> (Latour, 1991, p.129)

And so our descriptive process will continue, and as it does, the news process will slowly reveal itself as integrally defined through actors' associations, and their continuous attempts to translate both themselves and the network within which they are located. Our technologies will begin to speak out for themselves by our own ability to map their positions using the three axes outlined in this chapter, and by doing so deepening our understanding of technologies' relations with other nonhuman as well as human actors.

In the following three chapters the embedding of a new technology, PDP, represents a significant challenge to the existing network, and demonstrates the disruptive effects of radical *translation*, our next key ANT concept. It will also reveal how black box status can be successfully challenged and may even be lost altogether. We will see how the translation of the network at various different locations has a direct effect upon the configuration of existing actor positions, and more significantly, results in a reconfiguration of the news process, the associated news agenda and thus the content of the final news product.

4

VIDEO JOURNALISM (1)

How a technological innovation enters the news network

> To understand the path taken by an innovation, we must evaluate the resistance put up by the successive actors that it mobilises or rejects. Explanation does not follow from description; it is description taken much further.
>
> (Latour, 1991, p.121)

The following three chapters will explore the introduction and development of a particular technology, known as *Personal Digital Production* (PDP).[1] We will discover how PDP begins its life as the technological innovation of a single individual but that as soon as it is introduced into the regional television newsroom, it not only radically alters the news environment, but is also altered in the same process. This alteration is referred to in Actor Network Theory (ANT) terms as network *translation*.

The introduction of PDP into the BBC news network signalled the first stage of what has now become a more widespread use of video journalists throughout the BBC, which in turn has led to the development of new ideas of how to film and deliver news. This has culminated in the BBC's most recent pilot project in the West Midlands of providing a local television news service for the same types of audiences that currently listen to the BBC's local radio stations. We will focus on the central role that digital technologies play within this new service in Chapter 6.

Before we begin our own exploration of PDP, it is important to mention other significant studies that have been conducted into previous developments of digital news technologies and video journalism in the UK. One of the most interesting is Cottle and Ashton's own investigation of the BBC's early adoption of new technologies towards the end of the 1990s (Cottle & Ashton, 1999). Based in the BBC regional news centre in Bristol, their empirical study explores how journalists' routines and methods of working are altered by the introduction of the most recent digital technologies including the Electronic News Production

System (ENPS), which at the time of their research was to be deployed across all BBC news centres, as well as the early development of video journalism, which involved an increased multiskilling of BBC journalists. This is an important study that rightly suggests that the role of technology within news production has generally received relatively little theoretical attention. Cottle and Ashton argue that

> We need to engage in theoretically informed, detailed empirical studies
> of particular news operations if we are to begin to improve our under-
> standing of the complex interactions between changing news technologies
> and journalist practices, and their impact on news output.
>
> (Cottle & Ashton, 1999, p.26)

Cottle and Ashton's research reveals that BBC management initially identified the new technologies as both a leading force of change, as well as the means by which the corporation could seek to compete for the market share.

> The broadcasting industry in the UK is being transformed at an unpre-
> cedented pace. Digital technology will revolutionise the way television
> and radio programmes are made, transmitted and scheduled.
>
> (BBC Broadcasting House, 1996)

Cottle and Ashton show how at the specifically regional level, the BBC also promoted new technologies to both its own workforce and to the wider public as a means by which financial savings could be made, and radically different ways of programme making could be entertained.

> We have to use the opportunities offered by digital technology to
> redesign fundamentally the way we work in our programme making, to
> eradicate unnecessary administration from our business processes and
> to create and encourage opportunities for our staff to explore radical
> new directions in programme making.
>
> (BBC Regional Broadcasting, 1996)

Yet, Cottle and Ashton quickly discover that such radical promise heralded by the BBC in the adoption of these new technologies is not in fact borne out in the context of their own case study of multimedia news production. They suggest that this is perhaps not surprising given the somewhat contradictory aims that were embedded within the BBC's initial objectives, as well as its failure to account for the increased pressures of work relating to multiskilled and multimedia news production (Cottle & Ashton, 1999, p.38).

Cottle and Ashton argue that the adoption of these particular technologies is both socially and culturally determined. They identify a number of quite different factors including the commanding role of the BBC's senior corporate and editorial personnel, their interpretation of what the BBC as an institution should be, the place of news operations within that institutional framework, and the constraints and opportunities for change given existing arrangements and technologies of news production (Ursall, 2001). They are thus keen to move away from ideas about technological determinism and to locate the driving force of change elsewhere. The authors stress that new technologies involved in BBC production, though certainly facilitating multiskilled, bi-media and multimedia working practices, do not necessarily determine how these are actually conducted on the ground, nor the pressures experienced by the professional involved (Cottle & Ashton, 1999).

This is a significant realisation that will be further developed during our own analysis of the implementation of PDP. Although Cottle and Ashton do not use an ANT approach to inform their research, they conclude that the way in which the new technologies are adopted and used, and how they in turn may signal changes in both news practice and news content, is far from predictable, and must be carefully mapped on a number of interconnecting levels in different locations. Furthermore, they also recognise that existing working conditions into which the new technologies are introduced, also help to culturally shape the deployment of these technologies. It is this complicated process of identifying where change occurs, and the subsequent analysis of these locations of change that an ANT approach will assist us with once we begin to analyse how the new technology, PDP, developed within the BBC newsroom in Nottingham.

The translation process

To begin the story of PDP we need to understand what is meant by the ANT concept of *translation*. In the previous chapter we saw how certain actors such as the media hub, are able to achieve what is defined as black box status by the successful alignment and stabilisation of other actors. By mapping the media hub's network position using the three axes – the sociogram, technogram and chronogram – we were able to show how it managed to retain its status, even though these positions were forever being defined and redefined by different constellations of actors with whom it came into contact. Far from remaining constant, the resistances offered by other human and nonhuman actors were seen to continually test the durability of the hub's network position, illustrating that its black box status is not continuously guaranteed. In a contingent network such as the news network, black boxes that are closed may also be reopened if previous alliances forged with other actors are broken apart. The volatility of the network is ultimately characterised by such realignments, or translations. The concept of actor translation is central to any ANT description. As Latour states

> A good ANT account is a narrative or a description or a proposition where all the actors do something and don't just sit there. Instead of simply transporting effects without transforming them, each of the points in the text may become a bifurcation, an event, or the origin of a new translation. As soon as actors are treated not as intermediaries but as mediators, they render the movement of the social visible to the reader.
>
> (Latour, 2005, p.128)

Translation therefore describes any action in which *both* the actors involved are altered.

> Translation does not mean a shift from one vocabulary to another, from one French word to an English word, for instance, as if the two languages existed independently. I use translation to mean displacement, drift, invention, mediation, the creation of a link that did not exist before and that to some degree modifies the original two.
>
> (Latour, 1999, p.179)

The linguistic frustration, evident in this quote from the list of seemingly unsatisfactory synonyms is crucial to the notion of translation as active or performative. Almost as if Latour is unable to grasp the dynamism of the translation process tightly enough to fix it on the page, the description fails to hold, words seem to deaden it and the narrative cannot accommodate it. It is important to realise that the concept of translation is not peculiar to ANT, but appears earlier in the work of the French philosopher, Michel Serres, and it is to his definition that we might also turn to recognise this crucial performative aspect. In his description of Turner's watercolour, *The Iron Foundry*, Serres dramatises an obliteration of semiotic parameters.

> There is no longer any representation in Turner's foundry. The painting is a furnace, the very furnace itself. It is a disordered black mass centred on the lighted hearths. We pass from geometry to matter or from representation to work ... No more discourses, no more scenes, no more sculptures with clean, cold edges: the object directly. Without theoretical detours. Yes, we enter into incandescence. At random.
>
> (Serres, 1982, p.62)

The painting not only depicts the furnace, but also performs it. Although the translation process involves a semiotic representation of the furnace by the composition of the paint on the canvas in order to create the painting, it also explodes the parameters of that representation so as to become another matter altogether. Two simultaneous processes are occurring. One translation involves the semiotic reorganising of significations, interests and concerns. The other translation is the displacement of the object directly, no representation, no theory (Brown & Capdevila, 1999).

In the previous chapter, the description of the media hub's translation of the network and its attainment of black box status was seen to occur at the specific level of practice; that is how actors carry out the processes of news work thus affording to the hub its strong position, forged along sociogrammatic, chronogrammatic and technogrammatic axes. In this chapter, the introduction and embedding of PDP within the network will highlight how network translations don't just occur at the level of practice, but that such translations of practice themselves also translate eventual news products which means they effect the news content of those products, illustrating how actor translations of the news-production network occur simultaneously at the level of practice and product, and can no longer be convincingly ring-fenced off from one another. This will become clearer once we begin our analysis of PDP.

As Latour explains, a thing can remain more durable and be transported farther and more quickly if it continues to undergo transformations at each stage of this long cascade (Latour, 1999, p.58). The 'long cascade' to which Latour refers certainly stretches well beyond our own particular viewpoint within the newsroom, to less proximate network points, which may be unidentifiable. To attempt to define a network boundary it is often necessary to follow an actor back, to identify where it first became significant to that network, and thus to chart the translation process it has made up to that point. By examining the introduction of PDP within the Nottingham newsroom, to ascertain from where it originated, and to follow the translation process it has undergone, as well as to illustrate the separate but at times simultaneous translation of the news-production network, its boundaries and what we will refer to as its *mediators* and *intermediaries* will need to be clearly identified.

So what do we mean by these? To help understand the crucial difference that Latour makes between mediators and intermediaries we need to look at his most recent publication, *Reassembling the Social,* where Latour uses the terms to make a crucial distinction between what he considers to be the two types of social scientist, or researcher. For Latour, 'sociologists of the social' who do not explore what he considers to be the more dangerous terrain of network association, and the fluidity of both human and nonhuman actors, espouse a very different view of the world than do those who choose the rockier but more rewarding landscape of ANT. The safer world that the first group of analysts inhabit is critically defined by the distinction between these two terms.

> It is this infinitesimal distinction between mediators and intermediaries that will produce, in the end, all the differences we need between the two types of sociologies. To sum up the contrast in a rudimentary way, the sociologists of the social believe in one type of aggregates, few mediators and many intermediaries; for ANT, there is no preferable type of social aggregates, there exist endless numbers of mediators, and when those are transformed into faithful intermediaries it is not the rule, but a rare exception that has to be accounted for by some extra work, usually the mobilisation of even more mediators!
>
> (Latour, 2005, p.40)

Latour is arguing that ANT performs the controversies of a network by accepting that all actors within it occupy changing positions, hence the need to reject stabilised social aggregates thus allowing for the chance to interpret the world. The sociologist of the social, on the other hand, seeks to transform the world by establishing a priori positions that humans and objects occupy in stable and unchanging configurations.

The debate makes more sense if we substitute ANT's term black box for intermediary, and actor for mediator. Actor Network Theory argues for the jettisoning of an exploration of the social that requires most objects of its study to be defined as black boxes, already inscribed in the sociologist's notepad, and argues instead for a much more rigorous pursuit of actor translation, drama- tised by the rough and tumble of associated mediators all jostling for position, forging alliances, breaking open black boxes, perhaps even creating new ones, translating their own positions or being translated by other mediators in the process.

It will become evident from our own exploration of PDP within the news network, how an ANT approach exposes such contradictions and controversies that could not be as easily identified by a methodology that demanded the accep- tance of stable actor positions, or that wished for a preponderance of inter- mediaries rather than mediators. Most significantly, we shall see how the initial innovators of PDP, who will be identified as the story develops, seek to alter radically the process of news work by enhancing both the autonomy and the single authorship of news production that PDP affords.[2] Yet an exploration of the translation of the production process once PDP is introduced into the news network, and the subsequent shift this engenders in the perceived news agenda and in the news product, will provide a more detailed understanding of the complex interaction between changing news technologies, journalist practices and basic definitions of what constitutes news. What is even more significant for a developed understanding of television news production is that without the recognition of such an unsettled network whose translations render it continually fluid and unstable, the content of the news product, itself an actor or mediator in this process of translation, can also not be fully interpreted.

The story of Personal Digital Production

Previous studies of the adoption of new technologies in television newsrooms, such as the interesting comparative analysis of Spanish and UK digitised newsrooms by Avilles *et al.*, found that the technologies were more or less being adapted to existing newsroom structures (Avilles *et al.*, 2004). In contrast, the BBC's implementation of PDP demonstrated that there are quite significant changes to the news environment and structure, but just as Cottle discovered, these are not necessarily predictable nor can they be assumed. We will show that it is only by exploring the performative aspect of the translation process outlined earlier that adequate conclusions regarding the instability and fluidity of both the new technology and the network can be revealed.

This particular story of actor translation begins in 2001 at a conference in Amsterdam where the former CBS news producer, Michael Rosenblum, first introduces PDP to a group of BBC executives and managers of the regional directorate. Rosenblum carried out a demonstration of a small digital Sony PD150 camera and laptop editing kit to Fiona Macbeth, the then strategic development coordinator for BBC Nations and Regions (Hemmingway, 2005). He was subsequently contracted to conduct a BBC pilot project. Fifty-five BBC journalists, technicians and camera people were recruited. They spent three weeks together in a hotel learning to alter their existing perceptions of television production and to adopt what Rosenblum refers to as the 'new ethos of shooting and editing material' (Rosenblum, 2004).[3]

Michael Rosenblum is certainly the innovator of the PDP experiment, but if we adopt the first principle of translation, that the fate of a statement depends upon others' behaviour (Latour, 1987), Rosenblum must immediately enrol a number of other actors within the network for his experiment to be successful and his innovation to be accepted.

> We need others to transform a claim into a matter of fact. The first and easiest way to find people who will immediately believe the statement, invest in the project, or buy the prototype, is to tailor the object in such a way that it caters to these people's explicit interests.
>
> (Latour, 1987, p.108)

Rosenblum does just this. He managed to persuade the BBC management that PDP would enable the corporation to produce better television at a cheaper price and after a series of management consultations, audience focus groups and feedback from other news stations in Europe who had already adopted a form of PDP, Rosenblum was awarded a three-year contract to train 6,000 BBC employees from the BBC's regional directorate.

The Rosenblum ethos

In this particular story of network translation, it is critical to delineate points within the network where the specific actor, which in this case is PDP, can be observed in each of its different manifestations. The first point is located in another country, and also in another time frame. For the story could be said to have started back in 1988 in a Palestinian refugee camp in the Gaza Strip as it was here that Rosenblum first began to use his small digital PD150 camera to film the events of the Palestinian Intifada. He argues that it was only by living close to the heart of his story, and by observing the people he was filming over a long period of time, that he began to change the way he filmed and produced the news.

> If you live with someone for a month with a video camera, and shoot all the time, you know what you get? Intimacy. A real sense of inti-macy. You really start to get inside a story. Because now, instead of 'making TV' you are just there, observing and living an experience. And you start to use the camera in a very different way. Instead of making a movie about what a reporter does for a living, you start to record what it is that is actually happening. And instead of shooting a street saying 'here, only hours ago . . . ' you can actually be there when it happens.
>
> (Rosenblum, 2002, p.42)

The story then moves back to the UK and the next significant location we need to identify is located 200 miles north of the Nottingham newsroom in the BBC's PDP Training Centre in Newcastle-Upon-Tyne. It is here that Rosen-blum, having acquired his BBC contract, is allowed the freedom to persuade the recruited trainees, all of whom are BBC employees, to adopt this particular version of PDP working practice that he has developed during his time out in the Middle East. Rosenblum is not only the sole progenitor of the PDP model he also quickly becomes the promoter, distributor and trainer of the entire BBC PDP experiment.

It is worth pausing here to draw what may at first seem like a curious parallel between Rosenblum and the scientist Louis Pasteur, whose work Latour explores in *The Pasteurisation of France* (Latour, 1988a). This large-scale analysis of Pasteur, which Latour describes as a set of strategies, arrangements and mobilisations of different actors into a more or less coherent and more or less fragile network, of which Pasteur the person is only a spokesperson or an effect, known as the 'phenomenon' Pasteur, rather than the prime mover or individual genius, provides a prophetic parallel to how Rosenblum the individual comes to be represented by the news network during the PDP implementation process. As Latour argues

> An idea, even an idea of genius, even an idea that is to save millions of people, never moves on its own accord. It requires a force to fetch it, seize upon it for its own motives, move it and often transform it.
>
> (Latour, 1988a, p.16)

And so it is with PDP and with Rosenblum, who are both quickly translated by the network into which they become entangled. But this is jumping ahead. Let's first of all return to the second location of our story and watch how the translation process begins to take shape. The PDP Training Centre provides three-week intensive training courses in digital filming and editing. Yet the training provided is far more than a technical skills course. For both Rosenblum and for his PDP training team, the experience is regarded as nothing short of the beginning of the BBC's own technological revolution (Hemmingway, 2005). The messianic Rosenblum proclaims on the first day of the course

> I want you to forget everything you know, or think you know about television. I am going to liberate you. TV news has not been invented yet.
>
> (Rosenblum, 2004)

The close association of a technological innovation with the freedom to move outside existing working practices that may be repeatedly described in pejorative terms is a deliberate tactic of the successful innovator. As Akrich recognises in her own ANT analyses

> A large part of the work of innovators is that of 'inscribing' the vision of (or prediction about) the world in the technical content of the new object.
>
> (Akrich, 1992, p.220)

The introductory training sessions are thus dominated by a critique of traditional production practices emphasising how the new technology can assist in their elimination. A direct causal link is quickly established between technological implementation and a reconfiguration of news processes and news content (Hemmingway, 2005). Inscribing within the technology the ability to represent the world with more authenticity, Rosenblum argues that the eradication of established practices will lead to an enhanced vision of news both as a process and as a product.[4]

> This technology could be taken into a newsroom and made to replicate exactly what you did before but it's a waste of potential. These cameras and these edits give you the potential to re-define what television journalism really is. We will be able to introduce a sense of authorship into TV journalism. And that is something that never existed before.
>
> (Rosenblum, 2004)

The theoretical paradigm that Rosenblum deliberately constructs places technology and the unrealised potential of technology at the very centre of news production, and the single author as the empowered user of that technology (Hemmingway, 2005). News that is traditionally produced by a team of actors, each with core craft skills to contribute to the final product, is replaced by the notion of *single-authored* news production. The actor may be a journalist, a camera operator, a station assistant, a director or a VT editor. This systematic eradication of multi-authored news production, and the destruction of demarcated roles within the process, is crucially and deliberately linked to the development of the new technology.

> The technology sets the grounding and then people respond appropriately. The architecture of any industry is a function of the technology that makes it ... This is a very different way of not just going out with a camera and shooting something, but of organising an entire newsgathering operation. We are shifting the entire architecture of television.
>
> (Rosenblum, 2004)

This highly techno-deterministic philosophy of PDP production continually links technological development with the inevitable reconfiguration of filming practices. Each newsroom is to be equipped with 50 digital cameras and 30 laptop editing stations that will seek to eventually replace the traditional 5 camera crews and 4 videotape editors.[5] It is important to note that even at this stage of the translation process, Rosenblum considers his agenda to be significantly different from what *he* considers to be the BBC management agenda, although BBC management has never communicated to BBC staff its own aims regarding the introduction of PDP. Yet in interviews and training sessions Rosenblum continues to distance himself from the perceived corporate aims of cost cutting and staff reduction, that Cottle and Ursall both discovered in their research, using almost evangelical overtones to dramatise his role as the liberating prophet who has glimpsed the future of news production.

> I am not interested in cutting costs for the BBC. That's very cute but I'm not interested. I'm interested in creating a new grammar for television. This hasn't been invented yet. I can only do that by empowering thousands of people and unleashing them and I have to maintain their purity.
>
> (Rosenblum, 2004)

Fundamental to Rosenblum's philosophy is his reconceptualisation of news production and of time. As we discovered in the analysis of the media hub, perceptions of time are seen to vary considerably from one actor to another and from one network point to another. Throughout the specific translation process of PDP, notions of time are represented and conceptualised as they are constructed locally within the network, rather than existing as a fixed determinant surrounding the network from some other external location. As with in the previous chapter, actors are constituted as much by their specific temporal location, what we refer to as their chronogram, as they are by their sociogram and their technogram. And just as these alter depending on specific network locations, and are subject to change if actors become realigned, so it is with the chronogram. Networks are thus determined by the inextricable meshing together of the technogram, sociogram and the chronogram, and only by the mapping of actors along all three axes can network translation be performed. This becomes more significant as the story of PDP translation develops.

Establishing PDP's first chronogram, Rosenblum continually emphasises how PDP practice enables journalists to escape the limitations that time pressures pose when producing daily news. Rather than the relentless scramble to film and edit material on the day for the evening news programme, PDP's chronogram is perceived by Rosenblum to be altogether more forgiving, allowing up to two or three days to research, gather and film material, and up to two days to edit. Using conventional methods, a staff camera crew would take around one to two hours to film material, which would then be edited by a staff VT editor in less than two hours. Rosenblum argues that the PDP operation is more efficient for, while it may take up to three days to complete, it only involves one person. Rosenblum also forges a direct correlation between the liberating increase in the production time and the quality and content of finished news pieces.

> The limitations that you get in the field are not a function of the limitation of the imagination. The limitations that you get in the field are a function of the limitations of access to equipment and time.
>
> (Rosenblum, 2004)

Rosenblum's chronogrammatic pinioning of PDP will be worth recalling once it enters the news network and becomes located by other, separate chronograms all of which conflict with Rosenblum's initial vision. At this early stage, though, the lack of dependence on teamwork, liberation from time constraints or from limited access to equipment as well as the eradication of demarcated roles within the newsroom are all considered by Rosenblum to be essential for the embedding of PDP within the network, the reconfiguration of the production process and simultaneously the final news product. For Rosenblum the mutuality of these configurations is essential for the successful implementation of PDP. The process must be reworked in its entirety for the PDP single author to successfully transform news content (Hemmingway, 2005).

Thus Rosenblum, in not taking into account the network within which PDP will become embedded, makes a double mistake. In the first instance he wholeheartedly believes in the success of his own image as a cult figure of authority and genius demonstrated by successive references he makes to his trainees 'dressing up like him', or to his ability to 'liberate BBC staff' and to 'teach BBC management how to produce decent television' (Rosenblum, 2004). His second mistake is his belief in straightforward technological determinism. He does not realise the implications of embedding a new technology into an intricate, strongly forged, complex network with varied chronogrammatic positions, and numerous and ongoing actor translations that occur as a result of these shifting axes. Rosenblum does not realise that both PDP and also himself as innovator will be translated by the network.

Observing the three-week training course and the subsequent working practices in the Nottingham newsroom we can see how translation certainly takes place, but that, as Latour argues, there is always a trade-off between enrolling others in the process of developing an innovation, and acknowledging that this enrolment carries with it an element of risk.

> The paradox of the fact-builders is that they have simultaneously to increase the number of people taking part in the action so that the claim spreads, and to decrease the number of people taking part in the action, so that the claim spreads as it is.
>
> (Latour, 1987, p.207)

At this point we need to introduce another ANT term associated with the translation process: the *immutable mobile*, a particular concept that refers to certain actors that are able to stabilise or to help other actors achieve translation. The translation process involves making connections between sometimes very disparate actors, and of making sense of these connections. Certain devices can assist in this process. The immutable mobile can be thought of as a 'mobile actor', one that cannot be silenced or transformed, but that is able to perform all the silencing and the transforming itself. In Latour's writings, immutable mobiles often appear as statistics, questionnaires or charts, inscription devices that can be passed from one place to another within the network, and that transform it, without themselves being modified at all. To return to our PDP story, Rosenblum mistakenly perceives *it* to be an immutable mobile, adopting grandiose metaphors to explain PDP's overarching power to transform the production of television, once transferred from the training centre to the newsroom. At other times he describes it as an omnipotent invader or unstoppable virus that will contaminate every newsroom it enters.

> You know I compare it a little bit to Hong Kong which will ultimately eat up China. That's what this [PDP] is. This is a much more aggressive, dynamic, and creative system and people like it, and inevitably it will eat up the rest of it, it has to. .... .
>
> (Rosenblum, 2004)

Rosenblum's inability to recognise how PDP will be transformed as it is transferred is also compounded at every stage by his adherence to an ideology of technological determinism. Unlike the more complex social and cultural embedding of new technologies that Cottle recognised, Rosenblum believes that PDP will simply revolutionise television, not because people will adapt the technology to their own advantage, but rather the technology will force change upon people.

> The technology will militate for a new architecture. Inherent in the architecture is a grammar and that is unavoidable as the technology driving the architecture. Once the architecture shifts it brings with it a new grammar, there'll be more pieces, the pieces will run longer, you'll have more time to do things. All these things are going to happen and that's the grammar. Shift the architecture you shift the grammar. You cannot shift the grammar without shifting the baseline technology.
>
> (Rosenblum, 2004)

The Personal Digital Production training course

S: Isn't television a team game?

H: I get my best ideas by bouncing off other people. What do you think of this?

S: Exactly. We work as a team. Peter deals with everything editorial and Larry, the shoot-edit, deals with everything technical and we're a great team.

> (BBC trainees on the PDP training course)

By observing the PDP training course and talking to the 18 BBC employees attending it, we can soon detect initial concerns with PDP working practices, which focused mainly on the substitution of single-authored production for team working. The trainees were all selected from different BBC regional newsrooms where digitisation is being sporadically and inconsistently introduced. As Avilles *et al.* (2004) also discovered, sections of the BBC are not yet fully digitised and competing digital systems cause problems for cooperation between regions. The different experiences of these working practices prior to the exposure to PDP made for rather varied reactions, but the reluctance to adopt particular tenets of Rosenblum's agenda is consistently evident particularly during the first week of the course (Hemmingway, 2005).

Most of the trainees were keen to learn new skills, and the journalists in particular warmed to the idea of filming their own material. Yet the ethos of single-authored work, and the eradication of the production network with its demarcated roles, wasn't popular as most said they gained professional confidence and 'came up with better ideas' when they worked in a team. Technical staff and camera operators admitted they would be reluctant to make journalistic decisions about news without support from other journalist colleagues. A new output editor from BBC Newcastle, who was attending the first few days of the training course, expressed concerns that PDP practice meant that story ideas were commissioned without being discussed by a news team. With regard to the content of the news pieces, the trainees also felt that certain conventional filming styles, which were criticised by the PDP trainers, were an inescapable part of television life.

> We used 33 PDP pieces last month. We should use about three a week. I don't think Rosenblum's world is as realistic as he thinks it is. It's far too black and white. In his world no-one would ever do a piece to camera or stand outside a building or do an exterior shot.
>
> (Mark, news output editor, BBC Newcastle)

We can soon see that there was a correlation being drawn here between PDP filming techniques and story ideas, and more general definitions of news, which preoccupied the trainees. Although there were the separate fears that PDP may represent 'newsgathering on the cheap', as Cottle, Ursall and Avilles *et al.* all noted in their own studies, the more fundamental concern here was with Rosenblum's insistence on the reconfiguration of the news agenda, with the eradication of teamwork and the adoption of single-authored working practices. These two concerns were always discussed in direct relation to one another, illustrating recognition by all the trainees of a direct correlation between news values, production processes and the quality of the final news product. Yet towards the end of the three-week course some trainees' earlier scepticism was replaced by a willingness to embrace what they viewed as the benefits of single-authored news production, namely to learn new skills that had not been necessary in their existing newsroom roles, and that in some cases had been considered the exclusive professional domain of other members of staff.

> Being able to film my own material and getting to grips with the editing process has been a really exciting challenge.
>
> (Debby, trainee, BBC Norwich)

The PDP trainers also echoed this shift in trainees' acceptance of PDP working practices, a shift which they said occurred on every training course.

> There's a certain amount of scepticism from people when they first come on the course because they see it as cheap television. Wobbly shots, badly framed, there's a quality thing. They say you can't do it better than having a separate journalist, craft cameraman and craft editor. But I think, without exception, all are converted by the end of the course.
>
> (Paul, PDP trainer, BBC Newcastle)

On completion of the course the trainees return to their own regional news centres where they're encouraged to promote the idea of PDP to their own output producers and managers. What is interesting here is that we can see that in contrast to Rosenblum's somewhat trenchant philosophy that PDP will be adopted by individual news networks, remaining immutable to translation during the embedding process, BBC management had actually devised no consistent implementation strategy, and the trainees were left to develop PDP working practices as best they could to suit themselves and their individual newsrooms. One PDP training manager told trainees at their first session

> One of the things that we're hoping is to persuade as many managers as possible to start with a blank sheet and really restructure their newsrooms to take account of the opportunities that PDP has to offer.
>
> (Lisa, PDP manager, BBC Training Centre)

A number of the PDP trainers actually criticised what they perceived as a failure of BBC management to define a general policy for PDP implementation since the time that Rosenblum secured the contract in 2002. But what is perhaps more significant to our understanding of the translation process of this new technology is that, even within the artificially protected enclave of the Newcastle

Training Centre, PDP has already been translated. The actual use of PDP as a technology is far from consistent from one trainee to the next. Journalists grapple with most if not all of the filming and editing technicalities, picture editors use the laptop editing equipment with aplomb, but approach the actual filming process rather more tentatively than do their camera operator colleagues, whose technical skills flourish, but who struggle to find what is considered to be a news story. We can also find evidence of a number of varied and contrasting agendas among both trainees and also PDP trainers, and several different predictions as to how PDP will be implemented. Regional BBC managers, who believe that PDP practice should be defined by the staff of individual newsrooms, clearly do not share Rosenblum's more technologically determinist and thus holistic agenda. We now need to take a closer look at the implementation of PDP in the Nottingham newsroom so that we can understand more fully the complex translation process as PDP is transferred from one location, the training centre, to the next location, the newsroom.

The introduction of Personal Digital Production to the Nottingham Newsroom

> When artefacts come into contact with their users, they are carried on a wave of texts which bear testimony to the scars of their textualisations that accompanied their design and their displacement.
>
> (Akrich, 1989a)

To follow the translation story from the training centre to the newsroom, we need to try to establish the boundaries of our specific actor network. An actor-network topology is usually described in somewhat vague terms as logically grouped entities or elements associated and linked to each other via some form of relations. Charting the translation process of PDP it is thus imperative not only that the analysis of the network includes the two geographically separate locations of the training centre and the newsroom, but that we discover how relations between the two are constituted by actors within both. The concept of the immutable mobile, a device that facilitates translation without itself being transformed, has already been mentioned, but in this particular translation process immutable mobiles are quite difficult to discern. As this is the case, what other elements could we identify that would hold the two disparate but connecting parts of the network together, in order to facilitate the translation process?

Departing radically from Rosenblum's own technological determined prophecy, the most obvious connecting entity is the human actor itself. Having been subjected to a process of rather extreme de-differentiation,[6] stripped of their previous newsroom roles and individually defined operational responsibilities, the trainees return to the newsroom as a seemingly homogeneous group. No longer a journalist, or a videotape editor, or a camera operator, their translation process is constituted by the eradication of individual skills status, the adoption of an autonomous role in producing news, and having adopted a radically altered chronogrammatic axis along which to gather and report news. We therefore need to map their translation as they move from one part of the network, the training centre that has been deliberately designed to allow expression of these new responsibilities, to the newsroom, which is as yet unaffected by the PDP experiment or the 'new' actors trained to implement it.

The 'wave of texts' to which Akrich refers in this section's opening quote is constructed in this instance by Rosenblum as the innovator, and the trainees who have already begun to be folded into the new technology during the three-week training course. These actors' translation processes will continue alongside that of the technology itself, and we need to analyse both in order to faithfully convey the story of PDP translation.

In their earlier research of the BBC's Bristol newsroom, Cottle and Ashton discovered that with the development of new technologies, journalists were expected to be able to utilise a number of different skills, perform a number of separate tasks, and jobs were redesignated in line with the shift from single-media to bi-media, to multimedia production. A broadcast journalist might be expected to produce and present the early-morning bulletins, construct a report for the lunchtime bulletin from their desktop using ENPS and library footage, and produce regional subtitles for television news output. They may also act as a bi-media producer, constructing radio packages from transmitted TV material, and producing the regional news Ceefax pages. Technological development thus necessitated multiskilling, and as Cottle and Ashton discovered.

> The frustration of being professionally spread too thin, can also turn
> into a sense of resentment when expected to perform tasks that are felt
> to fall outside the remit of any aspiring journalist.
>
> (Cottle & Ashton, 1999, p.34)

It was against a similar background of professional redeployment, the move away from individual specialisation towards highly routinised, multiskilled, multimedia news production, that PDP was first introduced into the BBC digital newsroom. As we discovered in the previous chapter, the BBC newsroom in Nottingham, just like its counterpart in Bristol, had already implemented ENPS and its own digital news-production system incorporating the media hub, and Omnibus and Columbus. BBC Nottingham had also experienced a radical restructuring of journalists' roles in order to facilitate multimedia broadcasting, which included journalists having to perform what they perceived as more mundane tasks such as writing text for Ceefax and subtitling, as well as producing packages for both radio and television on a daily basis. This had created the same low morale among many journalists that Cottle and Ashton also discovered.

It is important to emphasise that the technological development of PDP within the newsroom was therefore fundamentally dependent upon utilisation within a complex production network. Previous multimedia developments and working practices outlined above, far from weakening the structure of the production network, had enhanced its significance. Multimedia working practices depend for their success on networks to facilitate mass dissemination of material. Personal Digital Production, whose operations are emphasised as being single-authored and autonomous, is thus rendered immediately problematic by the existence of the media hub and the operational network. As we saw in the previous chapter, the complexity of the hub with its ability to attain and retain its stable black box status, acts as an extremely powerful obligatory point of passage for all other actors, including the single-authored autonomy of PDP. So PDP's autonomy upheld so confidently by Rosenblum, is thrown into rather shaky relief by the complex and ever-changing sociogrammatic, technogrammatic and chronogrammatic axes along which the production network and all its actors already operate.

As we discussed in Chapter 3, the media hub is both a powerful central facilitator of news dissemination but also a technological gatekeeper. As equal an actor as any other in the production network, PDP is thus still unable to produce and disseminate its material autonomously. Even if PDP newsgathering, filming and package production can in theory be achieved autonomously, without recourse to other actors such as camera operators, the camera diary assistant and the VT editor, the PDP material must still be fed through the media hub to enable transmission. The hub's disproportionate number of associations, literally displayed in the constellation of its numerous screens and buttons, resists a retranslation by PDP. This black box remains intact and what we witness is a translation in PDP once it has entered the network. This digital matrix that is the hub is a highly significant actor in the production network and as we have already seen its black box status has thus far remained unchallenged by any other actor, whether they are a hub operator, a journalist or an output producer responsible for overarching editorial decisions regarding news content.

From the initial stages of PDP implementation, its single-authored operational capacity begins to seem rather more suspect once introduced to our complicated and interlinked network of humans and technologies. Furthermore, all the human and nonhuman actors within that network, while sporadically attempting to challenge certain network positions, demonstrate a general acceptance of it. They all obey the code. Black boxes remain closed. In fact, the restructuring process of the BBC news centre at Nottingham, undertaken to accommodate PDP working practice, was based entirely on this assumption that staff were equal participants in a team-working exercise, and that the team was defined by the configuration of the network as this training manager makes clear.

> The signal that it sent out to staff was, 'You're one great team. We're not separating out production and technical staff. We're all one big team. We all watch TV and all our opinions are valid as to what makes great television because that's the only qualification you need.'
>
> (Lisa, PDP training manager, BBC Nottingham)

And what becomes even more surprising is that the journalists in Nottingham welcomed the idea that an individual could use a small digital camera for the purpose of gathering and broadcasting news, not because it necessarily offered autonomy from the network, but because it signalled the eradication of previous professional practices, in particular the development of bi-media. These bi-media and then multimedia roles had been greatly and perhaps unrealistically expanded during the growth of digital production and were extremely unpopular with many members of staff (Cottle & Ashton, 1999). The same frustrations were evident in Nottingham.

> Technology has pushed the boundaries and it's constantly spreading people thinner; it's squeezing people's time. They've combined three roles for me now. I direct, play-out and vision-mix the programme, which is a challenge, but I am not sure it's the best way to make programmes.
>
> (Mark, director, BBC Nottingham)

This shows us that to roughly determine the boundaries of any network for the purposes of exploring a translation process, it is imperative that the traces of past translations also be taken into the account. In this case, had it not been for the outcome of the bi-media experiment, that was so unpopular with staff in Nottingham, the story of PDP implementation might have been very different indeed (Van-Loon & Hemmingway, 2005). The implementation of PDP is shaped by these past actor translations, now no longer evident, but whose traces remain enfolded within those actors now present and whose negotiations in the past have significant bearing on the negotiations of those actors now and in the future. Personal Digital Production's very first translation of the network occurred in the eradication of these bi-media working practices, which had been in place since the end of the 1990s, but had never been popular with journalists who found themselves working to tighter deadlines, having to satisfy more than one outlet and often involved in what they considered to be rather menial roles such as subtitling or writing Ceefax pages.

But the eradication of these past bi-media and multimedia roles was not predicated upon the embrace of the single actor as Rosenblum envisaged. Rather it relied much more upon the more traditional corporate philosophy of team working, directly conflicting with the philosophy articulated by Rosenblum that aimed to move BBC employees away from process-dominated production in the pursuit of what he considered to be 'better television'. Indeed, the head of the BBC in the East Midlands stressed that it was only possible to implement PDP by involving everyone in the process.

> What we did in Nottingham was set about defining a vision for the programme and saying every night we're going to concentrate on delivering these key things. And we got all the staff to buy into what these ideas should be. And we basically wrote on the wall a grid that contained things like exclusives ... and we had five or six things to deliver every night that all the staff had bought into.
>
> (Alison, HRLP, BBC Nottingham)

The news grid referred to in this quote remained on the wall in the Nottingham newsroom during the first few months of PDP implementation. An interesting example of what in ANT terms we would refer to as an *inscription device*, its purpose is to facilitate an actor's network translation, but very like the immutable mobile, it is an actor that should remain unchanged by the process. By its adoption, actors attempt to stabilise translation by the act of inscribing that process in a visual and fixed location. Latour's preoccupation with inscription devices centres around the way in which the scientists he observes record their results in order to fix the meaning of experiments so as to share, articulate and persuade others of their signification, even after the experiment has been performed and is no longer visible to actors who must still be enrolled in the process to ensure its success.

But the device also echoes Latour's frustration, outlined at the beginning of this chapter, with the need to fix the performative aspect of the translation process into some kind of narrative form. This exact process is shown to occur at the level of practice, with human actors attempting to establish control of translation by resorting to literary recording devices.[7]

> I will call an instrument (or inscription device) any set-up, no matter what its size, nature and costs, that provides a visual display of any sort in a scientific text ... What is behind a scientific text? Inscriptions ... This other world just beneath the text is invisible as long as there is no controversy.
>
> (Latour, 1987, p.69)

An inscription device can be an important way to settle controversy, before controversy has occurred. It makes other actors think twice about dissenting. It signifies that 'arguing is costly' (Latour, 1987, p.69). The same process occurs within the newsroom. The newsroom grid, deliberately created as a result of *collective* input from staff, is a device that attempts to fix the significance of PDP before other actors within the network adopt it. The managerial exhortation to staff to redefine the news agenda themselves, may seek to stabilise the translation process at an early stage, but as Michel Callon reminds us, it is a risky strategy. By allowing a plethora of actors to be involved in the translation process, the process itself may well become destabilised, and the network loses its convergent resilience.

> The higher the degree of alignment and co-ordination of a network, the more its actors work together, and the less their very status as actors is in doubt. This does not mean that everyone does the same thing, for networks usually include a range of complementary actors; rather it points to the way in which the activities of actors fit together despite their heterogeneity.
>
> (Callon, 1980, p.210)

The news grid may seek to fix the translation, and to imbue PDP with stable signification, but as so many actors are involved in the inscription process, it does not remain stable for very long. After only six months the news grid, rather than remaining immutable, becomes more and more unstable and unable to resist the exchanges that go on between staff about how and why PDP should be adopted, disappears altogether. Its eradication from the network signifies an inability to adapt to the translation process that is occurring, but such instability need not be considered radical or dangerous. Networks have many unstable actors within them, and as we have already seen in the previous chapter, also exhibit different degrees of instability. There are other actors who may exhibit a combination of stable and unstable characteristics that render their ability to resist others continually contingent on their exact position within the network.[8] The grid's disappearance does demonstrate how diverse are the individual perceptions of PDP and that PDP's significance in a well-defined and complex technological network capable thus far of withstanding drastic reconfiguration is, at this stage, also unstable.

> Considered from a very general point of view, this notion [translation] postulates the existence of a single field of significations, concerns and interests, the expression of a shared desire to arrive at the same result . . . Translation involves creating convergences and homologies by relating things that were previously different.
>
> (Callon, 1980, p.211)

If we wish to use this definition of translation, we now need to map how PDP gradually becomes embedded within the news network in such a way that a necessary degree of convergence is finally achieved so that the everyday routines can be carried out successfully. We will see how from the first three years of its implementation such stabilisation is only possible through a process of mutual translation. A resistance to it from other actors in the network translates PDP, but PDP also simultaneously translates the existing network, with considerable repercussions for other actors, and it is to this translation process and to a more detailed analysis of the agency of this particular technology that we now turn.

5

VIDEO JOURNALISM (2)

The translation of the news network and the
reconfiguration of news

We put up so many systems in place to try to be across all the nig-
gles and the training needs and the general depressive moods of
people – we have had to do an awful lot of background restructuring
to make some things happen that we wanted to happen.

(Alison, HRLP, BBC Nottingham)

Developing our exploration of the implementation of a new technology, known
as PDP, into the newsroom, we shall begin to see how its adoption causes significant changes to both the news network, and to the content of news. But
these changes are neither easily predicted, nor simply mapped and in this chapter
we will continue to use an Actor Network Theory (ANT) focus to find out
exactly what kind of changes occur and where they are located. The process of
translation introduced in Chapter 4 is further developed as we discover that
both the technology itself and the actor network with which it becomes entangled are both translated in often quite radical and surprising ways.

In the very early stages of its implementation in the Nottingham newsroom,
PDP working practices were organised fairly closely to how Rosenblum had
envisaged, and the major initial changes occurred at the level of resources.
Existing newsroom staff were relocated to three separate PDP bureaux, which
were set up in the local radio stations at Derby, Lincoln and at Leicester, so as
to create extra production roles and to allow the PDP operators who worked in
these bureaux more time away from the newsroom for filming, as well as the
extra time they needed to edit their pieces. The existing six craft camera crews
were reduced to three, releasing three craft cameramen to work as PDP
operators. Thirty-three edit workstations were brought into the newsroom to
replace the existing four full-time craft picture editors who were also employed
as PDP operators. The newsroom was thus quite radically restructured to enable
the majority of staff to be out gathering their material, with a significantly
reduced team located in the newsroom to produce and present the daily news

bulletins. Yet the perception among newsroom staff was that rather than creating a wider choice of better quality stories, this shift in resources resulted in the bulletin and main lunchtime and evening programme producers being left without the required flexibility of resources or satisfactory material to cover news bulletins throughout the day.

> You think it's easy, you've only got three crews, but actually everything now it is much worse because everything now has to be interlocked and so tightly to make sure you get what you want ...
>
> (Lisa, CDA, BBC Nottingham)

> I think they're finding that it isn't working but I think we needed to go through this process to find out that it doesn't work. You know what it's like – this doesn't give you flexibility but they say, well it should do because you've got all those PDP people doing stories – but they're not always there on the same day.
>
> (Lynne, production assistant, BBC Nottingham)

In the past the main lunchtime and evening programme producers were able to demand that their multiskilled reporters provide a lunchtime package and a separate piece for the main evening programme, as well as extra radio packages or interview clips. As we discussed at the end of Chapter 4, bi-media and multiskilling working practices had already been more-or-less abandoned, but before the introduction of PDP, there was still a tendency for the reporters to provide separate material for both the lunchtime and evening television programmes. With the implementation of PDP, this tendency rapidly began to erode and within six months it had all but disappeared. Widely welcomed by journalists, producers now found it a considerable challenge just to fill required airtime.

> The new technology has meant it's extremely difficult for the lunchtime bulletin – people are taking a very long time to turn around their PDP pieces and we are down to just one edit suite so we don't have any crews either to go out and film for lunch. We have had to rely on running reports from breakfast, but we're losing there too because there are no resources to film things for overnights.
>
> (Paula, lunchtime producer, BBC Nottingham)

Equally the reporters complained that the pressures of PDP working meant that showing willingness to lunchtime producers by providing them with material just wasn't a realistic option.

I have been in North Derbyshire starting to film something at 10.30am and the lunchtime producer has rung to say can you do something and you have to say, 'well no, I can't'. And you can't bash out an as-live and send it to them on a courier because you're on your own.

(Simon, PDP operator, BBC Nottingham)

Returning to our concept of the chronogram, that is the specific temporal axis that locates an individual actor within the network, we can begin to see how the specific chronogram of PDP as articulated by Rosenblum, and which is translated through to the trainees, directly conflicts with the separate chronogrammatic demands of those actors situated in the newsroom who are responsible for producing the daily bulletins. Once PDP enters the network, it renders problematic the diurnal obligation to fill airtime by what is perceived by production staff as the temporal luxury of PDP production.

This creates tension among separate actor groups, roughly divided between those working within the newsroom, and those PDP operators who are situated beyond the newsroom on externalised nodes of the network. Personal Digital Production operators who spend longer periods of time getting to know their story, collecting more in-depth, 'human interest' material that necessitates in Rosenblum's own words, 'time to get close', are thus placed in direct conflict with human actors within the newsroom whose entirely separate chronogrammatic position necessitates the ability to turn material round quickly so as to fill hourly bulletins. And directly related to this conflict between different chronogrammatic positions, what we're also witnessing is the beginning of a shift in journalists' definitions of news. For the PDP operators, the human-interest, longer, more-sustained exploration of an issue is considered to be newsworthy, while for the bulletin producer the one minute summary of today's bus crash or court appearance is considered news. These shifting concepts of what the news agenda should be, and their crucial relationship to the implementation of the new technology, will be discussed in more detail as they occur throughout this chapter.

To return to our exploration of the varying time scales that our different actors are working with here, it is clear that the two chronogrammatic positions that we have outlined are not only in direct conflict, but are also constructed by their relationship to other proximate nonhuman actors on the network in their specific locations.

To illustrate what we mean, let's take two different actors, in different network locations, both producing news material for transmission. In one location we may find the lunchtime producer who is struggling to fill an 11-minute programme with second-hand and out-of-date news material she has managed to gather from the earlier breakfast bulletins. We could say that she defines her time by means of her relationship with proximate technologies such as the media hub and Omnibus, which may hinder or assist her in reworking the material and re-editing the packages, depending on whether or not she can gain access to these technologies, as well as her own technogrammatic position in relation to these technologies, that is, whether she is adept enough to negotiate such technologies. Just as we saw in our analysis of the media hub in Chapter 3, journalists display radically different technological expertise and this allows them greater autonomy from such technologies – exemplified by the lunchtime pre-senter who was able to bypass the media hub and edit her headline sequence without requiring a port to be assigned to her. It is in this sense that we can begin to understand how technologies, just as much as human actors, display agency and can determine the outcome of specific news production tasks.

In our second location, situated on an externalised node of the network, and detached from the production of bulletins within the newsroom, the PDP operator's conception of time may also be linked to his or her individual proficiency to utilise the filming and editing technologies so as to produce adequate material that can be made into a finished piece. But this technological expertise differs from our first example, and is located in a different time frame. Here the operator needs a certain amount of time to set up the camera, to ensure the focus and the white balance is correct, as well as to check the sound levels on the microphone and to frame each shot. Similar technological proficiency is then needed to negotiate the digital editing system on the laptop – to ensure the sound levels are accurate and that the pictures fit together into understandable sequences.

These two actors are both working within the same network, and ostensibly share the same aim, which is to produce material for transmission. Yet due to their network position, and their proximity to the technologies with which they are inextricably folded, their chronogrammatic position and perception is wildly varied, as is their perception of the responsibility of their role within the net-work. This analysis of the separate temporal signification of human actors defined in part by their relationship with proximate technological actors reveals two crucial things: the variability of human agency, and the relationship that human actors have with the technologies they need to use. The examples also show us how a news network lacks convergence, and that this fluidity and volatility is being further exacerbated by the introduction of a new technological agent such as PDP.

Actors' varying temporal perceptions, as well as the actual extra time it was taking for PDP operators to edit pieces, placed increased demands on the pro-duction network that was soon recognised at the managerial level. In these early days, managers consistently argued that this would improve once staff developed their PDP skills and more material was regularly provided for transmission. Yet managers also recognised fairly early on that the professional and cultural changes that PDP demanded could not be implemented as quickly as they thought. There were quite obvious tensions between Rosenblum's chronogrammatic agenda and the actual time that the implementation process would take, as managers candidly admitted.

> You start off believing that you can make anyone a fully operational cameraperson, or journalist in three weeks – but it's just not true. I think we were a bit naïve about how it would work in practice . . . three weeks is just the beginning of a massive process.
>
> (Alison, HRLP, BBC Nottingham)

In response to the lack of resources for production, and the inflexibility this caused, as well as the longer turnaround needed to produce PDP items, there was also a discernible shift in the way that news began to be defined. It is in this particular context that PDP's translation of the network could be considered to be most successful. But it would be too simplistic to surmise that technology thus demonstrates a singular determining effect upon news content, for as will be demonstrated, the network in turn also reconfigures the technological actor.

The PDP operators did welcome the greater access to people and situations that the smaller cameras allowed, as well as the extra time permitted to follow a story.

> I am doing a piece about a football agent – following one guy around his world, looking after football players, and it took four days to film it – when would we ever have been given that before? I'm not the person to say whether or not it's worth that, but it's great that I can do it.
>
> (Rob, PDP operator, BBC Nottingham)

Yet the quote reveals a highly significant polemic that lies at the heart of PDP implementation and its role in the reconfiguration of the news agenda. Certainly the constraints of time and the expectations to produce news for more than one outlet in the days of bi-media and multiskilling were unpopular, but PDP did not simply mean liberation from tougher past practice. The eradication of core skills and roles was seen by most as extremely difficult, and honing editing or camera skills for a journalist was as much of a challenge as it was for camera operators to suddenly think journalistically about a story (Hemmingway, 2005).

> Finding stories is stressful – and looking at the computer all day is stressful – I'm normally out and about filming, but just sitting around trying to source stories is very difficult. I'm taking a lot more work home with me, as in my head, as I'm constantly trying to think up stories . . .
>
> (Richard, PDP operator, ex-cameraman, BBC Nottingham)

We can begin to recognise a tension here between the challenge of the new working practices and individual value judgements as to the significance of the material being provided as news. Departing quite significantly from Avilles *et al.*'s initial assertion that new technologies are being adopted to sustain past practice, with PDP implementation, the news process and the content of the final product were both rigorously questioned by those directly involved in its creation. The network thus became radically destabilised, and it is at this point that black boxes could have easily been reopened and actor positions reconfigured.

The important aspect of this destabilisation is that it occurs simultaneously in terms of practice and in terms of news content. Examining network translation where both the actor and the network are mutually contingent and altered by the process, allows one to realise how news content is inextricably linked with the microprocesses of news production. Furthermore, it also reveals how those actors involved in that production are active agents with the ability to reflect upon the translation of their environment as it occurs. They are not the passive recipients of technological transformations taking place in isolation from human actors within the same network. Hundreds if not thousands of network translations are continually reconfiguring both sets of actors, and in the process the signification of the final product, in this case the news programme, constructed as it is by both actor groups, is also reconfigured.

An example of a newsroom conversation between two journalists trying to explain to a hospital press officer why they will no longer attend press conferences, illustrates a reflexive examination of the new newsgathering practices that have become necessary as a result of the adoption of PDP.

R: I said we're trying to make interesting TV – it's not my job to stitch up your hospital or to promote it – it's my job to make interesting TV and that means access . . . and he didn't seem to get it. We are ignoring those on the day stories – we are ignoring them, as we're doing PDP.

C: And that's the whole point of it – they are very different.

R: Yeah that's the whole point.

C: And we must be getting something right because we have just had a letter from someone in Kent with no link to Nottingham, but just likes the programme as it's a good watch . . .

(Rob and Carole, PDP operators, BBC Nottingham)

This conversation shrouds within it a shared tension. The news agenda has changed: PDP operators are demanding greater access to real-life happenings rather than turning out to planned media events alongside their competitors. More time is devoted to longer more intimate projects, and consequently fewer 'on the day' stories are being covered. This chronogrammatic realignment that

PDP demands has concerned a number of journalists as they perceive this not only as a change in working practice, but as a reconfiguration of news. Journalists thus view the practice of newsgathering and filming as inextricably linked with how the final news product will be defined and the temporal implications of PDP practice are deemed to have a significant determination on the meaning of the final product.

> Our coverage has gone into longer featurey-type things and it can be interesting and do we really want to do that stabbing in a nightclub on Friday night? But having said that, if we don't do that, are we not telling people what's been happening in their region, you know?
>
> (Rob, PDP operator, BBC Nottingham)

This widespread unease regarding the reconfiguration of the news agenda to include the human interest, fly-on-the-wall, more feature-based type of coverage that the small PDP cameras are designed to permit becomes more significant over time. What we will see is that the news network, and with it the content of the news, is not only translated, but is then retranslated during the first four years of PDP development. It is these translations that will enable us to understand how news is constructed not by human actors alone, but by the complex relationship between humans and the technologies available to them.

Let's just consider one of these earlier translations to illustrate what we mean by this rather controversial statement. The example also shows us how earlier translations of the same actor also play their part in mapping subsequent translations that the actor makes as it become embedded more firmly into the network.

This particular translation occurred within the forward planning department, which is a subsection of the larger newsgathering department.[1] It was the reorganisation of the planning department in the very early stages of implementation that resulted in the most significant PDP translation, and the subsequent eradication of the role of the news organiser, an actor whose status was hitherto considered to be that of a black box. Many actors have argued that the loss of this position, as a direct result of PDP implementation, has had drastic implications on both the production process and the news content.

As we've already seen, PDP operators were expected to have extra time to research stories, thus liberating news coverage from slavishly covering items provided by press releases, local newspapers or planned promotional events. One BBC manager described past practice as being too dependent on news releases sent to the newsroom and journalists waiting by the fax machine to see what they could film for the programme. Regional news in particular had relied on a daily store of news items easily available for coverage. The forward planning department enjoyed a significant role in this newsgathering operation with planners handing out stories at the daily prospects meeting for individual reporters and camera operators to film (Hemmingway, 2005).

> One of my big hates was just going along to something that you knew was just there to fill lunch – and it was some press-release story and nobody got anything out of it – you didn't – the camera crew didn't – the VT editor didn't – so it's nice to be doing stuff that you know is being done, not just because there is nothing else ...
>
> (Simon, PDP operator, BBC Nottingham)

Yet if we analyse those actors in the forward planning department after PDP was adopted, it is quite clear that news stories were still being selected for logistical reasons regarding staff and resources rather than the so-called journalistic merits of the story, however those merits were being redefined. Personal Digital Production operators were certainly being freed up from the rota to pursue more intimate human-interest stories, but the planning department continued to set up the more reliable, press release based news stories to fill all the gaps in the under-resourced daily bulletins. It was just that now they were finding it almost impossible to resource these stories.

> Two or three years ago we had a lot of crews and we could set up a story, but now that tends not to happen – what tends to happen now is that if there is a crew free we will then look and see what they can cover, but we don't have the luxury of setting up stories in advance.
>
> (Liz, planning journalist, BBC Nottingham)

The Rosenblum ethos that PDP is designed to provide news that has been gathered in more detail, with more intimate coverage, thus representing the community more accurately, seemed immediately to fall foul of the interactions within the network that a subsequent lack of resources created.

> It makes it harder for the planners – because the planners have got to fit jobs to the crewing – whereas before you sent the crews to the jobs – I think that has now been reversed – they know what times the crews start so they know they won't get the jobs covered.
>
> (Lynne, production assistant, BBC Nottingham)

Having to accommodate PDP, with its contradictory prescriptions, meant that a destabilising translation of the planning department took place because extra actors, in this case cameras, could not be mobilised to stabilise the transition. Not only had PDP destabilised the newsgathering department, it facilitated the eradication of the senior news organiser post. The duties carried out by the news organiser were quickly reallocated to other staff. Output producers initially seemed to be fairly unconcerned by this as they had done the news organiser shifts and found them dull and tedious.

> I have been a news organiser. I used to think I was in a coma, so I lobbied to get rid of it ... when we really looked at it we found that the news organiser didn't really have that many responsibilities.
>
> (Neil, output producer, BBC Nottingham)

Yet elsewhere in the newsroom there was significant frustration that the loss of the role, described by one production assistant as the way to 'save money with the introduction of all this PDP stuff', had made logistical arrangements and covering stories for network much more challenging.[2]

> When network misses a story because we just haven't got anyone watching the wires or answering the phone, there will be hell to pay. And as far as the relationship we had with the local radio stations all of us alerting each other to stories, that's completely gone, all because of PDP.
>
> (Victoria, News 24 network reporter, based in Nottingham newsroom)

Concentrating on the traces of past actor translations to adequately describe present ones, it is significant to note that the news organiser role was itself once a rather precarious new actor in the network. Many journalists had vigorously opposed its introduction, which occurred nine years previously at the height of the days of multiskilling and bi-media practices. At that time many producers and reporters were deemed to be superfluous to the news process. They argued that output producers were capable of gathering news, and the camera diary assistant was capable of allocating crews and getting material sent back to base by dispatch riders or via ISDN lines. The newsgathering department was considered to be a waste of money and a way of creating another sphere of managerial influence having as it did its own level of managers and editors.

Yet once it was introduced, within a relatively short time the department had not only become a part of the network, but had managed to recruit and stabilise enough alliances that it had gained black box status. Just like the media hub, it couldn't have achieved this level of stability without surviving numerous translations of the other human and nonhuman actors with which it established stable alliances. As Latour argues

> Each element in the chain of individuals needed to pass the black box along may act in multifarious ways: the people in question may drop it

100

altogether, or accept it as it is, or shift the modalities that accompany it, or modify the statement, or appropriate it and put it in a completely different context. Instead of being conductors – or semi conductors – they are all multi conductors and unpredictable ones at that.

(Latour, 1987, p.104)

And such was the case with newsgathering, and the news organiser who soon became its *obligatory point of passage*. The news organiser not only collectively transmitted the status of the entire department from one actor to the next, be it a disgruntled journalist, the editor of regional programming, a camera operator who was forced to negotiate with newsgathering for a salary review, or the technical and architectural constellation of its own prominent geographical setting within the newsroom, but each actor added elements of their own, modifying it, incorporating it into new contexts, and strengthening it in the process. The newsgathering department became a black box precisely because

the only way to keep dissenters at bay is to link the fate of the claim with so many assembled elements that it resists all trials to break it apart.

(Latour, 1987, p.122)

Just like the media hub, enough actors in the network, whether human staff or nonhuman resources such as cameras and edit machines, were necessarily aligned to newsgathering in order to produce news, and its hitherto precarious existence was accommodated within the network, stabilised through these alliances to such an extent that it became a daily reality where reality is defined in ANT terms as the 'ability to resist trials of strength' (Latour, 1987).

That was, of course, until the introduction of PDP. The eradication of the news organiser role was facilitated first by the previous demise of bi-media working practices, which had become further reconfigured by the introduction of PDP, and then by managerial attempts to save money and free up staff positions, so that more PDP operators could be deployed. Yet it is significant to note that three years after the disbanding of the news organiser position, the network has still not stabilised and there is ongoing conflict between managers as to whether or not the role should be reintroduced. When asked whether she thought the role should be reinstated, one resources manager immediately referred the decision to the manager of output, illustrating the depth of tension surrounding the action.

You ought to ask Sally [output editor] that one – I mean, I think – the news organiser as it was should not come back and will not come back, but I think we still have a lot of big gaps ... that weren't properly plugged when that job was disbanded – I think you don't get rid of something like that role, which everybody thought God, what a dull job, and then suddenly everybody thinks, bloody hell the news organiser used to do that, you know we have camera diary making decisions they shouldn't be making, because there's nobody else there ... on a big story the thought was that well *News 24* can answer the phone – well *News 24* can't answer the phone because they are nearly always out, so again, so somewhere we need somebody who is doing those duties.

(Emma, operations manager, BBC Nottingham)

Yet although PDP was able to facilitate the eradication of a hitherto significant actor such as the news organiser, it too underwent significant translation during the same three-year period. This began at the microcosmic level of logistics where the autonomy of PDP was first challenged, and with that came further network translation soon afterwards. Let's chart this process to reveal the instability, not just of the human actors within our network, but of the technologies as well.

Personal Digital Production had only been implemented for a few months before managers decided that the chronogrammatic conflicts outlined earlier between the bulletin producers and planners who were responsible for filling airtime with limited resources, and the PDP operators working more individually beyond the confines of the newsroom in an entirely different time frame should be resolved. The planners had complained to management about what they considered to be breaches in protocol by PDP operators. The first occurred when a number of craft camera operators were redeployed as PDP operators. This meant that they were now closely intertwined with the news production process, where before they had worked on external nodes of the network and very often never even appeared in the newsroom. In their first weeks as PDP operators they were criticised by the planning department for failing to fill in a grid on the wall in the office saying where they would be on a daily basis.[3]

> There's no flexibility. We have to keep across it here because we need to know what stories they're doing – and in what order they're doing it so that we get stories for the evening programme. It's so important that people put where they are – but they're camera men and filling in a bit of paper – well that's hard work isn't it and they haven't got time to do it ...
>
> (Lynne, production assistant, resources, BBC Nottingham)

Similar frustrations beset other departments. The idea of autonomous film-making was initially encouraged, but other actors soon found that they couldn't keep track of staff and that any further contingencies could not then be covered adequately. Supposedly autonomous from the newsroom, PDP operators very quickly found themselves regularly having to account for their time so as to assist other actors.

> PDP people thought they were very independent and that they were doing their own thing. When it had been commissioned they would go off and do it, and they didn't put it in the camera diary because they were their own camera person … it was very difficult – they weren't letting you know – they could be sitting in Radio Leicester or Derby and you didn't know what they were doing. That's changed now – there is a lot more communication and it will get easier.
>
> (Planning journalist, BBC Nottingham)

This translation of PDP was engineered by the deliberate actions of journalists and production staff, who were acutely aware of the microcosmic negotiations occurring within the production network. The technology becomes embedded, but it is significantly redesigned, and continues to be redesigned as actors within the network make, break or negotiate ever-changing associations.

To explore the nature of the fluidity of translation processes, it is necessary to return to the ongoing debate about what constitutes news. In the first two years, staff continued to share misgivings as to whether the utilisation of PDP and the move toward longer more sustained human interest pieces could be defined as news. The reworking of programme items by the adoption of the news grid, which was supposed to encourage a reconfiguration of the traditional news agenda was considered by staff to be exceedingly unsatisfactory. Managers also recognised that this reconfiguration was their greatest challenge, but they initially insisted that the suspicions could be caused by a learned acceptance of a traditional news agenda that has never been rigorously questioned.

> I am keen that people have the debate rather than to say that there is a right or wrong to it. In my experience as a manager I find that people sometimes just want to be told – you know as if there is some checklist of ten things that are news and ten things that aren't and when I have had meetings with staff they will say – tell me – and I say, how can I tell you – you give me a story and we'll discuss whether or not it's a story – but there's this prescriptive thing that staff seem to be after all the time.
>
> (Alison, HRLP, BBC Nottingham)

One PDP operator who had previously worked as a news reporter felt that the move towards human-interest, feature length pieces as lead items on the evening news programme was too much of a departure from what he believed journalists and audiences had come to expect from news programmes.

> It's vague journalism. Sometimes we have had a few pieces at the top of the programme – lead stories – and I have thought, what's the story? It's been, like, graffiti is bad isn't it, and for the next four minutes we have had lots of shots of graffiti, and there's no other peg.
>
> (Simon, PDP operator, BBC Nottingham)

Speculation as to what audiences may or may not accept once PDP transformed the news agenda was also evident at the PDP Training Centre. The fear was that audiences would not understand why the content of news stories, as well as their style, had changed so radically, and trainees recalled recent experiments in their own newsrooms that in their view had not been greatly successful.

> What they did in Birmingham last week was they did a thing called *Your Midlands Today* so rather than have any news in the programme, it was basically just millions of PDP pieces; I mean about 25, 45-second pieces, and it didn't really work. And there was no news in it – people went, 'What happened to the news?'
>
> (Andy, PDP trainee, BBC Birmingham)

Where is Personal Digital Production now?

We have seen how the introduction of PDP has resulted in quite radical network translation, leading to the loss of certain human and nonhuman actors such as the news grid and the news organiser, and has also caused an ongoing reconfiguration and debate about what constitutes news. We have also seen how the new technology is itself beginning to be translated by the network, illustrated at the microcosmic level of logistics and the restructuring of the newsroom, as well as in practice where single-authored autonomous film-making was seen to conflict with the digitised media hub that necessitates that material is fed into a central server to facilitate communal viewing and editing.

To satisfactorily narrate the story of PDP translation, we need to revisit the newsroom after a significant period of time so that we can find out what other translations have occurred – to the network, to the technology and to the nature of the news content. It is important to recognise that with any story of actor-network translation, there can be no final summing up, no way to conclude the story, for the network is ever-changing, new resistances can present themselves at any time, and in connection with these, actors become realigned. Yet that shouldn't put us off. We need to recognise how this constant rein-scription process of both the human and nonhuman actors must be continuously accounted for if we want to develop a better understanding of how the news-room works.

> The only way to follow engineers at work is not to look for extra or intrasomatic delegation, but only at their work of reinscription. The beauty of artefacts is that they take on themselves the contradictory wishes or needs of human and nonhumans.
>
> (Latour, 1992, p.247)

The work of journalists is not dissimilar once we recognise their inextricable interlinking with a whole range of technological actors within the network, including digital technologies and other machines. Three years after its intro-duction, PDP has indeed taken on the contradictory needs of those actors who are directly associated with it. As a result the newsroom has been continually restructured, and the news agenda remains volatile and unfixed.

One of the most significant changes that occurred was with regard to the working practices in the PDP bureaux. Three separate dedicated PDP bureaux had been established at radio Derby, Leicester and Lincoln, staffed by a jour-nalist and a craft cameraman, both working as PDP operators. At the beginning of the process, each individual was expected to contribute four main evening programme items every week, but staff admitted that the deliberate placing of a journalist and a camera operator in each bureau was so that they could revert to more traditional methods of working as a journalist and camera operator, should a story arise that they felt should be covered by a team.

Another development has been the way in which the conflicting chrono-grammatic perceptions have been partially stabilised by a significant differentia-tion in the way in which certain PDP operators work. Those who are situated in the bureaux are now being asked by producers to film and edit material daily. They rarely enjoy the liberty of spending time on their research and filming, but often submit material that they have filmed and edited on the day for the eve-ning programme. This chronogrammatic translation has itself caused a rein-scription of actual filming methods, where operators are now gathering material in the more traditional and formulaic manner that was vehemently condemned by Rosenblum. It has also reinscribed the central Rosenblum ethos of using PDP to liberate the individual and by means of the technology to gain equality with all other members of staff. Rosenblum's vision was of a world peopled with hundreds of individual film-makers, all able to cover the stories as easily as the next person. But the restructuring of the Nottingham newsroom has ensured that there are certain *types* of PDP operators, and that a recognised hierarchy of these types with their different and separate privileges is communally accepted.

> Those in the bureaux do film and edit in one day, yeah it's certainly not unheard of. It depends on whether it's just clip, link, clip, link, thrown together in one-and-a-half minutes, forget art, let's just get it on.
>
> (Rob, correspondent, PDP operator, BBC Nottingham)

If we use our ANT terminology here, we can say that we are witnessing a translation of the PDP sociogram; it is now being used to film material for editing on the day, rather than being used for longer periods of time for lengthier news features. Thus its technogrammatic position also alters; the machine is literally used differently by the human actor. Far from Rosenblum's adage that the architecture of the technology dictates its usage and thus the final product, this determinist paradigm is shattered by an analysis of the technology in separate locations on the network. We can see that the technogrammatic architecture of PDP is as dependent upon network positioning as any other actor, and is therefore as contingent.

Furthermore, the BBC management structure in Nottingham has changed dramatically since the introduction of PDP. A new HRLP has been instated with his own very particular views of how the programme should look, and therefore how the available technologies should be used. His individual views of what constitutes news have further complicated the existing debate concerning the relationship between the technology, its use, and what news should be filmed and edited. As he explained within the first few months of his appointment

> I thought that the programme felt very featurey – that it didn't have a sense of what the important news stories were in the region and I'm not sure why that situation had arisen. Sometimes I felt that the lead was buried down the running order – and so when I came here I talked to a lot of people about news – and that I thought of *East Midlands Today* as a news programme – and that it needed to be a news programme but it wasn't being one.
>
> (Aziz, HRLP, BBC Nottingham)

A direct correlation is still being drawn between the programme showing too many feature length, human-interest stories and the technology that was being used to film the material. The PDP150 cameras have been replaced with Sony Z100 cameras, but the Rosenblum ethos of getting close to the human heart of the story that he had attempted to inscribe into the machines, which had been debated and challenged in the past, is now beginning to be completely eradicated by the new HRLP.

> I think when you are skilling-up a number of people to be VJs, there
> will be a period where there will be a dilution of that skill – when they
> are all learning and that probably did affect quality – I think that's been
> sorted now – I think in appointing VJs they were told to do a certain
> kind of story – rather than news stories – because I think people
> interpreted original journalism as telling people stories – and you can
> tell people stories but usually they fit into wider contexts – so when
> you do a news story – yes it is easier for the audience to understand if
> you reflect the effect it has through a personal story – but what is the
> news story – what are the implications for the rest of us? The con-
> textualisation was missing and instead you had the personal story at the
> expense of the wider story. This didn't just happen at regional level. It
> was just easier to film a person and tell their story rather than to film a
> news story.
>
> (Aziz, HRLP, BBC Nottingham)

This radical translation of the news agenda occurs at the top level of management, within a single actor, the HRLP, but as with any translation it cannot be entirely successful or become stabilised if the other actors don't come on board. We need to see how the HRLP manages to achieve this, so that we can develop our story of PDP translation and understand more fully how network change occurs.

As we have seen earlier in the chapter, a number of allies must be gathered together in order to stabilise any translation, and if the alliances they constitute are strong enough, that translation may then not only become stabilised but also achieve black box status. One of the most effective ways to do this is to use the traces of past translations, and to make these work to strengthen new alliances. The HRLP knows that many of the craft camera crews were extremely unhappy about working as PDP operators. He therefore reorganises the shifts so that those who did not enjoy PDP working are able to revert to being craft camera crews, working to craft editors and traditional reporters. Many staff members welcomed this move as we can see from the following quotes.

> Chris hated it – he joined because he was a cameraman – he wasn't a
> journalist and PDP working really wound him up – and Neil was the
> same – Neil got very ill with it – he practically had a breakdown with
> it – I think Chris turned round and said I am not doing this and I can't
> do this, but Neil didn't want to probably give up and he carried on

until it made him ill. Now Chris does ordinary crewing but he also goes out on the sat truck — he is quite happy to go out on the sat truck from a technical point of view. Neil will do what we call the shoot/edit because he doesn't mind doing a bit of editing and they feel because they go out on a story with somebody that they are much happier working that way.

(Lynne, CDA, BBC Nottingham)

I think there was an initial period of learning and now it's finding its own level — it will never go away and I wouldn't want it to go away — I am not a total Luddite — and I do see the advantages — PDP has fantastic access — we can get under people's skin in a documentary style that we can never do with a conventional style of filming so that's all good — but there were times when what should have been shot conventionally wasn't — it was being shot on a little camera and they suffer — some crass examples of filming cricket or football on a small camera which is just bonkers. But I do think there has been a slight wind change and everyone seems to be a bit happier about this.

(Richard, cameraman, BBC Nottingham)

And many of the reporters also welcome what they perceive as an increased flexibility introduced into the network by the mixed economy of working practices.

There is proof we are putting out fewer VJ pieces than we were — but I don't think we can be quite so prescriptive because if you have gone out and filmed something and there is an editor free — then why not use the editor to cut it — or you know if you have filmed something and there is no one to edit it — why not you edit it — I think we should look at it much more flexibly and say, just because someone hasn't done it all — doesn't mean that the skills aren't being used. I like to keep using them because I enjoy it and if I don't — I forget about them. And I like going out — I like to have the camera in the boot of the car — I did a piece yesterday about illegal immigrants and car washes but I used both a crew and got some shots as well — I mixed and matched the shots we had as it was that sort of story where you only get one chance to get the pictures so you might as well split up and get a range of shots. I think we shouldn't be saying that we have to work a certain way — and we don't.

(Quentin, chief news reporter, BBC Nottingham)

This most recent reconfiguration of the news agenda has occurred due to a number of factors, or network translations. Let's list what these are. First of all, the new HRLP has a clear focus and idea as to what constitutes news. Having come from a BBC national television background – he was a producer of the BBC's *Breakfast News* – he has realised that while Rosenblum's ethos of getting close to the heart of the story – spending time with people – and allowing them room and space to tell their individual stories may well have some value, the logistical arrangements to make this possible put too much strain on the network and he also believed that people watching the programme did not consider this type of treatment of a story to be news. He quickly communicated this to his output and operations managers, to garner strong alliances with pivotal actors, before attempting to persuade other staff in the newsroom. The strategy worked as the following quotes reveals.

> I think if we were completely honest, if we went back and had a look at things and we realised then what we know now, we would have rethought it – Aziz came in and – well its been a bit of a shock – a guy comes in and says you're not doing this or that – and this is crap – and you think you're working on a decent programme and the figures are ok and he says no the figures are not ok – everybody's figures are falling but your figures are falling faster than anybody else so we have to sort this out – so he came in with a specific agenda – it would be harder news at the top –with an OB, with relevance – so that's fine – what he wanted to do very early on was to establish that this would have to change because we were losing audiences – there is a haemorrhage there and we have to stop it. We seem to have done it – the figures have picked up.
>
> (Kevin, output editor, BBC Nottingham)

The news agenda is then also reconfigured because the HRLP realises that some of the working practices that PDP operators were being subjected to were not popular and were not practical. The greater flexibility he introduces by allowing people to work either as craft crews and reporters, *or* as PDP operators, gains him the required support throughout the newsroom to carry out the translation successfully. He may well be able to gain support more easily as he is a manager, and therefore enjoys a privileged and powerful position, but he also recognises that the staff working to him and to the programme need to share his vision of what that programme should contain, and therefore what the working practices should be.

> I joined the BBC to work in news and the staff were really pleased if we were going to be focusing on news stories again – so then what do you consider to be news stories – so we then had a big discussion with

all the correspondents and all the editors about what the main news stories were in the East Midlands region and then I added a couple of issues that I thought they didn't cover very well like business and arts . . .

(Aziz, HRLP, BBC Nottingham)

Other managers have also adopted this translation, by insisting that the original PDP agenda was never workable once the technology was implemented in the newsroom.

There is a move towards people working on the day . . . we always said that it would be a mixed economy and people were sold the PDP dream and they came back and they performed the PDP dream . . . but the reality was we said to them, everything is changing, everything changes all the time. They will always do mixed. Sometimes they work on the day with a crew, sometimes they work on the day turning stuff around for themselves and sometimes they don't do it on the day, they're doing a nice PDP thing that is for tomorrow, or the next day, or the day after that. So it's true, they do a bit of everything.

(Emma, operations manager, BBC Nottingham)

Conclusion

To understand the story of PDP translation it is important to try to include those past traces of actor negotiations that may be enfolded within actors in the present, to analyse how different actors on each internal or external node of the network all inhabit separate social, technical and temporal locations, and to recognise how the conflicting demands incorporated in these positions act as separate resistances to the new technology. What we have witnessed is that the PDP actor is not immutable, as Rosenblum predicted, but rather undergoes radical translation and reinscription, and that this process is ongoing. It is also imperative to recognise simultaneous network translation, as exemplified by the eradication of certain actor positions, such as the news organiser, and the more recent creation of separate PDP bureaux within which the technology is once again being reinscribed, this time in response to conflicting technogrammatic and sociogrammatic actor demands.

Initial resistances to PDP came from those actors unable to reorganise resources adequately until PDP operators had been fully socialised within the network. Hence we saw how a few planning journalists were quickly able to translate Rosenblum's omnipotent technological actor bent on network domination.

110

When most journalists and technical staff were asked how they thought PDP would develop during the next five years, we find a general consensus. Staff feel that the new technology has 'found its level' and ironically, in direct contrast to Rosenblum's ethos, many believe that it has now facilitated the ability to film what they consider to be 'hard news' rather than human-interest stories.

> I think that PDP is definitely here to stay – but at what level I just don't know. I think it will find its own level and we will use a mixed economy of crews and PDP. I hope we do anyway. I don't want to do PDP all the time.
>
> (Kate, PDP operator, BBC Nottingham)

> I think people thought when PDP came in that it was supposed to be used to do the fluffy bits, but they're not – they're doing strong stories and quite often the reporters on these stories will have to start off doing some PDP work before they get a craft camera crew to work with so it's working alongside – quite often it works like that – it's all gone a bit full circle – but I like the way we are going now – it is news – it is busy – I like it – I like being busy – getting back to being a proper news office that we were all those years ago.
>
> (Lynne, CDA, BBC Nottingham)

It is significant that most of the antithetical reaction to PDP is still based around the combined issues of story content and the reconfiguration of news, as well as the quality of transmitted material. As has been evident there is an assumed correlation between the two. This correlation finds justification in the overarching belief that news is still better covered by a team rather than by a single operator, indicating once again that there is a willing acceptance of a network to facilitate the successful production of news.

> One of the things that I am concerned about – and there are some great PDP pieces – it's team-working. Where you go out with a good camera operator and a journalist, you know you have that dynamic and then you go back and you edit with a good picture editor, and you have that dynamic, and you can throw in a good director or graphic designer – the really special stuff comes out of teamwork.
>
> (Mark, director, BBC Nottingham)

A further concept to explore so as to narrate this story of translation adequately is that of network *irreversibility*. This notion helps one to recognise whether or not a particular actor translation has been completed and the network stabilised. Callon argues that irreversibility depends upon a number of factors.

> I would say that the irreversibility of translation depends on two things: the extent to which it is subsequently impossible to go back to a point where that translation was only one among others; the extent to which it shapes and determines subsequent translations. Overall, however, it could be said that irreversibility increases to the extent that each element, intermediary and translator is inscribed in a 'bundle' of interrelationships. In such tightly coupled networks, any attempt to modify one element by redefining it leads to a general process of retranslation – the more numerous and heterogeneous the interrelationships, the greater the possibility of successful resistance to alternative translations.
>
> (Callon, 1980, p.212)

A conclusive translation process would therefore produce a black box. Trials of resistances have been successful, a number of significant alliances forged, and the unstable actor then closes these network associations around itself so tightly as to render further translation more dangerous to those actors attempting it than to its own position. The media hub is defined thus. Personal Digital Production is not. As we have seen the translation of PDP is still very much in progress. In fact, we still have not analysed what may be the most significant translation of PDP yet. This is exemplified by the BBC's new experimental project, providing local news to smaller audiences within a region of the country, similar to the reach of local radio. This service has only become possible to first of all contemplate and then to provide because of the development of PDP, and the increased use of video journalists within the BBC's newsrooms across the country. We will be looking at this project in more detail in the following chapter.

The translation process that has been explored in this chapter is a translation of observed network practice (PDP implementation) leading to a seemingly cohesive narrative account. Yet it would be to contradict translation as both performance and semiology to argue that the narrative acts as a completely faithful presentation of PDP's implementation. The beauty of translation is that it occurs at all levels of the network, including that of the researcher's observations and accounting. This text is folded within the context of the technology and the network it purports to describe. As Latour argues

> Translation is a term that criss-crosses the modernist settlement. In its linguistic and material connotations, it refers to all the displacements

through others actors whose mediation is indispensable for any action to occur. In place of a rigid opposition between context and content, chains of translation refer to the work through which actors modify, displace, and translate their various and contradictory interests.

(Latour, 1999, p.311)

The attempt to narrate a story of any network performance, of varied and multiple voices and of heterogeneous and contingent translations, all of which is still going on even at the point of writing, is certainly a challenge. But other researchers and social scientists have embraced this challenge before as a way to resist drawing highly theorised and often over-generalised conclusions to which the empirical findings never concur.

I seek an interpretive social science that is simultaneously auto-ethno-graphic, vulnerable, performative and critical. This is a social science that refuses abstractions and high theory. It is a way of being in the world, a way of writing, hearing and listening. Viewing culture as a complex, performative process, it seeks to understand how people enact and construct meaning in their everyday lives.

(Denzin, 2001, p.43)

As we have seen in this chapter, following and accounting for translations within the news network demands that the account of it is contingent and destabilised.

A network is a concept, not a thing out-there. It is a tool to help describe something, not what is being described ... a network is not what is represented in the text, but what readies the text to take the relay of actors as mediators ... whatever the word, we need something to designate flows of translations.

(Latour, 2005, p.131)

As the study of the news network develops, as human and nonhuman actors enter into more complex negotiations, as the observations made open up new controversies and reveal more uncertainty, our narrative will get shakier yet. This should be welcomed, not resisted. For it is in the very construction of these accounts, with their artificiality, their weaknesses and their uncertainty that the world of the news is revealed, not as a complete understandable and definable whole upon which a convenient label may be pinned, but as a mael-strom of micropractices that together, in association, in constant negotiation, go some way toward constructing what we know of as news. As Latour reminds us

The careers of mediators should be pursued all the way to the final report because a chain is only as weak as its weakest link. If the social is a trace, then it can be *re*traced; if it's an assembly then it can be *reas*-sembled. While there exists no material continuity between the society of the sociologist and any textual account — hence the wringing of hands about method, truth and political relevance — there might exist a plausible continuity between what the social, in our sense of the word, does and what a text may achieve — a *good* text, that is.

(Latour, 2005, p.128)

6

EXTENDING THE NETWORK

The BBC's local television project

One of the things we are going to learn is that there is no such thing
as technology transfer. That technologies don't originate at a point
and spread out. But instead they are passed. Passed from hand to
hand. And that as they are passed they are changed. Become less and
less recognisable.

(Law, 1997, p.2)

During this chapter we will continue to explore the translation process of our
digital technology, PDP or video journalism. As the quote suggests, any story of
translation involves multiple transformations of all the human and nonhuman
actors involved, and we will discover that PDP is once again quite radically
altered in various unpredictable ways throughout its ongoing translation process.
As our story develops so too does our network. No longer confined to the
Nottingham newsroom, this episode of the story takes us into other radio and
television newsrooms in various separate locations throughout the West Midlands. This is the story of the BBC's local television experiment: a pilot project
carried out by BBC Nations and Regions during a nine-month period from
December 2005 until August 2006. The aim of the project was to provide a
specifically local television service for six West Midlands' geographical areas
similar to those serviced by the BBC's local radio stations. Therefore the existing local radio areas were used as the subregions at which the six pilot services
were targeted. These were Birmingham, The Black Country, Hereford and Worcester, Shropshire, Coventry and Warwickshire, and Staffordshire. Five video
journalists and two producers were located at each location. The local television
trial was intended to use the existing infrastructure of both local radio and the
BBC's internet sites to create fully integrated multimedia production centres,
providing the whole range of the BBC's services for the local area.

If the project is successful, there might eventually be up to 66 local broadcasting stations in the UK, 48 in England and 18 in Wales, Scotland and

Northern Ireland. The primary technology used in the pilot was what has become known collectively as PDP or to be more precise, the now updated version of the PD150 camera, the Sony Z100 digital camera. It is the translation process of this particular technology and the further transformations that occur during this process to both the human actors and the machines with which they are associated that will be the main focus of our exploration of the BBC's pilot project.

In the previous chapter we discovered how as the technology becomes embedded in the news network, a complex and ongoing process of translation occurs, which includes the reconfiguration of the news agenda, the news-gathering processes and also the news content. As Law emphasises, translation is a verb that implies both transformation as well as the possibility of equivalence. The important point to recognise is that when something is translated it is to some extent transformed. A translated actor is thus not the same as the original, or better, it is both similar and different (Law, 1997). As we shall see from our exploration of the local television project a number of actors become translated. Some are changed quite radically, while others remain similar, only differing slightly from their original state. Throughout this chapter we will chart each of these translations and reveal how specific actors become altered by their association with one another, and how such alterations in turn transform the news-gathering routines and news content.

This is why an Actor Network Theory (ANT) focus is so useful. To return to the theoretical discussion we started in Chapter 3, remember that ANT is the study of how mediators mediate: how they join, negotiate and translate from one network to another. This is what distinguishes ANT from other approaches to media studies. It emphasises that *all* social activity requires mediation, and that all forms of objects and technologies are potentially mediatory depending on the networks in which they are engaged. This is fundamental to our understanding of the digital technologies within the news network. As we have seen, these technologies are just as likely to become altered as their human counterparts, to undergo translation and to become destabilised by other actor translations. In so doing, they may be able to transform the news agenda, or news processes or news content. But they do not do this alone. Technology does not determine the content of news. It is simply one actor in a network of hundreds of other human and nonhuman actors and it is only in mediation with all of these other actors that it has any determining effect upon news. It is our job to continue to try to unravel that complex process of mediation, as we have been doing throughout our exploration of the news process and as we shall continue to do now that we turn out attentions to the local television news project.

To begin with we need to outline the aims and objectives of the project, describe the structure and extent of its production network and familiarise ourselves with its significant practices, before we can begin to chart some of the most significant actors so as to gain a deeper understanding of how the translation of PDP or video journalism enables the emergence of a new form of television news.

The structure of the local television project

The nine-month local television project, which was based in the West Midlands' geographical area was, according to the BBC's own promotional material, an attempt to provide ultra-local news-on-demand for people where and when they wanted it. As the BBC's head of regional and local programmes (HRLP) in the region, David Holdsworth, described it the service would 'kick start something for local audiences and provide a new style of news not previously produced by the BBC'. At a very early project meeting with staff held in the centre of Birmingham, the BBC's controller of English Regions, Andy Griffy, described how the concept of local television news had grown from a previous experiment in the city of Hull where local news had already been successfully piloted.

> The starting point for all this was the Hull experiment. Hull is a broadband city. Ten-thousand homes can receive it so it gave us a great test-tube for something universal but the pace of this is now extraordinary. We gave people in Hull loads of digital programmes including *Walking with Dinosaurs* – but by far and away the most popular programme was local television news. It had a 70 per cent reach. There was also a growth of the Internet *Where I Live sites* which was all part of this – the power of the local was extraordinary – it's because most people only live within a 40 mile radius of their homes in terms of what interests them.
>
> (Andy Griffy, controller English Regions, 2005)

As we learned in the previous two chapters, for an innovation such as PDP or video journalism to be successful, other actors must be brought into contact with it and aligned with it. In ANT terms they must be enrolled so that the links they forge with the innovation strengthens it and ensures it remains successfully adopted and utilised. Recalling his analysis of the work of Louis Pasteur, Latour shows how the story of pasteurisation is not simply one of a genius and a single scientific discovery, but is instead one of a series of translations between many actors who become aligned with one another and who in their association with one another all enable the successful innovation of the pasteurisation process. Louis Pasteur is only one human actor among many in that network. Actor networks are motivated by the need for self-consolidation and

117

enhanced strength. And they can only acquire this in association with others. Indeed digitisation enables us to see how mediation is not actor-specific. Van-Loon argues that the digital medium itself expresses a universality of flow; anything can link to anything through digital interfaces. Text, sound and image are all exchangeable as digital data. And consolidation takes place when many actors engage with each other through similar or exchangeable protocols (Van-Loon, 2007). We can see exactly the same thing happening here in the early stages of the local television project. BBC managers realise that the experiment in Hull was successful. Therefore they deliberately enrol the same human actors and the same digital technologies into the new Midlands' local television network. They realise that consolidation will also enable the success of this project. They create a network, even if they do not use these terms, in order to allow mediation to take place in an intensively connected network of both human and nonhuman actors all of whom have traces of successful past translations enfolded within their present ones. Many of the same people are therefore employed who have worked on the previous television project in Hull, and the same digital technology is implemented, though both these human and nonhuman actors also undergo translation during the pilot project as we shall discover from our analysis of the evidence. Before we begin to explore the empirical findings, we need to briefly outline the practical details of the project and to highlight the significant areas where translation of both the digital technologies and the human actors associated with them are most likely to take place.

The local television service is to have two modes of delivery. On broadband the service will be 'on demand' where audiences will be able to access it via the BBC's existing *Where I Live* internet sites and click on single news stories in package format from whatever area they choose, in whatever order they choose. They are also able to watch the entire local television news hour as it is uploaded onto the sites after it has been transmitted on digital satellite television. The second mode of delivery is a televised satellite-news loop that is an hour in duration and within which each of the six areas produces a ten-minute news bulletin. This can be accessed by pressing the red button on the television remote handset, which will take the viewer through to *BBCi* – from where they will see a menu that will list the six areas and the times they are broadcast within the hour loop. This is watched in linear fashion and cannot be accessed on demand. Instead viewers either watch the entire loop, or alternatively make a note of the specific times that their particular area's news programme will be broadcast and tune in at those times for their own local news. During the pilot other modes of delivery are discussed such as uploading to mobile phones and viewing on Cable or Freeview television. These services have not yet been introduced but may well develop should the BBC decide to roll out the local news service across the UK.

The individual news pieces are shorter than regional television news items; no longer than one-and-a-half minutes and there is no presenter linking the packages together. There is more use of graphics to link items but there is a 'news in brief' section whose content underwent quite radical translation as the project developed. The other crucial aspect to this project and one that represents a significant translation of the utilisation of the technology was that from the very beginning there was a strong emphasis put on the idea that local news must also mean news that is produced not by BBC journalists, but by members of the community. The BBC views this as so crucial to the success of the local news project that they placed a target of 25 per cent of the total local news content to be produced by members of the community.

> The whole concept of citizen journalism will be a very big part of this. We need to think about communities of people making good films – but we also need to find ways to allow those people who can't yet make films to come forward – what we want to avoid is the usual suspects always coming forward.
>
> (Andy Griffy, controller English Regions, 2005)

This is a significant statement as it immediately associates the ability to hear the voice of the community with the technological know-how of that community. A large part of this project concerned itself with BBC journalists training ordinary people how to use the small digital cameras and laptop editing systems so that they could make their own independent films. Just as Rosenblum had done at the BBC Training Centre a paradigm is established here that places technological expertise at the centre of an enhanced democratisation of news. In other words, it is the relationship between the human and the nonhuman actor – the technology – that is seen to be absolutely crucial to the ability to construct news. And we shall see as our story develops, it is this aspect of the project that causes the most varied and disparate reactions from those human actors involved, as well as the most significant and varied transformations of the news agenda, of what is then defined as news and the content of that news.

As community journalism is one of the primary aims of the project a community producer is deployed in each of the six areas. Their task is to gain access to the community, create links and contacts, and gather local story ideas that can then be produced by members of the public, guided by the producer's technological filming and editing expertise. The producers are not meant to produce the news stories themselves, but to run workshops and training sessions to enable members of the local community to operate cameras and edit their filmed footage into what will be a news item fit for broadcast. Yet from the very beginning of the project many of the people involved were dubious about both the construction process and the content of the community items.

> I'm not sure community content has got a place. I think people delivering stuff to the BBC, certainly images coming into the BBC from all sorts of outlets is fine, and people making their own films with some help – possibly – but if it's on a news topic that is fine. But all this community content stuff is – here's my local drama group – it's featurey sort of stuff and I don't think it fits. It seems a bit of an add-on and it opens up that whole debate of what is community content? The only people who can basically gather, edit and tell a story with images are film-makers who are in the community who are doing it for a living or are doing it as a very serious hobby. The general public don't have the skills so the BBC should not make it a 25 per cent target.
>
> (Ian, local television trainer, BBC Birmingham)

Notwithstanding this note of anxiety from some of the people involved in the production of the community pieces for local television, BBC management stress that the role of the community, and the quality of the community content that is broadcast during the nine-month pilot, will be a significant factor when it comes to the overall appraisal of the local television project and will play an important role in the BBC's final decision as to whether or not the service will be rolled out across the UK. Once again, the paradigm that is constructed here places the technology, the small digital cameras and laptop editing systems, in a direct relationship with the ordinary person who is now able to construct their own news stories. Reminiscent of Rosenblum's original premise, the idea is that as the technology is so easy to use it *enables* the ordinary man or woman on the street to construct their own news, rather than having to rely upon small numbers of highly trained journalists who are lucky enough to have exclusive access to those technologies that are deliberately out of the general public's reach.

> What we're doing here isn't just about the pilot. This will massively change the future of news across the UK. It's about getting in touch with real people's emotions and if we haven't found ways to feed-in quality audio and video from them then we're missing a trick as the technology is there. Local television has to satisfy the Board of Governors, increase the reach of the BBC and show value for money. Then if it does all that it will be subject to a market assessment test to see if it has made a justifiable impact on the market, then it will be subject to public consultations. ITV is already trying this and they have launched local television in Brighton and Hastings. But they haven't employed

any more people, and more importantly there is nothing community based about it.

(Andy Griffy, controller English Regions)

Whether such a Utopian vision of the democratisation of the news-making process is actually realised during the pilot will be one of the major translations that our network analysis will help us to explore in more detail.

A further indication of the BBC's investment and interest in community produced items occurs just two months into the pilot, when six faith producers are deployed in each of the separate areas with a specific remit to assist the various local faith and religious groups in the production of their own material for local television.

Our remit is to use two Sony HC1 Cameras, which are high-definition camcorders, to do workshops with different people in the religious community – interested people tend to come to us – we run work-shops on how to use a camera for about two-and-a-half hours – they come back and then we do an editing workshop together where I ingest their tape into the computer and we look at their material. We do a rough edit together and then I bring it back and tidy it up and it pretty much goes out on local TV.

(Marsha, faith producer, BBC Birmingham)

As we begin to analyse the local television project in more detail, we will investigate whether or not these faith producers manage to access the commu-nity successfully and the crucial role that the associated technological actors play in their attempts to establish community connections.

Before we begin to look at the major actors involved it is important that we understand how the local television news project is produced and transmitted, as these technological arrangements begin to raise important journalistic issues as well as becoming central to some significant network translations once the pilot begins to develop. The local television teams are located in each of the six existing local radio stations, which are Birmingham, The Black Country, Here-ford and Worcester, Shropshire, Coventry and Warwickshire, and Staffordshire. They work alongside their local radio colleagues but they produce their own pieces that they film and edit in a single day, for transmission on that day. Once the items are completed, the editor of the radio station then produces a ten-minute bulletin from these individual pieces, as well as a *News in brief* section, a series of connecting graphics and some travel information. The bulletin is then fed into a central hub that is located in the BBC's regional newsroom in Bir-mingham, but which is situated in the corner of the newsroom away from the regional programme's own hub. The two hubs operate completely separately from one another.

The 'hub-and-spoke' arrangement, as it is known, that is designed for the local news project causes some strong disagreements among journalists in both the Birmingham regional newsroom and in the separate local radio stations. It is also an issue that even the project's technological team who designed the system do not find entirely satisfactory. Once again the discussion focuses on the complex relationship between unpredictable and ever-developing technologies and human actor expectations and needs. If we look at just two initial quotes, one from a producer in the Stoke newsroom, and the other from one of the hub's engineering team in Birmingham, it is evident that there are a number of crucial issues being raised that continue to cause tensions between actors and that are never really properly resolved throughout the duration of the project. Using our ANT focus, they also indicate where the most significant translations within the news network will occur and we will map these as our analysis develops.

> What I find frustrating is that I will put together a bulletin – what I think of as a bulletin – I have coordinated what I think is a balanced bulletin and then for somebody else to put it together – sometimes the order isn't right and at the beginning and the end there are little stings that are tagged onto the end and quite often they may be quite key to the story telling of the piece. There might be a little tease on the front, or editorially there might be a tag on the end where I have said, I will want a back announcement in terms of balance or in terms of an appeal if I want someone to get in touch with us, but quite often I will watch it but that's been hacked off because the hub team are just looking at timing.
>
> (Stuart, producer, Stoke)

> I think it's a technical thing at the moment – because we have to screen stuff – I mean on the hub at the moment we're like the gatekeepers – if you like – we act a bit like sub editors – we're like the last line of defence before something goes out. Because if you imagine all the video journalists are locked in on their own pieces, it's so easy to make a spelling mistake and it's so difficult to see yourself – and also technically as well. You can't be over everything. There is a limit to being multiskilled.
>
> (Darren, hub operator)

The significant issue that is being raised here calls to mind our earlier analysis of the Nottingham newsroom hub in Chapter 3. The video journalists in the local radio stations enjoy a certain amount of editorial and journalistic autonomy over their own pieces and the final bulletin they produce. But once it leaves their station and is fed into the hub the issue of who has ownership over the material becomes ambiguous. Once again, the black box status of the hub as a primary technological actor who acts as the *obligatory point of passage* seriously threatens the autonomy of the individual journalist. It is a frustration that is voiced by journalists throughout the pilot project, but which has quite different implications within the network than our analysis of the Nottingham hub revealed. This is because of the hub's unique position within the local television network that does not afford it consistent black box status. We will return to an analysis of these network implications of the hub-and-spoke arrangement later on.

In the first part of this chapter we have outlined the structure of the pilot project as well as identifying some of the main characteristics of the technological and journalistic arrangements so that we're familiar with our wider actor network and when we now come to use our ANT tool kit, we can reveal where the main network translations of our most significant actors may occur. To make things a little easier, let's briefly list what or who these actors could be.

Our main human actors will include our five video journalists working autonomously on their local news pieces in each of the six radio stations. Our six community and six faith producers will also be significant to our story, as will our six radio editors who produce their bulletins before sending the material to the central hub team in Birmingham. In this regional newsroom our local television-hub team will be significant, as will our regional-news team who are working alongside the local television team but producing their own daily regional news using their own journalists and their own technologies. Of our technologies, our PDP cameras or their equivalents, the Sony Z100s that are used by our video journalists are of crucial importance. So too are the Sony HC1 cameras that are given out to the members of the public. And the hub itself is a highly significant actor in our network, as are the satellites used for transmission and the computers that upload the internet material for broadband delivery. And let's not forget our members of the general public who are to become our amateur film-makers. They too play a crucial role in this particular story of network translations. We could go on, including the BBC governors and regional managers as well as journalists and producers and editors back in the Nottingham newsroom, they too are part of the same network and we will in fact return to these at the end of this chapter as they will figure in our continuing story. But let's pause for now and try to unravel all of the connections between these human and nonhuman actors that we have listed as we try to perform our story of local television news.

The community as an actor

As we have witnessed one of the most significant factors in our story of the implementation of PDP or video journalism, as it is more widely known, is which individuals get access to the cameras themselves, and how they then decide to use them. This has never remained fixed or constant, but has changed throughout our story. Having started life as Rosenblum's individual concept of the ability to bypass producers and editors and to have the capability for autonomous, personal, and in-depth film-making, this then developed from the BBC Training Centre in Newcastle, through the Nottingham newsroom, out to the individual PDP bureaux and now down to the Birmingham newsroom and adjoining local radio stations. Throughout all of these stages or network translations the architecture of the machine has stayed relatively the same, only changing in so far as updated models have replaced the original PD150 camera. But the working practices, and therefore how the machines are actually deployed, have altered along the way quite dramatically. And as those changes or translations have occurred, we have also seen how established definitions of news have altered in quite surprising ways that even our original progenitor Michael Rosenblum did not or could not have predicted. Yet even as we have explored all these alterations to both news processes and news content, the actual machines have only ever resided in the hand of BBC personnel. Now this has changed. As soon as the local television project was launched in August 2005, the network within which these technologies are being utilised grew considerably as every member of the West Midlands community, from Birmingham to Stoke, from Worcester to Coventry, now had the potential to take a BBC camera and film their own material. Yet what we will see is that this doesn't alter the network in a homogeneous or consistent way, but in fractious and haphazard ways depending on which part of the network we choose to look at. We need to explore some of these changes in detail to decide what translations are occurring and in what places in our network. We also need to recognise what is happening to our technology to understand how, in close association with its most proximate actors at specific points in the network, it is able to begin to once again reconfigure the news agenda. Yet with any successful network translation our technological actor does not alter in isolation. It too is altered and at the same time it also alters those other actors most closely associated with it. As Michel Callon explains

> Translations may change as time passes. Sometimes they are a product of compromise and mutual adjustment negotiated through a series of iterations. And when they are embodied in texts, machines, bodily skills and the rest, the latter become their support, their more or less

faithful executive. At one extreme the latter may be an isolated and homogeneous intermediary. At the other extreme, and more likely – they may be a hybrid cascade of intermediaries with articulated roles, links and feedback loops between the actors ... In either case a concern with translation focuses on the process of mutual definition and inscription.

(Callon, 1991, p.160)

It is to this 'hybrid cascade of intermediaries ... links and feedback loops' that we now turn in our exploration of the community as an actor.

In the earliest discussions regarding the community content of the local television project the general public were immediately categorised in terms of their technological capabilities. Three distinct categories were created: *the Cans, the Coulds and the Can'ts,* which referred to those who were able to use and had access to a camera and edit system, those who might be able to had they access to the machinery, and those who simply lacked both the access to the machinery and the technological capability to operate it even if they were permitted the required access.

As Chris Atton has noted in his illuminating exploration of the concept of citizen journalism, this crucial recognition that if the citizen is to be permitted real autonomy in the construction of news, they must first of all cultivate the required technological skills, is fundamental to a deeper understanding of the agency of technology within news production in general. The BBC rightly recognised that unless it enabled ordinary people to embrace these technical skills, the concept of citizen journalism would not be anything more radical than less-skilled people imitating the already accepted practices of the BBC.

If we return to our ANT terminology here, the individual person on the street was now being asked to translate their technogrammatic position within the network, in order to radically alter their sociogrammatic position from that of a *passive viewer* of the news, to an *active producer* of news. It is only if these radical translations are successfully performed that there can be any concept of a new form of citizen journalism that does not simply echo the practices of news as we already know it.

Rodriguez has conceptualised such media as 'citizens' media'. By this she means a philosophy of journalism and a set of practices that are embedded within the everyday lives of citizens, and media content that is both driven and produced by these people. Approached in this way, alternative media may be understood as a radical challenge to the professionalised and institutionalised practices of the mainstream media ... Its practices emphasise first person, eyewitness accounts by participants;

a reworking of the populist approaches of tabloid newspapers to recover a 'radical popular' style of reporting; collective and anti-hierarchical forms of organisation which eschew demarcation and specialisation and which importantly suggest an inclusive, radical form of civic journalism.

(Atton, 2003, p.267)

Although BBC managers do initially hierarchise the general public by means of their three technogrammatic categories, *the Cans, the Coulds and the Can'ts*, there is still a genuine, rigorous attempt throughout the nine-month pilot to bring training and development opportunities to those people who in the past may not have had the access or possess the relevant skills to construct their own news material.

We're encouraged to leave somewhat of a skills legacy with these faith communities and I don't see how I can do that if I go and I do the filming. And how much is it their story if I am doing the filming and I'm taking it away and I'm doing the editing. If it's someone else's story they should do it.

(Marsha, faith producer, BBC Birmingham)

But whether the BBC's objective to transform the *Can'ts* into *Cans* so as to enable more people within the local communities to construct their own news stories is realistic, and whether or not it is successfully realised throughout the duration of the pilot is infinitely debatable by those people working within the project, depending upon where in the network one is located. For instance, let's take two quotes from two community and faith producers. They both work in Birmingham's city centre where there is easy access to community groups, including amateur film-making societies or university media students. The first producer's opinion of the BBC's community content objectives is both positive and enthusiastic.

I made the point of saying it doesn't matter how old you are or what your background is – and there have been people who have never held a camera before now making little bits of television – they've done the best they can. And viewers are more understanding if they know it's been made by an amateur.

(Marsha, faith producer, BBC Birmingham)

The second producer also works in the same inner city area as a community producer. Her view is slightly more circumspect as she is not entirely satisfied with the quality of the films she says she is getting back from the community, even though she does still believe that the 25 per cent quota for community pieces is a realistic target.

> People are making content but they just need the skills to be shown how to make it better. They're making it and it's great content, but it's not really broadcastable, that is what we're finding. The BBC knows there is a lot of content out there, but they don't know how to use it so that it can be broadcast. So it's our job to say; 'Well ok great we need to film it like this!' And that is a big part of my job.
>
> (Patricia, community producer, BBC Birmingham)

If we then look at another two community and faith producers working in a different part of the network, in a more rural area where access to established community groups may be more difficult, and where the general level of media education is considerably lower, the perceptions and the working practices these individuals describe is very different indeed. And what is more, the technology is actually being implemented very differently with a far greater emphasis placed on the BBC producer constructing the film, rather than the public developing the required independent technical skills.

> If I am honest it is more leaning towards me making the films just because it is quite difficult to get people to take a camera off your hands and go away and shoot something decent. It's really time consuming and you're not going to get many films ... and your name's going to it at the end of the day so you don't want to be putting out rubbish basically. People are very interested to tell their story and I think it is perfectly valid for you to go in with a camera and work with people to tell their story.
>
> (Anita, faith producer, BBC Coventry)

> I don't personally feel comfortable giving a teenager a camera as I don't know what's going to happen to them. One got stolen from me so that was a difficulty. I think we should be the VJs and then we get a better piece. I love this job but it is too restrictive for one-and-a-half minutes and giving the cameras to the community I think is a waste of time actually. So in a way that devalues my job by saying don't give cameras out to the community but I think there is still a role to play in the community, but people get so daunted and it's not fair on me because I'm exhausted trying to get these people to come in and there's not the time you can spend with them.
>
> (Kathleen, community producer, BBC Coventry)

A number of important issues are raised here. The most obvious is that the producer's role as the general public's television trainer is seen to be compromised by a series of different factors to such an extent that this individual, situated as she is on a separate part of the network to her producer counterparts in the regional newsroom in Birmingham, is able to adopt very different working practices, which in turn also influence her own definition of what is community content and what constitutes local news. She cites the length of time it takes to train unskilled people to an acceptable standard, the one-and-a-half minute duration of the individual pieces as too restrictive and also therefore more difficult for untrained people who are not used to working to either temporal or spatial deadlines. She also highlights the very practical difficulties of allowing the cameras out into the community where one was stolen. All of these various practical, journalistic and technological factors combine together to create a perception of what this individual believes community content could and should be. The *logistics* involved in constructing the community content are thus a significant part of what she perceives that community content to be; the two are inextricably linked. Definitions of news, as we have seen before, are thus once more entangled with the construction process itself. This also signifies a translation of the BBC's original objective of enabling the ordinary person to film and edit their material. Once this objective is introduced into a complex network such as the local television project, it undergoes a series of translations depending upon where in the network it is situated. Here, in a more rural part of the network, out of the watchful eyes of BBC managers and other regional television producers, the operations of the community producers are very different from those who are working in the BBC regional newsroom in the centre of Birmingham. Yet, although they have adopted different working practices, and may have a different perception of what community content should look like, these producers still believe they are producing what can be defined in general BBC terms as community content.

> What I love is spending the time with people – just sitting down with them – that's when the stories come out. So it's actually been fantastic to be given that time but it could be used in a better way. I do most of the films myself now because I don't want to put out anything that isn't any good because it puts a bad name to the faith aspect of this project and the community aspect of this project and I can completely square it with myself when I sit down and make these films. Is this a community piece? Is this a faith piece? Yes because I have talked with them, I have worked with them and I have asked them what they want to do.
>
> (Kathleen, community producer, BBC Coventry)

The issues raised here lead us to further explorations of what is defined by different actors as community content, and in turn, what is defined as local news. As we can expect, rather than there being evidence of a homogeneous and consistent translation of local news criteria and definitions within the local television network, there is instead the *hybrid cascade of intermediaries* to which Callon referred earlier, again depending upon where actors are located within the network and depending upon the other actors with which they are associated. As we have already seen, the digital cameras, while remaining consistent at least with regard to their own architecture, are still utilised in more than one way by separate human actors and these different modes of operation themselves create different ways of defining news. If we look at a number of other human actors situated in various locations of the network, individual definitions of local news and community content become even more disparate. As is always the case, such definitions are intricately entangled with the associations established with other actors within the network at that specific point. Let's take a look at a couple of examples.

Working practices, technologies and definitions of local news

If we take two sets of quotes from four different actors all of whom are working on the local news project but whose daily responsibilities are entirely different, situated as they are on different nodes of the network, it is soon evident that there is no shared conception of how the local news service should be constructed and delivered, and in a more general sense, what defines local news. BBC management has always encouraged rigorous debate around these issues stressing that the pilot provides both a vehicle and a space for these kinds of debates to be aired, but what is happening from an ANT perspective is something rather more fundamental to news production. Instead of there being a group of homogeneous actors all of whom work towards a shared goal of producing a type of programme they all agree to be defined in the same way, if we look more closely at any news network we will soon find that there is only a series of disparate actors, both human and nonhuman, who act according to the *specific* associations they make with other actors nearest to them on the network and who they may or may not be able to translate or manipulate depending on the stability of their own network position. Any notion of homogeneity, of shared perspectives and consistent working practices, is soon dissolved once we take the time to explore the detail of these network connections. The local television project, itself a new and innovative part of our overall news production network, is thus a fecund territory to explore such connections as it is a network in the making; an innovation beginning to stabilise where all its actors are fiercely jostling for stronger and ultimately more stable positions.

If we take a look at the initial management objectives for the project it is clear that while the service is considered to be a departure from either local radio, or from regional television, and has therefore 'to feel different in its style of presentation', it is still to be closely associated with news and is defined primarily as a news service.

> The emphasis must be still on news. We are doing community projects but we must still assume that we are a news service.
>
> (Sarah, project manager, BBC Birmingham)

Other project managers also emphasise the fact that the local television service is a chance for journalists to try something new or 'to dare to be different'. Interestingly, one manager makes a direct reference to Rosenblum in his initial discussion of the project, stating that Rosenblum had been brought in by the BBC to try to make the regional news more radical, but that this experiment had failed to materialise, as we have also seen in our own analysis in the previous two chapters.

But once the local television project is underway, the discussion continues to rage around the issue of local news content. As it has in all the past translations of PDP, the transformation of news definitions is inextricably linked to the use and adoption of the new technologies, and the particular ways in which these technologies are implemented. As one journalist argues, the 25 per cent quota of community generated pieces is only a logical response to the ways in which people are now utilising technologies in their daily lives.

> I think ultimately we have got to do more of this really. When we see the big news events that have happened, like the London bombings, the stuff that makes it on the air first are people's mobile phone material, photos they've taken on the mobile phone, people with the little camcorders, and that's becoming more common. And we close our doors to that at our peril.
>
> (Stuart, senior journalist, BBC Stoke)

Here news is partially defined as the technological ability to record pictures quickly and to upload them to relevant broadcasting platforms. Both the technical skills and the form of delivery of the recorded material are in themselves primary defining constituents of news content. If we take another comment from a faith producer working in the Birmingham area, her definition of what local news should be is entirely different, though once again, it is inextricably linked to the technological ability of those who are producing the material.

The pieces are literally anything. They're personal expressions of faith, so they may have no traditional news value whatsoever. I've had a piece about Buddhist chanting, another on how a young man feels to be part of the Salvation Army. There was one piece that went out over Christmas that was just a gospel singer singing 'Oh Holy Night' with pictures of a nativity, and they're much easier for people to film and edit this way. So they vary and I think there is a nice sense of relief in a local TV bulletin, which can be really quite fast paced. The length of pieces is only a-minute-and-a-half but it's just a space for reflection. I personally feel that it's fantastic that the BBC is doing this because up until now how often do you see a real person saying this is what it's like for me to be a Buddhist, or a Jew or a Muslim. So I think it's amazing that that's happening.

(Marsha, faith producer, BBC Birmingham)

Here the perception that the local television service should be a primary news service is replaced by a more practical recognition that the stories may have no 'traditional' news sense but that if they are more simple personal expressions of faith or belief, they will be far easier to produce. Once again the translation that occurs is partially driven by the technology being used, but is equally determined by the human actor's relationship with both that technology and the other human actors with whom she is associated, in this case, the unskilled general public. It is this specific relationship that is also criticised by others within the network for its inability to produce anything other than lightweight, populist films that are devoid of news content. Once again the paradigm being constructed places technological expertise right at the heart of the news construction process. In this individual's opinion, without the relevant technical skills, the news production process and therefore the news content will inevitably suffer.

If you are to make 25 per cent from the community, if you are to make stuff that people have shot or edited themselves, actually you need your very best journalists working on that because that's harder to do than going and shooting your own stuff. The community producers they have recruited to that are quite junior people with very little experience and it makes it really, really tough to take someone else's material and turn it into a story. You need your best people on that really . . . So I think while there's some cracking stuff, and there is an outlet for it, I mean did you see the stuff from Coventry about the guy who did all the street dancing? Yes, fantastic stuff but then they say, 'Here's the news from Coventry today' and they lead with dancing and then there's the sport! It makes you think what on earth is this channel about?

(Ian, local television trainer, BBC Birmingham)

Towards the end of the project there is also a discernible shift in the management perspective that the service should only be delivering news driven content. Furthermore, there is an acknowledgement that there have been some problems generating the community material, not just in terms of the technical quality already mentioned, but also the skills required to produce a television piece with structural coherence and journalistic relevance to the viewer. Yet this is immediately countered by what is perceived to be a deliberate shift away from monopolistic BBC programming towards a more democratic and inclusive service. Thus the community content is now not only defined by what it is in itself, but also by what it might signify to the viewer about the BBC in more general terms as a viewer-friendly and politically progressive organisation.

> I think the content is as you expect more patchy – and quite a lot of it by normal broadcasting criteria – I don't necessarily mean technical here but in terms of storytelling or the level of interest or relevance it might have for the average viewer isn't very good – but the best of it is fantastic – I actually think the best of it is the best stuff you see – and the other thing that I have gathered from the qualitative research is that even among some viewers who don't choose to watch the community content, the fact that it is there influences their overall view of the service and makes them more appreciative of it being less of a top-down BBC offer and more of a community offer.
>
> (David, HRLP, BBC Birmingham)

What we have seen from these short examples is how our network is fractured and heterogeneous and that even the most overarching issues, such as what local news should include, look like or how it should be produced, are all defined by separate constellations of human and nonhuman actors depending upon their own specific network positions. Unfortunately, we do not have the space to continue to explore other important actor groups such as the relationship between the regional-news team and the local television team in the Birmingham newsroom, or the working practices of the video journalists situated in the six local radio stations, and their local radio colleagues. But as we can now expect, all of these different actor associations within separate but related parts of the network will reveal disparate working practices and utilisation of technologies and varied perceptions of local news and the local news project. Further research is needed here, should the BBC's pilot be successful and local news is extended throughout the UK. Yet what we must explore now in the light of our continuing analysis of digital technologies, is the role of the local television hub and the implications of it occupying such a primary, yet also curiously ambivalent position within the local television network.

The local television hub

As we have seen from earlier journalists' reactions to the hub-and-spoke arrangement, there is a shared frustration with the production process whereby the individual local bulletins are fed into the central hub and edited together to make the final hour-long programme for satellite transmission, as well as being uploaded onto the BBC's *Where I Live* internet sites for broadband delivery. Most of the video journalists and the local radio editors feel there is confusion over who has editorial control over the material and some find their individual items being altered by the central hub team, without being asked to sanction the changes. This frustration is exacerbated for those journalists who were present at the initial planning meetings where editorial ownership was discussed at length. At this stage the main producers of the project stressed that the six individual radio editors would have editorial control over how their bulletin should look.

> The hub team will certainly know what makes a story work, but the radio editors own the bulletins. And while there will be a conversation both ways, what the radio editors say will go.
>
> (Sarah, local television project producer, BBC Birmingham)

Yet as we can see from a number of interviews during the project with both video journalists and radio editors within the six local areas, this practice is not to their mind satisfactorily executed on a day-to-day basis.

> The hub team do have a very difficult job. I can't imagine how stressful that must be for them. But sometimes you watch it and it's not the bulletin that you imagined and if they're short of something they might stick something up that I'm not happy with it, like a standby, and it's just very difficult to not have the ownership. I would like to compile the bulletin and feed it from here. The initial idea was that the hub would be your editorial linchpin. But why have an editorial linchpin in the hub who are not happy with the piece – it's been done by that point.
>
> (Stuart, senior producer, BBC Stoke)

> The major frustration of the whole project is that as we get more skilled, as the VJs get more skilled and creative and more technically able, we can make things look jazzier and snazzier and really give them a bit of gloss. But we can't assemble a bulletin here. It has to go to Birmingham back to the hub, and the kit they have means all they can do is a cut-and-paste job on what the material is, and so basically what we had was some links and some VT which were just kind of banged

together in the hub. It looked OK but it should have looked a lot
better and it's no one's fault apart from the people who first bought the
kit I guess that it didn't look any better.

(Duncan, editor, BBC Coventry)

Interestingly even some members of the hub team are not entirely satisfied
with the arrangement, and share similar frustrations with the technological
limitations of the editing package installed in the hub, though they do recognise
that there are significant related factors such as the amount of revenue allocated
for the pilot that has determined some of the technological limitations of the
machinery that has been installed.

The pilot is an editorial pilot so we have put in technology that will get
us on air but we haven't put in technology that's sustainable because we
don't know what we want to scale-up yet. We don't know what we
want to do. So really in terms of technology in terms of the pilot, it's
in, it's working, but one of the things we need to concentrate on is
taking the piece of content and being able to publish it to many more
different platforms without too much intervention. So we have broadband and we have satellite, during the length of the pilot. But we might
have 3G mobile phones, or Telewest on demand, or potentially making
it so we can download it onto the Apple Ipod, so there are a number of
other platforms.

(Adrian, technical project manager, BBC Birmingham)

If we now consider some of these issues through an ANT focus, we can begin
to recognise certain significant differences between the network position of this
hub, and the more stable position of the Nottingham media hub, which will in
turn help us to understand the crucial but at times very fluid and unstable role
that technological actors play within the local television project, as well as news
production networks more generally. To begin with we might want to argue that
the Birmingham hub still occupies a strong position vis-à-vis the human actors
within the six local areas. Each local team has to feed material into the hub, it
certainly acts as a gatekeeper or an *obligatory point of passage*. But it is also clear
that there are problems with the technology itself. In the previous quote, Adrian
is making a significant distinction between the hub's sociogram and its technogram when he states that the pilot is an 'editorial' one and the technology has
been installed in order to 'work'. He recognises that this particular hub is technically not wholly adequate for the job it is required to carry out. It therefore
does not occupy a consistently strong network position as its technogram, that is
its technical capabilities, are not strong enough to sustain its sociogrammatic

position within the network. As others have also commented, it is only capable of simple video edits; for example, it cannot perform video wipes, or edit sound levels. Therefore its sociogrammatic position within the network, which is that of an editorial gatekeeper, an actor who can perform complex editorial tasks in order to stabilise its position as gatekeeper, is thwarted by the limitations of its technological architecture.

But what does this tell us about technologies in a more general sense? How can we square this local television hub's rather ambivalent network position with that of the Nottingham hub that had acquired black box status within the network? The most crucial aspect to this particular analysis is that we can see just how fluid technologies can be. They play a crucial role in the gathering, production and the transmission of news, but their position does not remain static or consistent. They are as malleable and as inconsistent as their human counterparts. It is precisely because of the local television hub's *specific* network position, which is that of an experimental and limited piece of economically affordable technology, that it occupies the network position it does. It is certainly not in a stable position. It is nowhere near attaining black box status. Indeed many actors talk about the pilot as sustaining it, but that should the project be successful, there will be significant and even multiple translations of the hub, as the technological options for whatever final decision is made about the delivery to the different platforms on which local television might appear are myriad.

> I think there'll be regional hubs, but there is no reason why if we go purely to an on-demand service, that we don't have a massive server. We have a server, which all the clips go through; we have to schedule for television but for broadband, for the internet, and if you did it on-demand, you'd do it the same way. All you would do is effectively, once you've edited a piece it goes straight into a computer server and then you say, 'Right this one is for cable', so you encode it for cable format and send it off to the cable people who will serve it out . . . Or one of the other options you could do here is say why don't each local team just schedule what they're doing, send the clips off to a central area, and then the central area looks after all the stuff technically and editorially, and then they would schedule their own bulletins.
>
> (Darren, hub operator, BBC Birmingham)

As each of these possible future translations of the hub are considered, we need to note how they are always determined by the close association with other significant actors positioned at specific points within the network.

For instance, in the following comment, note how the technological arrangements are being considered in close association with the recognition that the regional news programme will still be being produced and transmitted. In this person's opinion, the regional programme as an entity is a more stable actor, occupying a stronger network position and therefore it will force translation of the local television hub. The hub's technogram will therefore be translated by its weaker sociogrammatic position vis-à-vis the regional programme and therefore its development will take a very different course than if it were allowed to take precedence over the regional programme and translate it out of existence. This too could of course happen as our network continues to shift and change. But at this stage this is considered by most to be unlikely.

> At the minute the technology lends itself to a hub-and-spoke arrangement. With the advance of technology whether we require a hub-and-spoke arrangement technologically is one question, but whether we require a hub-and-spoke arrangement editorially is quite another question. The 6.30pm news programmes are still going to be around for many, many years to come and you can't just throw 40 more cameras in a region and ignore what the half-hour regional programme is doing. So even if it is technically possible for everyone to have total control of his own destiny, editorially how do you then glue it into what the 6.30pm programme is doing? Because they have their own structure of journalists and camera crews, and what we don't want is two lots of camera crews turning up at every story. So the hub-and-spoke arrangement is down to two aspects: one is the technical capability, the other is the editorial desirability.
>
> (Adrian, technical manager, BBC Birmingham)

The other aspect of such radical and unpredictable translation of the hub is that we mustn't forget how each change will in turn alter how the news is gathered, produced and transmitted. And just like these possible technogrammatic translations, the translations that could occur to the news content are also multiple, depending upon the relationship between the human and nonhuman actors that will become entangled with one another, as both of the following comments suggest. Both predict a possible future news production set-up and both illustrate how human and nonhuman actors are inextricably interlinked with one another. But they both envisage very different specific actor translations. To take one example, in the first quote the duration of the local bulletins is seen to be a predicted translation, while in the second quote the satellite transmission is translated so far that it is eradicated altogether.

> I think you should just package it in the radio station when technology really takes over. It would make more sense to make your own ten

minutes and send it as a ten-minute section . . . and why ten minutes as well, that's another issue, surely if you're in Birmingham, you know the newspapers get Monday thin, Tuesday thick, Saturday thick, Sunday thicker, and TV has been very bad at that. We have always had 26.40 minutes when you may have loads of news, and you've got 26.40 minutes when you've got no news! Sometimes we might only have 18 minutes of news today but we're going to fill it out with some rubbish! And other days we have 35 minutes but we are going to drop some of it or squeeze it in too tight because we don't have enough room.

(Ian, local television trainer, BBC Birmingham)

I don't think the hour-long segment is the future. That's one of the limits of the technology that we have got. On digital satellite it's really separate whereas on broadband you can watch what you want. When it goes onto cable you can watch what you want. I think the on-demand thing will be the key thing, not it's on a loop you can watch this at ten to the hour with people watching the whole thing through. I just don't think it's ideal and it won't last long like that.

(David, assistant editor, BBC Birmingham and The Black Country)

Before we conclude our analysis of the role of the local television hub, we need to summarise what we have discovered, and to explain why our findings are more widely significant. To begin with, this brief exploration has taught us that it is dangerous simply to assume that the same technology will behave in exactly the same way if it occupies a different network position. Our two hubs, one in Nottingham and one in the Birmingham newsroom, share similar if not some of the very same technical characteristics and seem to be performing the same role within the network. Both act as *obligatory points of passage* as both are responsible for collating digital material and disseminating it to other parts of the network. They also share similar relationships with the most proximate human actors with whom they come into contact. Both engender the same frustration within those human actors who resent a loss of autonomy and ownership of their material.

But we must remember that to investigate the role and function of digital technologies in newsgathering and production processes, we must always consider the relationships they establish with other actors. And it is here that our ANT focus provides us with the detailed theoretical tools to examine each network position and each technological or human actor as we come across them at *specific* locations within the network. We have seen that, unlike the hub in Nottingham, the local television hub is an innovation that has not yet stabilised, as it has not yet managed to forge those alliances to which Latour refers to enable it to achieve its own translation of the network. Instead this local television hub may well be translated in a number of different ways, depending upon which other actors – human and nonhuman – it may come into contact with throughout the duration of the pilot project and more crucially, whatever developmental phases may occur in the future. We have touched on a few of these in the comments and observations of working practices illustrated throughout the chapter, but there may be many other associations that the hub may forge, and therefore hundreds of other constellations of actors created, all of which will translate the technology or be translated by it, altering both the news process and ultimately news content.

What we have witnessed is that a technology may certainly possess agency, but that it is only by a successful alignment and a cohesive association with other human and nonhuman actors that the technology may attain a stable position within a network, and that unless it can achieve this and the black box status that this affords, each translation caused by any number of actor groups will have effects upon both the workings of the network and the products of that network. We therefore cannot say that technology determines news content, or equally that it is superfluous to an analysis of news. Neither can we say that a technology remains constant and thus has a constant effect upon news practice. All we can say is that to examine news technologies in detail, we must understand the complex and ever-changing relationships they enter into with other actors within the network in which they operate, so as to try to understand how they behave as a result of the associations that they establish.

Callon (1991) talks of translation as a triangular operation involving a translator, something that is translated and a medium in which that translation is inscribed. Translation is thus dependent on more or less intermediaries. And it is important to realise that these intermediaries are not like structural pipes that simply transport the social product (Law, 1994). Instead they become the message too, and everything is translated. As Law urges, a satisfactory ANT analysis of any process would have us 'attend to the noise in the actor-network machine, its ragged complexities, rather than to attend to its gleaming purity' (Law, 1994). This is what we have attempted throughout our brief exploration of the local television project, and what we would continue to strive to do should we extend our research of the project, to map whatever future manifestations of local television may come into being.

Conclusion

So what can even a rudimentary exploration of an innovative new project such as the local television pilot tell us about the role of digital technologies such as the hub or the digital cameras, as well as the role of human actors in news production processes? To begin with it simply shows us how technologies possess agency. They are able to manipulate and translate networks, sometimes to extreme degrees, to alter newsgathering and news production processes. Remember how the implementation of PDP in Nottingham finally led to the eradication of the news organiser role that was once considered to be a stable actor position, even a black box.

Here we have seen that the role of the small digital camera, passing from the hands of trained BBC personnel into the hands of an untrained general public creates a number of different translations of the newsgathering process, which in turn helps to determine changes in news content, which are different depending upon where they occur within the network. For instance, we have seen how the news content of the community pieces in the more rural areas, where BBC personnel are more reluctant to surrender their cameras to people on the street, is quite different from the content of community pieces independently produced by the public in an inner-city area with the more detached assistance of BBC producers. Yet both of these processes create what is defined as local television news, and both are produced by a unique constellation of human and nonhuman actors.

Our story of PDP and its translation of the network, as well as its own translations within the network, cannot be concluded. In so far as the local television pilot project is concerned, there is now a period of time whereby both BBC management and independent assessors will consider the market implications of introducing local television, the related political and economic issues, as well as decide whether or not it is a service that is considered to be in the public's interest and a service they might expect the BBC to provide. I leave others to examine those developments and to explore the fascinating political or economic ramifications of whatever decision is reached. What we need to do, before returning to our close examination of Nottingham's news production network in the following chapter, is to summarise how an actor-network analysis of news processes can help us gain a deeper understanding of the heterogeneous and unpredictable ways in which news is produced.

An ANT focus helps us to recognise a network of associated actors, both human and nonhuman, all of whom possess agency and all of whom are able to manipulate, alter and translate a network. We recognise that this process is ongoing. We also recognise that in order to talk of *effects* upon news processes or news content, we must look at how each individual actor is associated with other actors and how only by following and unravelling those associations themselves can we begin to understand how humans or technologies affect news. Let us just take one last example to demonstrate how our translation process of PDP, the development of video journalism, and now the local television project, together create a significant translation back in the Nottingham newsroom to the existing internet service.

Almost as soon as the local television service was taken off the air in August 2006 and BBC managers began their lengthy assessment process, a new service was immediately introduced in the Nottingham newsroom, known as *Slice and Dice*. This service allows viewers to access the transmitted regional half-hour news programme simply by going to the East Midland's BBC *Where I Live* internet site where all the programme items have been uploaded and can now be viewed on demand. As one online journalist pointed out, this would never have happened without the local television pilot.

> You could speculate that now local TV is finished and is being con-
> sidered, *Slice and Dice* has come in. It is different as it's regional TV but
> presented in a different way, whereas local TV was local with a differ-
> ent audience and preparation. But you could say to a certain extent this
> is offering the same thing. It's offering video content on the web, just
> as local TV was offering, except one is more focused and one is just
> sliced and hashed.
>
> (Eric, online journalist, BBC Nottingham)

What we are witnessing is the ongoing story of network translation. Our network has for the duration of this chapter expanded to allow us to explore the local television pilot. But it is the same network that we have been examining in the previous three chapters, with the same actors jostling for position as well as some new actors appearing as our network develops. With every story of translation there cannot be a satisfactory conclusion, for there can be no final, conclusive view of our network. As we argued in the previous chapter, this should not make us lose faith or believe that our analysis is therefore fruitless or redundant. It should fill us with wonder and equally with a determination to dig still deeper, to explore with an even sharper focus the hundreds of actor asso-ciations we can see before us.

As I have asked you to do from the very beginning, if you use an ANT tool kit with which to unravel a complex world such as the world of news, you need to take that leap of faith and not lose heart. Actor Network Theory does not allow us to make easy conclusions, or convenient generalisations about our objects of study. For it turns our objects of study into actors who continue to act even after we have lost interest in them. Law urges us to let these objects and our own theorising of them be liberated from our usual need to pin down or neatly conclude our analyses.

> I think we might imagine that, like its objects of study, ANT cannot be
> told. Cannot be told as a single narrative. As an overall story about the
> growth of a centred network with its successes and reverses. And

140

instead imagine that it can only at best be represented as a set of little stories that are held together (if they are) by ambivalences and oscillations. Perhaps there is no single and coherent pattern. Perhaps there is nothing except practices. Perhaps there is nothing other than stories performing themselves and seeking to make connections, practical and local connections, specific links. In which case? In which case we are no longer in the business of epistemology. Of trying to find ways of telling about links that exist between bits and pieces of complex objects. Instead like the general practitioners and surgeons and the laboratory assistants, we are in the business of creating links, of making them, of bringing them more or less successfully into being. Which means in turn that we are no longer trying to find good ways of narrating and describing something that was already there. Instead, or in addition, we are in the business of ontology. We are in the business of making our objects of study. Of making our realities, and the connections between those realities.

(Law, 1997, p.17)

In the following chapter we will continue our journey through the newsroom, making those connections to which Law refers as we begin to explore what is the highly performative and temporally splintered world of the *live news event,* and examine those specific technologies and human actors that combine to construct and transmit live television news.

7

THE SATELLITE TRUCK AND LIVE
REPORTING

Talking about reality as multiple depends on another set of metaphors. Not those of perspective and of construction, but rather those
of intervention and performance. These suggest a reality that is done
and enacted rather than observed. Rather than being seen by a
diversity of watching eyes while itself remaining untouched in the
centre, reality is manipulated by means of various tools in the course
of a diversity of practices.

(Mol, 1999, p.77)

Throughout this book we have explored the complex and varied relationships in
which humans and technologies become embroiled once they join together in
the construction of news. Nowhere are these relationships more significant than
in the process of reporting live from a scene beyond the cosy confines of the
newsroom or studio. If we recall our intrepid CBS newsmen, who reported the
live shooting of Lee Harvey Oswald using what would be considered today to be
prehistoric and impossibly unwieldy technical equipment, for them the individual relationships they managed to make with the technologies they were using
were just as significant to the news event as anything that was unfolding before
their eyes. As Bob Huffaker recalls

As Nelson and I kept reporting through that long Saturday, we were concerned not only with facts, but also pictures. KRLD's news man George
Phenix was shooting with his big Auricon optical-sound camera, and
Nelson and I were trying to get as much video as possible on our live
cameras. Rather than breaking into the day's sad and unrelenting news
with brief shots of Oswald's passing, we taped them for later broadcast.

(Huffaker et al., 2004, p.45)

The descendants of these archaic, technological actors that played such a significant part in the coverage of one of the most momentous news stories of our

time, still perform an equally important role in the digital, technologically converged world of television broadcasting today. They may well bear little resemblance to the cameras and machines of yesteryear, but the role they play in news production is perhaps even more significant. Today's digital technologies have certainly become easier to use and more widely available to newsrooms. In so doing, some of the practices of news reporting have also changed. Indeed, as Huffaker argues, such technological developments have in some cases not just altered the particular style of live news coverage, but degraded it.

> Today's television makes so big a deal over being live that reporters stand at deserted scenes long after the action is over. We stayed at scenes only when there was a reason, and we left when nothing was to be reported. Instead of wasting time someplace merely to be live, we went when things were happening. We reported on the spot if events were urgent, and when they were over, we hurried in with film to develop and stories to write.
>
> (Huffaker *et al.*, 2004, p.45)

This is a crucial point. It is this ever-growing preoccupation with the *notion* of the live news event that has contributed to these technologies' positions as such prominent actors within our news network. And it is on a full exploration of the various roles they play, and the complexity of the associations that they have established with human actors within the production network that this chapter will concentrate. For it is certainly true to say that technology has developed to allow live coverage of fast-breaking, unpredictable events. But it would be wrong to assume that this is what live reporting is all about. It is just one of its many functions and manifestations, all of which are made possible by the continued entanglement of technologies and humans.

Therefore to fully explore all of the microprocesses involved in the construction of news, we now need to depart from simply mapping specific actor translations as we've been doing so far, to embrace a slightly more developed idea of *performance*. To help us understand what we mean by the performance of actor networks we will take a brief look at the empirical research of the philosopher, Annemarie Mol. Her work uses an actor network focus to analyse how certain diseases are often given very different medical diagnoses and therapies, depending on where the individual patient chooses to go for treatment. Mol's empirical interest in the combined medical and social diagnoses of these diseases, and the varied, often radically different ways in which they are treated, leads her to venture much further into the world of performance and multiplicity than we have done thus far.

We have seen that Latour's Actor Network Theory (ANT) certainly recognises the translation process as highly performative, and thus unstable or fluid, but in his work there is eventually a move towards resolution and with it some form of stabilisation once the translation process has occurred. As we have seen, black boxes are clearly evident by their strong actor associations, alliances are created and can remain fixed, and after all the drama of the translation process, there is a notion of resolution and conclusion.

Yet such defined points of resolution, and the static objects they seem to create, are misleading. Surely in a network of heterogeneous actors, the notion of any kind of resolution or conclusion is unthinkable? Yet in his empirical work, Latour seems to fail to follow the trajectory of his own logic so as to fully appreciate the implications of the performance of endless translations. It is as if he will not grasp the nettle and assert that even the 'finished' experiment that he is observing is itself merely a contingent actor and thus there can be no final settlement of controversies. We have seen this with our own exploration of the development of video journalism within the news network; there is no finished state of being for this particular technology, and therefore for all the other actors that are entangled with it. As we discovered in the preceding chapter, we cannot conclude the story. It has no definite end. So in order to understand the implications of our unresolved network of actor associations, we now need to depart from Latour, to give us a better grounding for our exploration of the ongoing performance of the news production network.

Varied perspectives versus multiple realities

This may seem to be a curious subtitle in a chapter that purports to examine the processes of live television reporting, but the difference between these two states is crucial to our understanding of what happens in the construction of live news events. We will use Mol's empirical work to help us get to grips with what may at first seem like a rather complicated, even philosophical, distinction. By so doing, we will soon discover that this highly theoretical distinction between varied perspectives and multiple realities is in fact a fundamental concept that manifests itself in the everyday realities of news reporting and producing.

To explain the crucial distinction between what she refers to as 'perspectivalism' on the one hand, and 'multiple, fragmented realities' on the other, Mol cuts an elegant theoretical knife between the two, challenging us to rethink our own perceptual relationship with the hitherto safely defined subject. She argues that perspectivalism may have challenged the strangulating version of a single truth, but it doesn't manage to go that one step further and embrace the concept of there being multiple and simultaneous realities, it merely demonstrates that there is more than one way of perceiving a *single* reality.

> Perspectivalism broke away from the monopolistic version of truth. But
> it didn't multiply reality. It multiplied the eyes of the beholders. And

this in turn brought pluralism in its wake. For there are mutually exclusive perspectives, discrete, existing side by side, in a transparent space. While in the centre, the object of the many gazes and glances remains singular, intangible, untouched.

(Mol, 1999, p.76)

What Mol is saying here is that an object does not occupy a stable or singular state. There is therefore no constant reality upon which to fix our separate and different gazes. And if this is the case, our relation to the 'it' – the subject – that cannot be defined – must therefore be redefined in some other way. That other way is through performance. Let's illustrate what we might mean by this rather complicated idea. If we look at Mol's empirical work we find that in her exploration of the diagnosis and treatment of a particular disease known as lower limb athero-sclerosis, Mol shifts the focus away from simply representing the actor network translations, to reveal instead the multiple realities of the object itself. Her form of analysis allows us to investigate the uncertain and complex lives of objects in a world where there is no closure or conclusion; where there is no recognised and stable singularity. It allows us to explore what she refers to as the continued *enactment* of objects. And as part of this, it allows us to recognise the multi-plicity of those objects, the ways in which they interact with one another (Law, 2004). The crucial difference between Mol and Latour is that Mol accepts that the medical inquiry and intervention she explores *may* lead to a single reality, but that this 'does not necessarily happen' (Law, 2004, p.54). In thinking of this Mol finds it helpful to distinguish between 'construction' and 'enactment'.

The term construction was used to get across the view that objects have no fixed and given identities, but gradually come into being. During their unstable childhoods their identities tend to be highly contested, volatile, open to transformation. But once they have grown up objects are taken to be stabilized.

(Mol, 2002, p.42)

With enactment we are able to attend to the *continuing* practice of crafting. Enactment and practice never stop, and realities depend upon their continued crafting. Mol rejects any notion of construction or of closure. She argues that if we attend solely to the practice of objects we may find that there are no objects ever routinised into a reified solidity. Instead there are simply ongoing stories of performance.

In performance stories, fleshiness, opacity and weight are not attributes of a single object with an essence that hides. Nor is it the role of tools to lay them bare as if they were so many aspects of a single reality. Instead of attributes or aspects, they are different versions of the object, different versions that the tools help to enact. They are different and yet related objects. They are multiple forms of reality. Itself.

(Mol, 1999, p.80)

And it is these multiple realities to which Mol refers that we will explore as we look at live television reporting. We will examine four separate live news events, known as 'outside broadcasts' (OBs) that take place during a week's programming of *East Midlands Today* and we will identify the key human and nonhuman actors involved in the process.[1] Each actor's separate socio-grammatic, technogrammatic, and often conflicting chronogrammatic positions, will be identified and analysed to show how the live news event presents more than an elaborate version of perspectivalism, which is a series of different per-spectives that are simply created by ever-changing actor network positions, but that the live television event demonstrates rather a more radical illustration of multiple realities, which are continually and simultaneously performed. It is to this multiplicity of objects, both human and technological, that we must pay attention if we are to fully explore the implications of what is perceived to be the 'live' news event. The performance of various multiple realities, some of which remain crucially invisible to other actors within the same net-work, and the practical inability to resolve these performances so as to fix actors in stable network positions, is what will alter our perception of what constitutes the 'real'.

What is 'live' reporting?

News is geared towards an ideal collapse of temporal and spatial difference. The often-witnessed scramble of reporters all trying to report 'live' from the scene, is a deliberate attempt to eradicate the spatial and temporal delay between the news happening in the world and the transmission of the news event that reports it. The complete collapse of such parameters rarely happens. When it does, it makes great television; the assassination of Lee Harvey Oswald, or two Boeing 767 planes flying into New York's World Trade Center on 11 September 2001. Viewers watched these events unfold 'in reality', on television, literally before their eyes. There was no perceived temporal or spatial lag between the news occurring and continuously developing, and the produced media event. In the case of the World Trade Center, the first plane crashing into the first tower not only provided the spectacle, but also prompted cameras to film the second event as it unfolded before them. In ANT terms we can say that the chrono-grammatic position was identical for both the viewer and the viewed subject and as such viewers were also unable to prepare themselves for what they were watching (Hemmingway, 2004).

Both the real and the associated media events of 11 September are extremely rare. In regional television news in particular, the combined collapse of space and time rarely if ever occurs. Stories are usually planned events, and the opportunity to rush out to 'live' news and film it as it is taking place is highly unusual. The SNG truck, which is a mobile vehicle that can be driven to anywhere in the geographical and editorial 'patch' covered by the particular programme, is thus used to provide an illusion of reality; the 'live' event taking place as the viewer turns on the programme, the news unfolding as they witness it, both sharing the same chronogram, with the production processes neatly and deliberately eradicated in transmission so that they become literally invisible.

Yet as we will see from our analysis of a week's 'live' transmissions, this so-called 'live' event is anything but a snatch of reality as and when it happens. Instead it is a highly constructed few minutes of an illusory reality, created by the network's ability to mobilise a myriad of human and nonhuman actors together often over external and invisible nodes of the network, to produce what only seems to be a singular, spontaneous event.[2]

The live event is not only specifically constructed, both in terms of its technological architecture and in terms of its operation, but is also wholly dependent upon the contingencies of the network. The perceived singularity of the live, where the viewer perceives the events to be simply happening before their eyes, within the same chronogrammatic frame as their own, is just one of its many multiple realities. Other realities are taking place simultaneously, unbeknown to the viewer. These may involve technologies communicating with one another, and/or other human actors intertwined with these technologies. Thus, to fully understand the live news event, we need to examine the empirical material, using our ANT focus so that we can *perform* the fragmented realities of its production, and reveal how the singular event does not exist alone. The live event is deliberately designed to *seem* singular, devoid of fragmentation and encompassing the same temporal framework as the viewer.

To argue that the live broadcast is merely a highly constructed event is not a particularly startling observation, and is actually more akin to the perspectivalism to which Mol initially refers. What is more crucial is that the live is only perceived as a singular, unconstructed 'real' event by means of the viewer's acceptance of and adherence to the concept of a single, stable subject, viewed in its singularity, devoid of any associated technological apparatus evident in its visual dissemination. It is as if the singularity of the live event is achieved in spite of itself, simply by relying on the conceptual embrace of the traditional stable subject by the viewer. This is similar to the fixed subject with which Mol grapples.

Yet the empirical evidence in this chapter will show us that this concept of the singular reality is only one of many and it is performed alongside various other, conflicting and fragmented realities, all of which are inscribed and reinscribed by the network. Furthermore, it will reveal that it is only by means of the simultaneous coexistence of and relationship between these multiple realities, involving both technological and human actors, that any perceived singularity can ever be achieved.

The satellite truck – architecture, perception and operation

The satellite (SNG) truck occupies a strong position in the network, and at certain times may even enjoy precarious, temporary black box status. It is one of the newsroom's most significant technological actors, but unlike the media hub, its network positioning is also more changeable, as are the relations it enters into with other actors. This is in part due to its technological architecture, but it is also due to the positions it may occupy vis-à-vis other actors, which can result in it being in direct socio- or technogrammatic conflict. We will explore this more fully as we analyse the empirical research.

As a result the SNG can on the one hand be considered to be one of the network's most convergent actors, able to create a myriad of multiple actor translations simultaneously, thus affording it temporary black box status. Occupying this network position, it can also be seen as another *obligatory point of passage* as it too establishes strong alliances between actors and acts as a technological gatekeeper for the transmission of news material. Yet although the media hub is also exposed to interpretative fluidity, as we discovered in Chapter 3, the SNG incorporates even more continual operational flexibility, and its role and its autonomy are more often challenged due to reinscription by certain actors of its multiple sociogrammatic, chronogrammatic and technogrammatic positions.

The SNG occupies a distinct geographical network position, invisible to those actors within the newsroom. It is highly mobile, literally orbiting the newsroom, as it is continuously placed at different locations in the 'editorial patch' by deskbound producers whose conception of it is simply as a production tool to gather and disseminate news to fill airtime. Unlike the media hub, whose autonomy is in many ways guaranteed by its constant visual presence within the newsroom, and its ability to force actor translation by its insistence on the dissemination of material through its central and collectively accepted technological apparatus, the SNG and those human actors working on it are more open to conceptual reinscription as they are geographically distant from the centre of the production network, and not party to significant production discussions. But as we'll discover, such *perceived* reinscriptions are often dangerously inaccurate and in themselves can contribute to the actual strength of the SNG's human actor positions.

Before we attempt to perform the SNG's plethora of actor functions, and to analyse the relations they have to one another, we need to outline what these are so as to recognise its multiple operational, technological and conceptual network positions. It's also helpful to briefly describe the truck itself and the two engineers who operate it (see Figure 7.1).

The SNG is a mobile satellite vehicle manned by two operators, known as SNG1 and SNG2. The SNG2 position is sometimes referred to as the 'wet end', as they are responsible for laying the cables out from the truck, operating the camera and acting as a point of contact for the live guest or the reporter performing the live event. They are predominantly working outside the truck, hence the reference to *wet* as the possibility of getting rained on, and could be positioned some way away from, and often out of sight of the truck. The SNG is used daily and all the technicians and engineers carry out the operational shifts. Usually a more technically trained engineer will take the role of SNG1 as this involves liaising with satellite providers, locating the satellite, possessing a working knowledge of the infrastructure of the entire van in terms of moving the satellite into position, keeping in contact with the satellite-link provider, as

Figure 7.1 The Satellite Newsgathering Vehicle (SNG).

well as liaising with the technical manager and the director in the gallery back at base during the programme in which the live is to be transmitted. The SNG1 is also in constant contact with the camera diary assistant (CDA) in the newsroom who is responsible for identifying the truck's locations and communicating with the operators, through the technical manager, to ascertain what is expected of them at each location to which they are sent. The SNG operators spend their eight-hour shift predominantly on the road, rarely returning to base once they have been dispatched at 11.00am in the morning. They are expected to provide a live facility for both the lunchtime bulletin at 1.30pm and the evening pro-gramme at 6.30pm, though these may well be at different locations.

Just like the media hub, the SNG itself is in a strong position within the network as it is technologically complex and many actors do not understand its operational capability at the technical level, depending instead on other actors to facilitate their use of the vehicle. There is some disagreement between staff over whether the SNG's technical infrastructure can be fully understood by journal-ists and producers as opposed to technically trained engineering staff. One of the main objectives of managers is to try to eradicate the perceived divide between what are referred to as the 'techies' and the journalist and production staff, and the operation of the SNG is immediately placed centre stage in an organisational struggle to de-differentiate between actors on the network, and demystify the complexity of its operations as the following quote demonstrates.

> I think it's just vitally important. You will remember how easy it is to just segment off the engineering staff from journalists and the time when the engineering staff really know what the programme is about is when they're out live. They're either working as a camera crew or they're working on the sat truck, so I think just about everybody can work on it. Well no, there's SNG1, which is the highly technical bit where they get the satellite link up, but there's SNG2, which is known as the wet end where you run out with cables which you and I could do quite frankly, so at the very least every member of the team can do SNG2, so every member of the team is given a shift on that.
>
> (Emma, operations editor, BBC Nottingham)

Yet even between managers, the perception of the SNG quickly begins to lose focus. As we have seen, the operations editor views the SNG as first and foremost a resource with which to grapple with conflicting role distinctions between staff.

> The whole point of me taking over the production side of things, because let's be honest, I wasn't appointed for my detailed knowledge of engineering and technical equipment, but I did very simple things

like I made the technical manager, instead of hiding downstairs, sit upstairs next to the producer. They did moan about it you know, but I made them come to the morning meeting and their very presence means that we take the technical side of things very seriously. And as a producer you should be telling the technical manager what you want to do. They can make the necessary adjustments and get people in early if they need to, and I think there are far less cock-ups.

(Emma, operations editor, BBC Nottingham)

It is also perceived as an economic resource whose use must continually justify its operational cost. The editorial perception of the live as contributing to an interesting or significant television experience is not even considered.

Question: Do you have a directive to say there has to be a live every night? Yes, it is a major disappointment to me if I see that truck sitting in the car park at any point during the day really. It should be out at lunchtime and in the evening for the 6.30pm. All I think is, if it's sitting here, there are two members of staff sitting here on their backsides, and there is a live opportunity that we're missing, so there is a directive.

(Emma, operations editor, BBC Nottingham)

In direct contrast, the output editor who is responsible not for the management of operations, but for the management of the *content* of programmes perceives the SNG as facilitating an appropriate live feel to the programme thus enhancing the content. To use the SNG in any other capacity, such as to merely justify its own costly existence, is strongly rebutted.

Speaking as someone who used to do the live when I worked at Central, I am not a big fan of the pointless live. I think we went through a phase of we have this technology and let's get someone out there live. Particularly in the winter months when there is really not very much to see, to throw a reporter out there in the blackness to say something that is much more interesting if he had filmed it three hours ago when he had some pictures doesn't seem very sensible to me. There are times when a live can really give it a bit of energy and adrenalin and that's great . . . there is no directive that there has to be a live for each bulletin. We hope that there is a reason for getting all that technology in place.

(Sally, output editor, BBC Nottingham)

These conflicting managerial views already illustrate the fluidity of the SNG's position in relation to other actors. The operations editor needs to manage technical and production staff and try to eradicate perceptual differences between them so as to enhance professional cohesion. She is also acutely aware that her staff and her equipment must be cost effective. In contrast, for the output editor the content of the programme is ostensibly the most significant factor, although a self-reflexive adherence to past practice as a reporter also colours her perception.

We may be tempted at this point to say that all this reveals is the kind of perspectivalism that Mol strenuously urges us to move beyond. Therefore we need to take some time to map our entire network, which includes ranges of perceptions, various operational action, human and nonhuman actor agency and human actor self-reflexivity, so that we can begin to reveal the more significant *performance* of multiple realities that both involve and are practised by such a fluid actor as the SNG and to argue that this indicates something more significant than merely multiple perspectives.

Returning briefly to the operations editor's urge to demystify the perception of the SNG's technological complexity, it is significant to note that the observation of those engineers who are actually responsible for operating the truck reveals yet another viewpoint. Most of them complain of a lack of understanding by journalists and producers of the time it takes to set up a live, and what technology is needed in order for the satellite link to be established so as to transmit material live, or send back recorded pictures.

> You can't cable over the road ... if there's a public highway ... you can't ... sometimes the journalist will say 'there's a great shot over there' and you'll say, 'yes it is a great shot, but we can't do it. Your mikes will reach, you can be over there and the camera here, put the extender in, but we can't go over there' ... it's a hard learning curve for them.
>
> (Boris, SNG operator, BBC Nottingham)

Yet shrouded within this sense of frustration is also an acute awareness that their own superior technological capability affords them a strong actor network position. Rather than seeking to de-differentiate between technical and non-technical human actors as does the operations editor, the SNG operators seek to deliberately maintain this discrepancy in order to retain their powerful position. Indeed operators often exploit the journalists' or producers' inherent lack of technical understanding to actually dupe them into believing they're receiving live material when in fact they're not. This is only possible because of the unique geographical position that the SNG occupies as an actor on the periphery of the production network, invisible to other actors, yet whose technological capability ensures a strong actor position.

We had a classic one last week! They said; 'let's have a closing shot' and so I found a closing shot but it was miles away and I was convincing them we'd do it live. So I prerecorded it and then after the weather, we had it in the tape machine and we ran it off tape and cut to it and of course they all thought it was live. [Laughter]

(Ian, SNG operator, BBC Nottingham)

It's also significant to note that those operators who consider themselves to be more technically adept, deliberately stress how their communication is between machines rather than human actors. The media hub operators share a similar discourse; human actors are displaced by the ability for the machines to communicate thus enjoying a particularly strong form of agency. The media hub operator expresses relief that the network facilitates for this discourse between technologies; the reporter is deliberately bypassed, perceived as a subsidiary actor whose presence is more often than not considered to be a hindrance.

We communicate with the sat truck not the reporter unless the reporter was just sending bits and pieces and telling us what bits to dub. Sometimes there is a reporter here looking at what's coming in and you let the two talk to each other. But it's much easier if we just talk to the truck.

(Tony, media hub operator, BBC Nottingham)

Yet there are also conflicting views among those technical staff with regard to who are the most significant actors in the network able to facilitate the operation of the broadcast. In direct contrast to the previous quote, an experienced SNG operator, whose technical capability probably outweighs most other actors, emphasises that while the technological knowledge is vital, for him the success of the live operation hinges upon the relationships between the specific human actors at all points on the network.

You just try to be as helpful as possible, and that's the thing really. This is a people job, you're dealing with people at the end of the day, the technology is fine but at the end of the day it is people at the end of it, and it's the people skills that are equally important as the technical skills. You could be as clever as to be able to strip this truck out and to put it back, but if you haven't got the people skills, it's awful because you're just hitting brick walls.

(Boris, SNG operator, BBC Nottingham)

So what does all this mean? Obviously we already have a number of stark contradictions, at this stage mainly at a purely perceptual level. The actor network reveals that even within certain departments, be it management or resources, who are directly responsible for operating the SNG, the perceptions of the SNG position, its relationship with other actors and its significance within the production network, are all wildly varied. We could easily begin to chart a similar selection of freeze frames to those in Chapter 3, to illustrate the varied sociograms and technograms these individual actors occupy to reveal the ultimate negotiability of the SNG and its status vis-à-vis other actors with whom it is in continual contact.

But the argument must now develop further than to simply assert that a technological actor, even one who enjoys temporary black box status, such as the SNG, is still malleable. We have already learned this from our analysis of the media hub's status and how its position is dependent upon the ongoing tensions between its technogram and sociogram. What we now need to show by a closer analysis of the operation of the SNG, is that the varied technogrammatic and sociogrammatic positions it occupies reveal it to be a multiperspectival and fluid actor whose position may be open to translation should any of the alliances that go to make up each technogram or sociogram become destabilised.

That's all very well. We have done this throughout our exploration of both the media hub and the development of video journalism. Now, there is something more significant occurring. For these varied positions are not only *perceived* to exist by other actors, they are literally *performed* alongside one another and each separate performance contributes to the multiple realities to which Mol referred in her analysis of the disease, atherosclerosis. If we recall the quote, she argues that

> Perspectivalism broke away from the monopolistic version of truth. But it didn't multiply reality. It multiplied the eyes of the beholders. And this in turn brought pluralism in its wake. For there are mutually exclusive perspectives, discrete, existing side by side, in a transparent space. While in the centre, the object of the many gazes and glances remains singular, intangible, untouched.
>
> (Mol, 1999, p.76)

It is thus significant that our television viewer only catches a glimpse of *one* of these realities, that of the actual broadcast, and as we'll see, it is indeed a fractal reality, certainly in so far as it reveals little of the news production process, which has been deliberately eliminated by the process of transmission. It also reveals little of what the viewer might define as the 'real world' as so much of the media event is highly constructed so as to create the illusion of the news occurring at exactly the same time as it is witnessed by the viewer. By analysing the operation of the SNG over a four-day week these simultaneous performances can now be brought to life so as to reveal, not the *many eyes of the many beholders* to which Mol refers, but instead the *multiple realities* that such a simultaneously strong yet fluid technological actor as the SNG enacts.

Interviewing Nottinghamshire's Chief Constable for the lunchtime bulletin

Our first illustration of the operation of the SNG reveals a number of important characteristics with regard to how the SNG is used by producers in the news-room, technical staff operating the SNG out in the editorial patch and the public guests invited to take part in the live broadcast. It also illustrates how the technological agency of the SNG itself contributes in different ways to the per-formance of a number of simultaneous realities.

The context

Of the four outside broadcasts that we'll examine, this first one is perhaps the closest to illustrating the SNG's capacity to cover news as it happens. Having said that, the story had already come to light the previous evening with a leak of a soon-to-be-published report from Her Majesty's Inspectorate of Constabularies (HMIC), the statutory body responsible for the regulation of the efficiency of police services in the UK. It stated that due to a lack of confidence in the Nottinghamshire Police Force it was to draft in a senior officer from another force. The new officer would assist the Chief Constable in improving the effectiveness of policing in the county, with particular regard paid to the increasing number of high profile murders that had occurred in Nottinghamshire during recent months. The report was published the following morning and the senior officer was named as Chris Simms, the Deputy Chief Inspector of the West Midlands Constabulary.

The SNG was already located out in the editorial patch when the camera diary assistant (CDA) informed both Ian and Dave (the SNG operators) that they were needed at the Nottinghamshire Police Headquarters to do a live interview with the Chief Constable, Steve Green. The interview was to be used as part of a lead story for the 1.30pm lunchtime bulletin. This was the first media oppor-tunity Green had had to comment on the report and the decision to draft in assistance from another force.

The operation of the first live broadcast and the performance of separate realities

The SNG arrived at the Police Headquarters at around 12.30pm. The SNG1 operator, Ian, began to line up the satellite and chose a location outside the main building from where the interview would be conducted. At this point Ian had only talked to the CDA. There had been no discussion between the truck operators and the producer or lunchtime presenter, Priya, who was to conduct the interview from the studio in Nottingham. Unusually no reporter was sent out to meet the Chief Constable and conduct the interview at the location. Instead it was to be done from the studio 'down the line' by the bulletin presenter, Priya.

At this point the SNG operators are the essential actors who facilitate the technological capability of conducting the live, as well as making sure the guest, Steve Green, will be available at the desired time as Ian explains.

> The producer doesn't want to know ... at about ten past I will bring the satellite signal up. I will talk to London to do that. I will check with London that they can see me, they will send the signal straight up to Nottingham – again, internal wires – it is always there now within the BBC. Then I will check with the technical manager that he can hear my sound, he can see my pictures, he can hear me, I can hear him; that talkback between us might not ever get used, but it is there for an emergency, it is just useful to have. Once it goes beyond that, production will step in.
>
> (Ian, SNG1, BBC Nottingham)

At this point, the SNG acts as an *obligatory point of passage*, as it is the technological capability of the truck that will enable the interview to be successfully conducted. The story relies entirely upon the ability to get a satellite signal, and for the technical operators at the location and the technical manager back at base to communicate with one another.

> Once we get the guest, we will show the guest. We have to remember that as a truck and as a cameraman, we are the eyes of the studio, so if the guest has arrived then I will try to get a picture of the guest. If there is no picture coming into the van, then I will go to a test signal, because the producer would rather see a test signal from us than black. Black is a fault even if it might not be. But a test signal says, I am the truck and I am still there, and if there is a problem, then I am across it.
> Q: So it's just to stop the production people from getting too unhappy?
> Yeah, it's just that I'm saying; 'I am still here! Yes, something has gone horribly wrong, but it's my problem. It is not your problem.'
>
> (Ian, SNG1, BBC Nottingham)

Not only has the content of the most significant news story of the day been supplanted by the technological capability of obtaining satellite clearance to establish both audio and visual signals, but there is a clear recognition by the technical operators that the hermeneutic understanding of that technology is already varies widely between the producers at base and the operators at the location. At this point the SNG has achieved temporary black box status. By establishing a stable relationship between its technogram, that is its ability to receive the signal in order to show the Chief Constable on screen, and its sociogram, which is its essential positioning at the location in order to facilitate a lead story to be aired successfully. Other actors, in this case the producer and presenter, are folded into the technology and literally silenced by it.

This act of silencing is also visually represented by the choice that the technical operator can make to put up either the black screen or the test card to be viewed by those producers, presenters and gallery staff back at base, knowing that these two signals denote separate representations of the technology to the production team, and therefore to their understanding of the progress of the story out at the location. That these representations may be incompletely or even inaccurately interpreted by the production team, affords both the SNG actors and the SNG a strong alliance. A secondary aspect of the SNG's technogram, that of it being geographically distant from and therefore invisible to the production team, also assists in determining this strong position. Far from being in a vulnerable position on an external node of the network, this separation between the SNG and the newsroom enables the engineers at the location to establish the strongest alliance with the technology as they are the most proximate actors to it, and thus control its signification in relation to other actors who are situated at more distant points from the SNG. This affords significant power to the individual SNG operator, articulated further by his explanation of how he is able to manipulate the signification of the SNG by means of the technical signals he chooses to provide to those actors back at base.

It's also interesting to note the emphasis that the operator places on the ability of the truck to 'go wrong'. Ironically, while the SNG has achieved black box status at this particular instance by the strength of its technogram, it also maintains this position by an ability to create in those actors distant from it, and technically ignorant of it, a perception of it 'going wrong' at any time. The articulation of this perception of other actors is repeated by the SNG1 operator time and again, and serves to further emphasise his own individual position. For if there is a perception that the SNG is likely to be exposed to unpredictable and regular error, and that those back in the newsroom cannot do anything about it, the SNG1 is then perceived to be the only actor who is able to rectify the situation.[3]

It is only when this position is temporarily established that a blatantly hierarchical perception of the relationship with other actors in the network is articulated by the technical operators. Far from agreeing with the operations editor's perception that there is no longer a conflicting relationship between the 'techies' and journalists, the technical actors perceive that the retention of their dominant position is wholly determined by their developed hermeneutic relationship with the technology itself.

> *Techies* understand what production is all about – it's more difficult to get production to understand – they don't come out on outside broadcasts. You know, the journalists who come out on OBs understand better; we have become journalists but journalists haven't become *techies* so much.
>
> (Ian, SNG1, BBC Nottingham)

> Some of our journalists that come from a technical background as well, like Jeremy, he understands, but the ones that are purely journalists, don't do technical, don't even like technical, they're the worst.
>
> (Tara, SNG2, BBC Nottingham)

The enfolding of those human actors (SNG1 and 2) with the technology that will facilitate the performance of the news story continues throughout the live operation. It is also cogently and continually commented on by both SNG1 and SNG2. This self-reflexive awareness of their relationship with the technology creates the first separate reality: a reality that is invisible to those human actors back at base and to viewers watching the actual broadcast, but which demonstrates that the strongest alliance that the SNG operators establish is between themselves and the truck, not between themselves and the production team who are reliant upon them for the success of the broadcast.

The separate reality is thus performed and articulated by the SNG operators, held in constant tension by their relationship not only to the technical complexity of the truck's architecture and operational capability, but also to their continual belief that things may go wrong. We must note that there is a subtle difference between the SNG's *own* perception of the potential for error, and the perception of this that they foster in *other* actors back at base. It is in the SNG operators' own interests to permit those actors to perceive that potential as far greater than it may in fact be. The SNG operator's adequacy is thus judged by other SNG operators almost entirely by the capacity to cope with unpredictable technological failure, or technical contingency that will occur by the very nature of the fact that the broadcast is live.

> You do have to understand the technology and the more you know about it the better because if something goes wrong and you think it through logically like, Boris has a good understanding of how it all goes

together and how it works, and how if you press a button, what that button does. So when something breaks down he can work his way through in his head to the point that it has failed and try to figure ways around it or how to fix that problem. You don't necessarily have to know, you know, how many capacities are in a box or whatever, but having a good understanding about the chain of events that happen to make things work is very important. As I say, to get up the satellite anyone can do it, because it's just about following procedure, but that's not what makes Boris so good at his job, or the others like Paul. They know how to deal with stuff when it goes wrong, because that's the test of being a good SNG operator.

(Tara, SNG2, BBC Nottingham)

Once the Chief Constable has arrived the SNG2 operator is responsible for ensuring he is standing in the right location and that he is able to talk to the presenter back in the studio in Nottingham from where the interview will be conducted. Again the SNG operator's individual perception of reality is that the communication pathway is controlled entirely by the technological capability of the truck, and is seen almost as a privilege that may be granted or refused at the will of the SNG operator.

This is what I hear in the truck and what the journalist hears in their earpiece and what Tara hears in her earpiece, but the two are split. The wet end is Tara, the front end, which means that I can talk to Tara and the journalist won't hear me. We can hear anything that is happening in our studio via the satellite, because this dish receives as well as chucks out. If all that goes wrong, I can phone using that GSM phone and go to an ISDN line that is on the desk in the studio and then press divert, and then put GSM on which means they can then hear the clean feed via the phone, which is very clever.

(Boris, SNG1, BBC Nottingham)[4]

The SNG's technological capability to create separate audio pathways, thus enabling actors to obtain separate levels of knowledge of the live operation, exemplifies its technogrammatic multiplicity. The truck, unlike almost any other actor with the exception of the media hub, enables a variety of tasks to be performed simultaneously, but actors do not share the same technogrammatic or sociogrammatic positioning even while performing those related tasks.

I can talk to everyone from here, I can talk to the studio. I can talk to the guest, talk to my colleagues and I can talk to my colleagues separately, which means if there is something wrong I can talk to them without letting the guest know. It is also very useful if you have an inexperienced camera operator because you can count in your camera operator without your guest knowing. As this job is more experienced than that job [wet end], you might put an inexperienced person at that end, you could put someone fairly inexperienced that end and literally say left a bit, right a bit, up a bit, and the guest never knows.

(Ian, SNG1, BBC Nottingham)[5]

In this particular live broadcast, SNG2, who is considered by Ian to be an inexperienced camera operator, is thus controlled by the technical capability of the truck to silence the guest. (As we saw from the previous quote, SNG1 could also have silenced the journalist, had there been one present.) The SNG1 operator thus occupies the strongest actor position, virtually folded into the technology by being in closest proximity to it, and having the greater level of technical understanding. Those actors who are situated geographically further away such as the guest and the SNG2 occupy weaker positions. They each have a separate and varied understanding of the technology. Their sociogram and technogram are thus defined by a lack of technical knowledge and thus in the performance of this particular reality, they occupy less stable positions and may be manipulated or controlled by SNG1. What is significant is that the SNG's technogram creates a crucial division between those actors performing the same reality and the SNG1 by its own multiple functioning capability. What we are seeing here is that the SNG (the truck) fragments the reality being performed as it creates multiple actor translations so that each actor occupies a separate position with separate sociograms or technograms.

Once the link has been established, the guest has been situated in the right location and Ian is content that the SNG2 camera operator is in place, he contacts the gallery so that the director and Priya, the lunchtime presenter, can introduce themselves to the guest. What is significant in this short exchange between the production staff and the guest is that it involves a deliberate 'setting up' of the live. It also indicates how the guest is acutely aware of the dual realities beginning to crystallise between the construction of the live event, and the actual performance of it in the transmission of the bulletin. The guest is what we might call 'media savvy' and this begins to have a bearing on the situation as the construction develops and the actual physical environment also becomes inextricably linked to the success of the performance. To demonstrate what we mean, let's take a closer look at a recording of the initial interchange between the guest, the presenter and the programme director.

Green: Can you see me as well as hear me? It's raining out here.
Director: Is it? I thought you might be in your office.

Green: Well to be honest when we started setting up it wasn't raining – but it is now – we've got to a point now that if we start reorganising we are just not going to get there – set up on time.

Director: OK, no problem – you will be talking to Priya who is our presenter and I will be getting her to have a quick chat with you.

Green: OK, no problem.

Priya: OK Steve can you hear me?

Green: Yes I can Priya.

Priya: Are you well?

Green: Yes, can you keep talking to me Priya . . . hello?

Priya: Oh, you're back again now – I think we lost you for a second.

Green: Is that OK?

Priya: Yeah that's fine. Do you want to know any of the questions?

Green: Yes please.

Priya: Well we're going to ask you questions – well, like the reputation of the force, whether it's going to damage it having this person drafted in, whether you think it will affect the management of Nottinghamshire Police?

Green: OK, that's fine.

Without dwelling too long upon this issue of the live event as a deliberate construction, illustrated further by the deliberately false intimacy shared by the guest and the presenter, Priya, it is significant in that it provides an example of another reality, performed simultaneously with the technological operations that we discussed earlier. Indeed, while this exchange between Priya and the Chief Constable takes place, SNG1 (Ian) is attempting to contact the media hub operator to ascertain whether or not the Radio Nottingham producer wishes to use the SNG to conduct a live interview once the television interview has taken place. Priya continues to rehearse the live with the Chief Constable and an added contingency comes into play as the rain thickens.

What we have is at least three simultaneous realities being performed at this point. Ian is attempting to make contact with the radio producer. Priya, the director and the guest talk about the interview. SNG2 tries to wipe moisture from the camera lens so as to improve the shot, and the rain beats down. The most flexible actors are the SNG and the SNG1 operator, exemplified by their ability to slot easily between the different realities so as to attempt to clarify a situation, which Ian does now when he cuts across Priya, literally silencing her by cutting off her microphone from the interior of the truck, to talk directly to the guest.

Ian: Mr Green.

Green: Hello.

Ian: My name is Ian. I am in the truck. You may be aware of this but in theory at least, radio would like to do an interview with you straight after telly, are you aware of that ... in theory radio would like to do an interview straight after TV.

Green: Yeah, well my intention was to ring them up and speak to them directly over the phone.

Ian: Oh right – Oh I see!

Green: Advantage of that it will be drier. I didn't want to be engrossed with them and be late for you so I have put them off until after I have done this interview.

Ian: Ah I see – there's a cunning plan – the impression was you would be doing it with us – we'll see what happens.

Green: Well the advantage would be that if it carries on raining I certainly won't be. But as soon as I walk back into my office I will ring them.

Ian: Ah thanks, OK. Bye for now ... [To the researcher] It's organised chaos. [Pause]. Ian to technical manager in the gallery – just to let you know, he would rather do radio on the phone in his office because it's raining – I will try and tell Lynne [camera diary assistant].

Thus Ian obtains clarification not from other actors on the production network, with whom it should be easier to communicate, but from the guest who makes a unilateral decision to conduct the interview over the phone, based entirely upon the fact that he doesn't want to get wet. Ian then conveys that message to the technical manager in the gallery as well as to the camera diary assistant upstairs in the newsroom. Thus, even though he is geographically dislocated from the production network, he communicates production decisions to other relevant actors who are geographically more proximate but have so far failed to contact one another. Yet, just at the point where it seems as though the enfolding of the SNG1 operator with the SNG creates an infallibly strong actor alliance, even reaching beyond its own boundaries to the production network back at base, the unforeseen contingency of a bout of rain and a guest who doesn't like getting wet radically alters the situation.

From our observation of this live broadcast it is clear that there are multiple, sometimes conflicting, realities being simultaneously performed. As Latour asserts, boundaries are also not clear but are themselves performed. The SNG develops temporary black box status both as an *obligatory point of passage* and by occupying a strong technogrammatic position. It achieves the translation of other actors all of whom occupy different and separate socio- and technogrammatic positions within their own separate realities. Yet just as it seems as though the black box may close around its own forced alliances, the fluidity of the SNG status is brought into stark relief as the guest refuses to perform the live radio interview and instead retreats to the comfort of his office to make a phone call. The significance of the performance of all of these realities is that they are then totally eradicated for the viewer in the actual transmission of the live broadcast. As Latour argues

> Our argument is not just that facts are socially constructed. We also wish to show that the process of construction involves the use of certain devices whereby all traces of production are made extremely difficult to detect.
>
> (Latour & Woolgar, 1979, p.176)

The viewer only witnesses the apparent singularity of the live event and in that transmission is unaware of any other reality. The viewer also establishes a traditional subject/object relationship with the media event in which they observe what is happening 'out-there', in the 'real world'. But by observing the performance of multiple and fragmented actor relations, this notion of internal and external is itself eroded. The SNG does not remain a stable actor, around which multiple perspectives vie for prominence. Remember Mol defines plur-alism (as opposed to multiplicity) as

> mutually exclusive perspectives, discrete, existing side by side, in a transparent space. While in the centre, the object of the many gazes and glances remains singular, intangible, untouched.
>
> (Mol, 1999, p.76)

The SNG does not remain untouched, nor does it remain stable. This is recognised once we accept that the definition of an object is also the definition of its sociotechnical context: together they add up to a possible network con-figuration. There is no inside or outside. There is also no definition of a stable reality for it is the very performance of multiplicity that enables the transmis-sion of such perceived singularity. Or as Latour argues

> Reality cannot be used to explain why a statement becomes a fact, since it is only after it has become a fact, that the effect of reality is obtained. This is the case whether the reality effect is cast in terms of 'objectivity' or 'out-there-ness.' It is because the controversy settles, that a statement splits into an entity and a statement about an entity; such a split never precedes the resolution of controversy.
>
> (Latour & Woolgar, 1979, pp.179–80)

Yet as we saw at the beginning of the chapter, and as we shall see from our further analyses of the live event, Latour's somewhat cosy confidence in the eventual settlement of controversies refuses to acknowledge the ongoing performance of these separate realities, or the drama of enactments *without* closure or resolution.

A fascination with technological actors – the satellite truck, the Xmobile and a selection of cameras

We might, instead or as well, imagine versions of method assemblage that craft, sensitise us to, and apprehend the indefinite character of the non coherent-in-here and out-there.

(Law, 2004, p.14)

In this section we will analyse two separate broadcasts, which highlight the use of various technologies to create the actual content of the live, and which further problematise the traditional notion of a defined external and internal reality in both the viewing experience and the production operation.

The first broadcast is transmitted immediately outside the Nottingham television studios in the adjoining car park, using the SNG, the SNG1, two extra camera operators, the regional political correspondent and the two main programme presenters. The second example is a short live broadcast at the end of a lunchtime bulletin involving the SNG, SNG1 and SNG2, the weather presenter and a guest who talks about observing the first signs of spring across the region. Both these broadcasts have little or no hard news content, but are dominated by the construction of realities through the use of an assemblage of technologies.

The first live broadcast is separated into three sections. In each the political correspondent, Jonathan, is seen outside the main Nottingham BBC building, a recognisable landmark to those watching the programme, accompanied by a large Land Rover with an election motif sprawled across its body and a large grey X painted on the bonnet. This is BBC Nottingham's 'Xmobile'. As Jonathan explains in the first live section, which immediately follows the programme's opening titles, the vehicle will be travelling across the region during the coming general election campaign and viewers are invited to come out to talk to Jonathan about the issues that they think need addressing by the politicians.

Programme Transmission:

Jonathan: 'This is our very own *Xmobile* as X marks the spot!' [Pointing to the X motif on the vehicle as he walks around it.] 'Coming to your own town in the next few weeks, I'll be there to hear about what issues interest you! You can easily find out where I'll be by logging onto the BBC website – the address is on your screens now!'

In the final section of the live broadcast Jonathan is once again situated outside the BBC building with the Xmobile but this time he is accompanied by the two main programme presenters who come out of the studio to meet him and to admire the vehicle. This section, in which the three of them chat lightheartedly together, once again encouraging viewers to make contact with Jonathan, concludes the main programme and the closing shot comprises a high, wide view of the building incorporating the vehicle and the presenters and Jonathan waving good night.

Once again the main SNG1 operator, Ian, is ostensibly responsible for ensuring the successful transmission of the live sections of this programme. But this time this responsibility is also shared with the programme director who is situated in the gallery and who directs the sections of the show that are located inside the building. The technological complexities are further enhanced by the use of two separate camera operators outside, which are directed by SNG1.

The purpose of this live operation is to present the election vehicle, and to encourage viewers to become involved in the process of making television. Once more, viewers are unaware of the technological logistics of the presentation of the election vehicle as the SNG literally reveals this technological prop, while itself remaining invisible. If we consider the socio- or technogrammatic position of each of the actors involved in this example they are constantly shifting depending upon what part of the programme is being transmitted. While the programme is on air, the SNG1 occupies a weaker position than the main programme director in the gallery, as it is the director who at this stage has overall responsibility for transmitting the programme. When the live section is transmitted the programme director literally hands over to the SNG and the two SNG operators. While this section is being performed, although the SNG and SNG1 again occupy strong positions, they are reliant on the successful communication between camera operators, the reporter and the two main programme presenters who actually walk in and join the live transmission. The SNG1 position can therefore only remain stable if communication with all actors, human and nonhuman, is continually achieved and managed.

There was some question as to whether I would be able to cope with the sound of three presenters and cut the two cameras because I cut the two cameras outside, effectively directing outside. It wasn't perfect but it was OK. And actually that is something I do. I am quite happy to do a second camera if we have the time. There was Neil, the cameraman, and Andrew was the second cameraman and the high up top shot – that was Andrew – and there was Lynne keeping people away – that's the way we normally do it. Keep it simple. We have one cameraman who is shooting it like it is a conventional single camera and you have a second single camera almost locked off but not necessarily – that is the cut-away camera. And that way everybody just assumes they're on air all the time.

(Ian, SNG1, BBC Nottingham)

Once again the SNG1 occupies a position of strength due in part to his proximity to the technology and the ability to only reveal partial information to other actors with regard to who is on air at what time. If we were to conduct a freeze frame of each actor's positioning at the very point of the live transmission, these would reveal a plethora of realities according to each actor's socio-technogrammatic positioning vis-à-vis one another.

Just briefly, consider the position of the internal director. He hands over the technological control to the SNG1, and ushers the presenters out of the studio to join Jonathan at the Xmobile. Once this is done he is unable to intervene further should a technical error occur with the SNG unable to get a stabilised satellite signal, as he no longer has any presenters to cut back to in the studio. His position is utterly exposed, as he is solely reliant on the presence of a presenting team in the studio. The SNG1 position is then stabilised by the alliances he establishes between the presenters, the reporter and the team of technical actors, the two cameras and the SNG. However, should he lose the satellite signal, his position is also immediately radically altered and there is no contingency with which he can work to rectify that situation, as he cannot hand back to the internal director, as there is now no internal reality to present, devoid as it is of the programme presenters.

SNG1 also directs the live filming so that the cameras are all used to maximum effect and a variety of shots are presented to the viewer. This is significant as there is little or no news content to engage the viewer. The viewing experience is hence solely reliant on the two technological actors – the SNG and the Xmobile. The multiple realities that are performed by all of the actors are themselves reliant on the rapid associations they enter into with one another at a given time. An assemblage of technologies and humans, all of which rely on creating alliances with one another in order to occupy a temporarily stable position, thus replaces the notion of a delineated external or internal position that defines a stable subject and object in relation to one another.

The second example once again illustrates the use of technologies to create visual content. The use of the weather live is an established tradition whereby producers use up airtime if they're unable to find enough news to fill the required duration of a bulletin. Again, it is highly constructed and does not reveal an unknown or happening event. It is practised many times before being transmitted 'for real' and usually involves a light-hearted interchange between the weather presenter and an invited guest, followed by the delivery of the weather details.

This is a weather OB, which obeys Ian's rule of thumb about regional OBs that they're either at the top of the show, and sometimes big things happen, or they are at the bottom of show and they're weather – and they are very rarely in between – and nothing's happening at all.

(Ian, SNG1, BBC Nottingham)

What is significant in this example, which involves the weather presenter, Lukewsa, and a park ranger, situated in a woodland location in Leicestershire, is that the SNG is parked 30 metres away from the location requiring a long length of cable to be 'run out' to the place where the live will take place. Once the location has been selected and the cables have been laid, it is soon discovered that the park ranger is not a very confident talker, and the location is also visually dull. At this point SNG1 is contacted by the lunchtime producer who tells him that they have an extra minute on the live as a news story has been dropped from the bulletin. At this point a crucial decision is made to attempt to make the live visually more interesting.

So to make what is one weather presenter and one guest and almost nothing else to see apart from a few bluebells, a little more interesting, we will try to use a second camera. What we will do is we will do this as simply as possible; we will run it as if there is only one camera so that cameraman who is Mark, will think he is on air, and then Andrew will offer cut-aways; probably bluebells, which are part of the subject today; it's Spring and this is the reason we're here and offer an end shot to take and he may well offer me a wide shot of the presenter and guest doing the interview; a wide shot with bluebells and trees and even a cameraman in there too and I will direct it here.

(Ian, SNG1, BBC Nottingham)

As we saw in the previous example, the SNG1 manipulates the two camera operators' positions by making them think that they are filming and on air all the time when in fact they may not be. The geographical distance between the SNG and the live location once again makes such manipulation possible.[6] By doing this, the SNG1 is able to create visual interest by providing a wider selection of shots, cutting between the two cameras from inside the truck. What in effect creates the live experience is the utilisation of the assemblages of technologies thus adding a richer visual dimension to the event. So two cameras are used and a sequence in which SNG1 vision mixes between the two from inside the SNG, offering separate shots, is practised three times before the actual event. But, as in the previous examples where the technological operations of the live were eradicated in the actual transmission, here a partial glimpse of the actual technological process by means of a shot of the second camera operator is provided for the viewer. This signifies that the SNG1 recognises that not only do multiple realities perform throughout the live process, but that in desperate situations, where the constructed live is visually uninspiring, a separate reality, that of the technological performance of the *actual live* is more interesting and should therefore be revealed to the audience.

Technological hermeneutics

In our final example of a regional outside broadcast, the emphasis lies in recognising the fluidity of actors' chronogrammatic positions during the performed reality as well as the development of a highly refined technological hermeneutics that illustrates the successful enfolding of human and nonhuman actors. It also reveals the deliberate manipulation of live and recorded events within a single programme, facilitated by the multiple technological functions of the SNG.

In this instance the SNG is located at a hotel in Kegworth, a small town in Leicestershire where the then Liberal Democrat leader, Charles Kennedy, is holding an election press conference. The conference is itself a staged media event. There are no members of the public present, just representatives from the regional print, radio and television media. The press conference takes place at 3.30pm and lasts for approximately half an hour. After this the Liberal Democrat leader conducts longer separate interviews, one of which is to the BBC's regional political correspondent, Jonathan, and then he leaves for the local airport. He has spent approximately one hour at the hotel.

In contrast, the SNG vehicle arrives at the hotel at 2.30pm. The camera diary assistant tells the SNG operators that they're expected to remain at the location until 7.00pm, which is the end of the evening news programme. There is a resigned, if not slightly annoyed, response to this plan that echoes Huffaker's original observation concerning the use of live broadcasts.

> OBs are utterly pointless – most news OBs are anyway … my dad as a punter, who is in his 70s, said; 'Why is this guy outside the Home Office as if the people in the Home Office are still working when they go home at four or five or six?' But then he's a civil servant so he'd know that. But anyway, we will send a package in advance so they can check all the astons and stuff – and that will already be there. Then about third item in they will hand over to Jonathan and Jonathan will say 'Here I am at a hotel that nobody is at anymore – Charles Kennedy has left hours ago, and everybody else has left, but hey – let's put our flash Land Rover in front of it and make it look as though something is

happening – his Xmobile – so basically it's just another pointless live, like yesterday.'

(Ian, SNG1, BBC Nottingham)

What is significant is that in this live broadcast not only is there an attempt to deliberately manipulate the viewer's conception of time, presenting Jonathan at the hotel, introducing his own package (which has been edited some hours earlier), before returning to him accompanied by the Xmobile to conclude the live, but that this temporal dislocation between *presented* time and the actual time in which Charles Kennedy addressed the press and spoke with Jonathan is again facilitated entirely by the technological functionality of the SNG. For in this example both the editing and transmission facility of the truck combined is utilised so that a completely edited news package can be sent to the media hub via the SNG for inclusion in the programme. The live elements where Jonathan introduces himself at the location and then his own prerecorded package, are used to 'top and tail' these, thus confusing the viewer by presenting two distinctly separate chronograms as one: one of the edited package and one of Jonathan introducing it and reporting live after it has been played out from back at base. The package is filmed by Jonathan and a camera operator during the morning and is edited on the Avid Editing Suite (see Figure 7.2) inside the SNG once the truck arrives at the hotel.

Another neat irony is that even though the SNG could transmit the finished package live from the location straight into the main programme, the production team in the newsroom prefer to have the piece sent over in advance as they are wary of relying on the live capability of the truck; a fear that is encouraged by the SNG operators as we discussed earlier in the chapter.

> They don't like doing it live back at base, but if it's the only way they're going to get the piece ... but they prefer you to send it back and then they can put it in their running order. It's basically a reassurance thing.
>
> (Tara, SNG2, BBC Nottingham)

> They have no control over it if it's played in live. They want to clip it up at the top end and they know exactly how long it is, they might say it's one minute twenty, and it might be one minute eighteen, but they're grateful for anything they can get.
>
> (Boris, SNG1, BBC Nottingham)

The reporter and SNG operators are thus situated at the hotel location for approximately five-and-a-half hours within which time they edit together a two-minute recorded news package that includes sections of the interview with

169

Figure 7.2 The Avid Editing Suite inside the SNG.

Charles Kennedy that has been conducted by Jonathan. It also includes a range of opinions by the local people of Kegworth who are noticeably absent from the stage managed press conference. But the actual live elements that introduce the package and that conclude this section of the programme are once again reliant on the technological assemblage of the invisible SNG and the highly visible Xmobile and added props: a plastic table and chairs, which are unloaded from the back of the Land Rover and set up alongside it to illustrate how Jonathan will appear to the public in their own towns across the region. The insistence on these visual props is vital as there is no news element to this live component, but rather a specific and deliberate blurring of the distinction between the live and edited elements of the section facilitated by the SNG's multiple technological functionality, to persuade the viewer that the entire section is happening here and now right before their eyes.

A second significant observation that we can make during the performance of this live broadcast is the complex development of the hermeneutic interchange between human and nonhuman actors who facilitate the live element. SNG1, Ian, is reliant on knowing what SNG2, Andrew, has prepared for him in terms of cables, audio feeds, microphones and cameras. Ian has had no time to be involved in the *setting up* of the live element as he has been busy editing the required two-minute news package. Thus, unusually his position is weakened by a lack of proximity to the technology and a fragmentation of his techno- and sociogrammatic position, taking on the separate and added role of a video editor, rather than retaining his single function as an engineer. Yet his ability to function in this dual role, performing simultaneous roles, is once again dependent on a hermeneutic awareness of the technology. In other words, he quite literally reads the signs.

> I edited the package that you saw. I was sending that from the truck to base whilst *East Midlands Today* was on air. So I didn't have time to muck about with what Andrew was doing. I looked up and I saw the camera on camera three and I looked to the left and I saw the radio mike receivers were on, and I looked out and I saw a green cable. He at no point told me what he had done and I had no time for him to tell me what he had done. I just knew what he had done by the indications in the truck and I knew where I would find what I was looking for, and I just pushed the button and, more importantly, the right fader on the desk. The clues were there – the obvious one was the camera –that shows camera one and camera two and that's fairly obvious. But the other ones, these had lit up, which are my radio mike receivers so I knew he had gone for radio mikes. Both had lit up so I knew I had two radio mikes and there's only one person there so almost definitely he's given Jonathan double radio mikes, and then the green cable means that there is no audio coming in apart from the radio mikes, so it's not fibre. So he had never told me what he had done, but I knew it.
>
> (Ian, SNG1, BBC Nottingham)

What is significant here is that this is a three-way symbolic conversation between both SNG1 and SNG2 and the technology itself. While Ian prides himself on being able to ascertain what has been set up by his successful interpretation of the technology, SNG2, Andrew, has provided Ian with this by his own awareness of the technical functioning available to him. And the ontology of that functionality itself is of course essential, for either human actor to be able to interpret what the other one may or may not have done. A three-way interchange combines both human and nonhuman actors in a hermeneutic assemblage of technological perception, reaction and performance, in order to successfully transmit the live element of the show.

Conclusion

> But there is a more radical possibility too. We might, instead or as well, imagine versions of method assemblage that craft, sensitise us to,

and apprehend the indefinite character of the non coherent in-here and out-there.

(Law, 2004, p.82)

From a detailed observation of a number of different live broadcasts significant findings can be made both with regard to the role of the SNG and those related actors responsible for the performance of live events, and also with regard to the way in which news production may be understood more fully on a more theoretical level. Returning to Mol's substitution of multiple realities for pluralism, and echoing the sentiments from Law's quote above, the related performances of the SNG and associated actors teach us first of all that there is no clear distinction to be made between the varying roles of human and nonhuman actors, nor between external and internal sites in the production network. It also reminds us that in the eradication of these sets of polarities, it may be impossible to discern who or what constitutes a subject and who an object in a given network. To use one example, at one point the SNG1 occupies a distinctly strong position as he enjoys the closest technological and geographical proximity to the SNG, which has become a temporary black box. Yet at another point he is rendered unstable by the occurrence of technical errors over which he has no control and from which he cannot disentangle. At other times he is only able to stabilise his position by reading the signs deliberately left by other actors to assist him. The SNG1's sociogram and technogram are continually shifting due to his position vis-à-vis other related actors, and vis-à-vis the shifting sociograms and technograms of the SNG itself. The SNG1 thus occupies numerous different positions, sometimes able to manipulate, dupe or silence other actors in the network, at other times commanded by them to undertake a particular course of action so as to achieve a certain outcome decided upon in his absence.

So what does all this tell us? Returning to the example of the perceived simultaneity of the two planes crashing into the Twin Towers and the media event that brought this to our attention, even here we can begin to recognise that we are not actually witnessing a singular reality. Instead we witness a coalescence of multiple realities, enfolded within one another and made singular by the very invisibility of their separate and fragmented performances. It is helpful in an attempt to disentangle these to use Law's complex exposition of the composite elements of presence.

Method assemblage becomes the enactment of presence, manifest absence, and absence as Otherness. More specifically, method assemblage becomes the crafting or bundling of relations or hinterland into three parts; a) whatever is present; b) whatever is absent but is also manifest in its absence; and whatever is absent but is Other because,

while it is necessary to presence, it is not, nor cannot be made manifest. Note to talk of crafting it is not necessary to imply human agency
or skill – the various ethnographies we have explored suggest that
people, machines, traces, resources of all kinds – are all involved in the
process of crafting.

(Law, 2004, p.84)

The same is true of the live media event. There is never a singularity of
presence that exists within a stable temporal or spatial framework, but rather
the performance of multiple realities, at times made partially or fully manifest,
or otherwise deliberately defined as Other and absent, so as to preclude the
possibility on the part of the viewer to witness a fragmentation of that perceived
singularity. As we have seen throughout the SNG examples, these variations of
presence, absence and Otherness are also evident within the production process
itself. In this way it is not possible to identify a constituted ontological 'it' that
we may call the production process.

The idea of the universal transportability of universal knowledge was
always a chimera. But if the universal disappears, then so too does the
local – for the local is a subset of the general. Instead we are left with
situated enactments and sets of partial connections, and it is to those
that we owe our heterogeneous responsibilities.

(Law, 2004, p.155)

Thus ANT itself can only be seen to contribute to the performance of the
myriad of actor alliances that together and in constant relation to one another
may be considered to constitute, in so far as this does not indicate stasis or
closure, the news production network. And by recognising the multiple, conflicting and often intertwining realities that are performed continually within
that network, as we have seen in this chapter, it is now necessary to move
beyond Latour's analysis of laboratory practice with its highly visible translations
to begin to reveal more opaque and often messier assemblages that go to make
up the news production network. As we have discovered in our analysis of the
live event, the invisibility of the production network is significant as it offers
both human and nonhuman actors opportunities to strengthen positions and to
establish stronger alliances with other actors. Many of these opportunities
involve certain behavioural characteristics, which we have already glimpsed in
the actions of the SNG1 operator and his manipulation of less proximate actors.

But it is the distinction between human and nonhuman actors – which Latour
does not accept and therefore does not address in satisfactory detail – that will
be the focus of the following chapter. During our exploration of human-actor

behaviour it will be demonstrated that multiple realities, including others not as yet mentioned in this chapter but once again involving the SNG and the live event, continue to dramatise themselves throughout the network, enfolding those human and nonhuman actors together wherever we attempt to fix our ethnographic gaze. It is only by accepting that a desire for fixity does not lead to successful exposition but rather to deep misconceptions, and by allowing a developed version of ANT, involving a trenchant struggle to recognise the dramatisation of multiple realities in several intertwining and conflicting locations, so as to continue to destabilise the coherence we may at first wish to attempt to locate, that the true performance of news production may be allowed to flourish.

8

HUMAN ACTORS, INTENTIONALITY AND ACTOR NETWORK THEORY

The strategy which ANT is in the process of constructing involves fabricating an approach that denies the primacy of the human subject, and treats humans and non humans as a priori parts of an undifferentiated universe. This is a strategy of de-differentiation, and it requires a viewpoint and a vocabulary that hardly exist.

(Boyne, 2002, p.32)

TV news journalists and their 'programme visualisation' contribute to the routine production of a news subgenre defined in terms of a number of shared experiences, conventions and appeals. These are inscribed daily into the programme composition and form and, along with other considerations, are likely to be implicated in the choice and selection of news formats. In this regard, journalists deserve increased attention in the empirical examination and theorization of the production domain.

(Cottle, 1995, p.281)

During the last five chapters we have explored how constellations of human and nonhuman actors are enfolded together in the production of news. We have used Actor Network Theory (ANT) as the means with which to study these microprocesses of news production, to reveal how the news product is constructed by a myriad of actor translations that occur as a result of the complex alliances between humans and machines. We have argued that because of this 'reality' is not definable within traditional epistemic distinctions. For Latour, truth and reality are and always have been conditions that must be specifically produced and continually maintained through networks of practical social activity (Ward, 1994, p.88). Our own research has also demonstrated how news facts are *constructed* just like the scientific facts analysed by Latour and Woolgar in the Salk Laboratory by means of establishing strong associative actor bonds to sustain effective translations that in turn may or may not create sealed black boxes over which controversy becomes silenced. The stronger and more encompassing the network, the stronger the truth claim becomes. ANT's aim is to

> ... avoid the twin pitfalls of sociologism and technologism. We are never faced with objects or social relations, we are faced with chains which are associations of humans ... and non-humans. No one has ever seen a social relation by itself ... nor a technical relation.
>
> (Latour, 1991, p.110)

We have continually witnessed these chains of association within the newsroom. To begin with, by actors' acceptance of the media hub as an *obligatory point of passage,* or by the complex and ongoing implementation of Personal Digital Production (PDP), with its effective translation of certain other parts of the network, resulting in the demise of the news organiser and a partial and at times radical reconfiguration of the news agenda. We have also come across these chains of association in our exploration of the complex enfolding of human and nonhuman actors in the delivery of the live news event. In all of these instances we have revealed how the associations established between humans and machines construct the news. By charting the separate technogrammatic, sociogrammatic and chronogrammatic positions of individual actors, we have witnessed how some level of network stability, essential for the production of news facts, is established only by this ongoing and fluctuating relationship between the technical, social and temporal.

The adoption of ANT as a method for reading news has provided us with an important means with which to carve out the neglected area of *practice* wherein news is constructed from beneath the more traditional readings of media as primarily producing *effects* upon a stable and separately defined society. As we have argued earlier in the book, traditional readings of media that necessitate essentialised and often deliberately unproblematic notions of the technical, the social, the cultural or the literal have tended to neglect the complex connectivity of the media process at this level of micropractice.

The use of ANT to attempt to mess up the demarcations of media, society, technology and culture upon which these readings have hitherto relied so as to argue that either media *is* society, or has purely societal *effects,* was explored briefly in Chapter 2. Returning to the earlier studies by Couldry (2003), Boyne (2002) and Law (1986) that look at the effectiveness of ANT to address the issue of human actors in a network, it is worth pausing for a moment to recall where the frustrations with ANT as a methodology are specifically located. Once we have provided a brief outline of these arguments we can then move towards a fuller exploration of ANT as a method for reading human actors within the network, paying particular attention not so much to human *subjectivity,* as is the primary focus of these authors' studies, but to the issues of human *motivation* and *intentionality*.

While the authors mentioned above have all expressed relevant concerns that ANT does not adequately address issues of human subjectivity and consciousness, it is not with regard to subjectivity but more precisely with regard to human strategy, motivation and intent that this chapter will grapple so as to reveal certain specific weaknesses that ANT may have as a method. We will then seek to offer a specific way out of what may seem at first to be a rather serious methodological quandary should we choose to adopt ANT as a tool for reading news work, by providing our own new development of the application of ANT as a method. We will spend time analysing our human actors within the network in some detail and argue how, in a departure from Latour's own applications of ANT, they must be differentiated from their nonhuman associates if the news process is to be fully unravelled and explained.

Actor Network Theory and the human subject

As we saw in Chapter 2, Couldry's recent interpretation of specific media institutions as extended social networks has led him to extol ANT's efficiency in providing a refreshing new approach to media; to act as a significant counter force to more established texts within the media studies tradition. Yet in his adoption and adaptation of ANT there is clear uneasiness with what he argues is its insistence to under-represent the role of human actors.

> ANT remains an important antidote to functionalist versions of media theory and an inspiration towards developing better versions of a materialist approach to understanding what media are and their consequences for the social world and social space ... but we need to think about how people's cognitive and emotive frameworks are shaped by the underlying features of the networks in which they are situated. If expressed in these terms, there is a great deal to be learnt from ANT in its understanding everyday practices around media.
>
> (Couldry, 2003, p.4)

His criticism of ANT's human subject focuses on what he believes to be its inability to define the human other than in direct correlation to the technological.

> ANT is interested in the celebration of human agency in terms of its entanglement with technology, and not any other dimensions of human agency – all this, in spite of the fact that from other perspectives

networks are at most the infrastructure of human action, not its dynamic content.

(Couldry, 2003, p.5)

As we also discussed in Chapter 2, Boyne's exposition of the human subject involves a delineation of what he argues is Latour's careful reconfiguration of the human, moving towards a position where the subject is celebrated for being hybrid and unstable.

> Latour's view is that we cannot grasp the human unless we restore it to its element of quiddity, its 'share of things'. He argues; 'So long as humanism is constructed through contrast to the object that has been abandoned to epistemology, neither the human not the nonhuman can be understood'. So what are the consequences of this approach to the human subject? The subject is inevitably and permanently hybrid. This does not amount, for Latour, to the death of the human, but it does mean that the human is not a stable form.
>
> (Boyne, 2002, p.29)

Boyne argues that Latour doesn't completely deny the human subject, but instead places it and associated human traits such as subjectivity, feelings, perceptions, impulses, fear, pride and curiosity, into one corner of a black box, insisting that the size of an actor is only determined by how much is held in that box, and whether or not it can be kept there successfully (Boyne, 2002). Once more the Nietzschean principle of human power as simple, brute force is evident in Latour's definition of the outcome of competition between subjects as determined by who can 'muster on the spot the largest number of well aligned and faithful allies' (Latour, 1990, p.23). Boyne argues that Latour's reconfiguration of the human is a logical development of his overall denial of the fundamental dualisms of subject and object, individual and society, social and natural, which he believes underlie modernism.

> The position outlined here replaces the modernist symmetry between subject and object, in which the human subject is a paranoid construction always under threat from the other side of the divide, with a symmetrical world in which machines are not simply machines, organisations are not simply organisations, and human subjects are not simply human subjects. Machines, organisations, goods and subjects are all hybrid quasi-objects. They exist between hard nature and free society.
>
> (Boyne, 2002, p.30)

Boyne's exposition of the debate regarding the status of the subject within sociology, in which he recalls the earlier 'Science Wars' and Collins and Yearley's scathing attack on ANT, develops most significantly in the endnotes of his chapter. Here he considers Latour's relativism and how this contributes to a fuller understanding of the human subject within ANT. Recalling Latour's own criticisms of the terminology of ANT, and his insistence that neither the word *actor*, nor *network* should be used anymore, Boyne points out how Latour's view that social ontology does not reduce to the agency-structure divide can assist us in an understanding of the status of the human subject.

> His view is that social ontology does not reduce to the agency-structure divide but is more a matter of circulation founded on the dissatisfactions which attend focus on both the micro and macro levels: dissatisfaction with one leads to the other in a never ending circulation. This circulation provides actants with their 'subjectivity, with their intentionality, with their morality'. Circulations are summed up into local focuses . . . In this context, 'Subjectivity, corporeality is no more a property of humans, of individuals, than being an outside reality is a property of nature.' It is fundamentally a 'circulating capacity, something that is partially gained by hooking up to certain bodies of practice'.
>
> (Boyne, 2002, p.40)

What he means by this is that to attribute what are traditionally accepted *human* traits such as motivation or intention *only* to the human actors within the network is to refuse to acknowledge the circulatory practices of the network, and to once again plunge into the uncontested waters of essentialist paradigms. And it is with this central contention that we will attempt to engage throughout this chapter.

As we have already seen criticism of ANT's refusal to recognise the ontological disparity between human and nonhuman actors is echoed by those within the field of the sociology of scientific knowledge and as Boyne describes the debate came to a somewhat dramatic head in 1992 with Collins and Yearley's (1992) attack on what they deemed to be the regressive nature of ANT.[1]

A more detailed exposition of the debate between those who favour a human-centred approach to an understanding of science, and those who attempt to throw off the mantle of established epistemologies to inhabit a different space, wherein a search for a new vocabulary is determined by the desire to treat both humans and nonhumans symmetrically, can be found in Chapter 2. As Boyne discovered in his exposition of the status of the subject within ANT, the relegation of the human subject with its properties, powers, internal organisation and fate to the far margins of social scientific concern, has serious implications for how the commonplace split between nature and society, human and machine, may be readdressed in the sociology of science and that many such as Collins and Yearley, will continue to espouse these dualisms as ontological givens (Boyne, 2002).

However, it is now necessary to challenge such frustrations with ANT and its relationship to the human subject, to argue that such criticisms are perhaps somewhat misdirected. For is it not the case, as we have demonstrated by many instances cited in the past five empirical chapters, that by using ANT to map the constellations of actors within a network, we are more than capable of charting human subjectivity? We need only recall how in the previous chapter, the SNG operator deliberately used his stronger technogrammatic position vis-à-vis the satellite truck to acquire a more powerful position than other proximate human actors, to recognise how human subjectivity is revealed, even if it is also enfolded within associated technological actors.

There is certainly an understandable resistance to the use of ANT to investigate human behaviour as we have outlined above, but this reluctance is often overplayed. In this chapter we will reveal that it is not the *subjectivity* of the human that remains under-represented by an ANT analysis, but that the weaknesses of ANT as a methodology occur when attempting to explore the *motives* and *intentions* of human actors. In fact, we will demonstrate that the specific *subjectivity* of the human can be readily revealed if only we remain faithful to the very mechanics of ANT.

The empirical evidence of the previous five chapters demonstrates that human and nonhuman actors are defined within what we have referred to as specific techno-, socio- and chronogrammatic axes and that their actions are constructed, if nonhuman, and constructed and recognised by both themselves and by others if human, from their specific location within these axes. This is a crucial difference and it is here that our own analysis of the disparity between human and nonhuman actors begins to conflict with Latour's relativistic approach to human traits being in continual network circulation and therefore unable to be corporeally situated as we outlined above.

Human actors are able to reflect upon their actions. Technologies may well recognise processes, as recognition can be a simple process of action, selection, practice and feedback mechanisms. Such a process is more than possible for a machine to achieve. But whether we can successfully argue that technologies are able to demonstrate self-reflexivity, and as such, be capable of intentionality and motivation, is quite another thing. We will see that it is this specific disparity between human and nonhuman actors that must be recognised and incorporated into ANT if we are to develop it as an effective method for reading news work. It is my belief that such a development, as this chapter will illustrate, is not only highly possible but is also necessary if we are to adopt ANT as a pertinent means by which wider social practices such as the construction of news facts may be explored.

While ANT may insist that the human subject remains undifferentiated and the human and nonhuman folded into one another so as to suggest symmetry between actors, it is still necessary for us as researchers to define and to interpret each actor, whether human or machine, by means of our three socio-, techno- and chronogrammatic axes. As we have seen time and again, human actors are not immune to network translation. The significant difference is that they are self-reflexive and aware. They may thus utilise their techno- or sociogrammatic position to gain stability or power as we witnessed in the previous chapter when the SNG1 operator used his heightened technological expertise to maintain a stronger sociogrammatic position within the network, or in Chapter 3 where the presenter maintained her stronger sociogrammatic position by bypassing the media hub to operate the technology autonomously.

Thus by using the specific concepts that ANT provides, and that have been used as a method for reading news practice thus far, we can begin to make clearer sense of the strategies, power struggles and public expressions of control, disaffection or affirmation between human actors involved in the process. These concepts become an integral part of the ethnographer's toolbox. The limitations of ANT are still evident. It still refuses to properly address the notion of power as anything other than the display of force, and it remains maddeningly fuzzy in its delineation of human motive or intent. We will address both of these limitations, but this need not necessarily be a hindrance to the pursuit of a clearer understanding of news practice using ethnographic observation, if one holds fast to the underlying principles of ANT.

Continuing to chart these three axes and by applying ANT's most significant concepts we will now analyse the production process over a period of a single day, and will illustrate as in previous chapters how news facts are constructed by means of the alliances created between all actors on a network. The difference will be that instead of relying on the visible actions and materiality of the human and nonhuman actors, this analysis will now wrestle with issues of power, manipulation, discourse and subjectivity. It will concentrate specifically on the interplay between human actors, to explore how the techno-, chrono- and sociogrammatical axes are continually constructed, translated and realigned by humans in the network.

We will thus challenge the limits of ANT by providing a detailed analysis of human intentionality and motive. By so doing, we will also seek to develop the application and relevance of ANT as a methodology for reading human behaviour. It is always possible to enhance ANT for it is itself constituted by its own ongoing associations with new actors, at both the methodological level of observation and application, and the theoretical level. While challenging its

current limitations, we will therefore illustrate how the inclusion and exploration of such a methodological critique can further develop an understanding of
the practice of human actors within the news network, and offer important
insights into the construction of news at the level of microprocesses, as well as
permit ANT to comment upon itself as a fluid and developing methodology.

Actor Network Theory, intention and power

> Since it is impossible to take only one of the many ontological positions
> in order to account for the way scientists bring in nonhumans, we the
> analysts have to entertain the whole range. One way to do this is to
> extend our principle of symmetry to vocabulary and to decide that
> whatever term is used for humans, we will use it for nonhumans as
> well. It does not mean that we wish to extend intentionality to things,
> or mechanics to humans, but only that with any one attribute we
> should be able to depict the other.
>
> (Callon & Latour, 1992, p.353)

This quote is taken from the response to Collins and Yearley penned during the
so-called 'Science Wars'. It reminds us that any attempt to investigate or decipher human intentionality is erroneous if it does not, at one and the same time,
investigate those nonhuman actors with which it is immediately and continually
associated. Leaving aside Boyne's issue of circulation and whether or not human
traits should be accepted as being situated, this argument does initially seem
logical. Indeed human behaviour in this study has only ever been analysed in
conjunction with associated human and nonhuman actors. That being the case,
in what way can we argue that human intention or motive remains neglected by
an ANT analysis? An answer to that question lies in Latour's limited and somewhat inflexible definition of power, which we will now examine. Remember
Latour argues that

> When an actor simply has power, nothing happens and s/he is power-
> less. When, on the other hand, an actor exerts power it is others who
> perform the action.
>
> (Latour, 1986, p.264)

As we saw in Chapter 2, Latour views network *mobilisations* – a term that can
equally be used to describe human or nonhuman action – as an example of the
play of *forces*. For Latour, power is something that cannot be owned or stored,
but is rather the result of the collective action, or force of the actors in the
network.

> A dictator is obeyed, we say, because 'he has got power'; a manager is able to move his headquarters because, as we like to say, 'he is powerful'; a dominant female monkey is able to grab the best feeding sites because she 'holds' a powerful rank ... Power is, on the contrary, what has to be explained by the action of the others who obey the dictator, the manager, or the dominant female. If the notion of power may be used as a convenient way to summarise the consequence of a collective action, it cannot also explain what holds the collective action in place. It may be used as an effect, but never a cause.
>
> (Latour, 1986, p.265)

This is reminiscent of Nietzsche's definition of 'The Will to Power' as being not something 'out there' that must be discovered – but something that must be created and that gives a name to a process. For Nietzsche the more powerful a force of life becomes, the greater its capacity to impose the 'truth' of its vision of existence upon the world (Nietzsche, 1968, p.299).

The French language uses two words to define power. It is as if Latour has taken the first French word for power, *puissance,* to mean force, and has ignored the second meaning of the French word *pouvoir,* also meaning power, but as potentiality.

Law's frustration with Latour's insistence to define power merely as force, and to further assert that power is not demonstrated other than by means of the result of observable *collective* action, urges him to argue that actors possess a particular form of agency, which includes the notion of *power over* and *power to* which can be stored.

> Indeed as lay people we work routinely on the assumption that both 'power over' and 'power to' can indeed be stored, even if the methods by which they are stored are never entirely secure and we know our store may spring a leak. If this were not the case we would never open bank accounts, we would never accept promises at face value, and neither would we say (surely with some reason some of the time!) that Prime Ministers have 'more power' than back benchers.
>
> (Law, 1986, p.170)

Law develops the notion of stored power by examining some of the strategies that human actors use to exercise discretion in the deployment of *power to* and *power over.* In so doing he negotiates a tricky path between an evaluation of actors' so-called human characteristics, and an insistence that this is not a redefinition of Latour's term, and that the notion of power and agency can equally be applied to nonhuman entities.

183

> I want to say that an actor may be pictured as a set of relations which in some measure has the effect of (a) characterising, (b) storing and (at least in some instances) (c) offering a degree of discretion with respect to power to and power over. In tying agency to power and relations in this way I am seeking to elide the agency/structure dualism ... I am suggesting that it is difficult to imagine the one without the other. I am also suggesting, to be sure, that agents are not co-terminus with people. Other entities may also be agents.
>
> (Law, 1986, p.171)

Yet a less problematic and perhaps more logical refute of Latour's insistence on power being defined only by collective performance, can be made if we return to the actual mechanics of ANT itself. By using an actor's individual sociogrammatic, chronogrammatic and technogrammatic position within the network as our defining axes, the notion of individual agency and the storing of power can be further examined. As we have seen in previous chapters, for example where either the position of the media hub or the satellite truck is examined, stability by means of network positioning along these axes, in the case of the media hub so as to create black box status, can be achieved equally by nonhuman actors. If we then concentrate on the delineation and exploration of each of these *specific* positions, as we did in our analysis of the media hub, PDP and the satellite truck, the differences between human and nonhuman actors become very clearly illuminated.

Thus these core concepts that ANT itself espouses reveal as inadmissible the insistence that human and nonhuman are indistinguishable. They may be utterly dependent and folded into one another, and as we have seen, it is only through means of the association of the human with the nonhuman, that either actor can be fully defined, but they are still different. By recognising the very *specificity* of actor positions that these three axes define it is possible to reveal more clearly how each separate network location provides actors with radically different power configurations, and that human actors are both aware of and able to use these positions strategically in order to stabilise their associations with others. It is thus both their subjectivity, and their intentional agency that sets them apart from nonhuman actors.

Latour's definition of power as pure force or forged associations is reductionist. It fails to recognise the plurality of motivation of actors situated in different nodes of the network and assumes that these nodes are simply empty vessels. There is no realisation here that some nodes may transport information more quickly, or may react more effectively than others: that humans can be more responsive than computers. The symmetry insisted upon by this strangulating definition of power as exerted force reduces the network to a mere exhibition of unmotivated and unintended action. Yet by examining human behaviour through various journalists' discourses and the various strategies they employ in the production activities of a single day, we can challenge Latour's notions of collective power and show how human actors employ discretionary tactics, exhibit motive and intention, and react differently to the network than do their nonhuman counterparts.

Journalists, interactions and the daily news production process

The empirical analysis is gathered from observations, interviews and participation in the news production process of a single day. The human actors consist of:

- Chris – the main programme news producer
- Steve – the lunchtime producer
- Priya – the lunchtime presenter
- Mark – the programme director responsible for directing both lunchtime and evening news programmes
- Kevin – the assistant news editor who is responsible for setting up future stories, as well as overseeing the overall programme output
- Anne and Dominic – the two main evening programme presenters
- James – the reporter responsible for reporting on two court stories that are anticipated to conclude on this particular day.

Other actors involved are the two SNG operators on the satellite truck, and the technical engineer in the gallery who is responsible for communicating with the SNG operators.

To analyse the construction of news facts, and in particular the role of human actors within the network, it is necessary to return briefly to earlier ANT concepts that Latour and Woolgar devised for articulating the process of the construction of scientific facts in the Salk Laboratory. One of the most important was the scientists' use of various *inscription* devices in order to record and materialise their findings so as to recruit other actors thus fortifying their position on the network.[2] As Latour argues

> We go from a conversation between a few people to texts that soon fortify themselves, fending off opposition by enrolling many allies. Each of these allies itself uses many different tactics on many other texts enlisted in the dispute.
>
> (Latour, 1987, p.43)

Just as in the laboratory, numerous inscription devises are evident throughout the newsroom. Their purpose is to stabilise translation by means of literally visualising times, events, stories or locations all of which are granted added significance by the fact they are inscribed and therefore fixed. Actor Network Theory argues that it is only through the use of inscriptions that actants are moved throughout the network and temporary stability achieved.[3]

> Thanks to inscriptions, we are able to oversee and control a situation in which we are submerged. We become superior to that which is greater than us, and we are able to gather synoptically all the actions that occurred over many days that we have since forgotten.
>
> (Latour, 1999, p.65)

The first example of the inscription device is the *prospects news grid* that is stored electronically on the Electronic News Production Service (ENPS) and is available to every member of staff. Outlining all possible story ideas for the day, and stating which reporter is allocated to each story, the grid is divided into two sections, separated by a thick black line. Anything that appears below the line is not ready for transmission and may need further filming or planning, or has not been agreed as a story idea. Anything that appears above the black line has been commissioned, which means that it can be filmed and edited and transmitted on that day. The news grid can be accessed and amended by anyone working in the newsroom, although the main people who utilise the grid are planning journalists who are responsible for finding news stories to 'fill the grid' and the producers who read and print off the grid ahead of the first daily meeting at 9.00am, known as *the prospects meeting.*

The first example, on this particular Thursday, of the significance of the news grid occurs at the prospects meeting, attended by the main programme producer Chris, Steve, who is producing lunchtime, and the morning presenter, Priya. Usually there is a journalist from the sports department as well as a senior management figure and a planning journalist, but on this day the meeting is somewhat under attended.

In light of this under attendance, Chris spends very little time discussing the prospects in this forum, which as we shall see from a later analysis of the behaviour of actors in public arenas, usually acts as a significant multidiscursive area where individual human actors demonstrate their use of power and strategy to gain stabilisation or even translation of individual network positions. We might speculate that on this particular morning Chris sees no need for any kind of overt manoeuvring, due in part to the lack of attendance by other staff, and therefore he simply uses the *news grid* to steer the meeting to a swift conclusion.

> We'll just take what's above the black line then and the rest is pretty
> self explanatory. I don't think we need discuss the stories – it's all there
> on the grid. Let's just go and get on with it.
>
> (Chris, programme producer, BBC Nottingham)

In this instance the inscription device acts as a significant *immutable mobile*. It is
used by a single actor to forge an important alliance with the rest of the production
team, urging them to agree to the content of the grid, limit discussion and instead
to disperse and 'make news'. Yet the grid itself has already determined to some
extent what news will be 'made' for as the meeting is not attended by other significant actors, which might result in Chris spending a considerably longer time
interacting with it, the grid remains unchallenged. The grid has allowed Chris to
oversee and control the situation and the meeting is swiftly concluded without
debate. Yet from this example alone, Chris can be seen to be exercising strategic
agency. Working within our ANT axes, his sociogrammatic position is secure
enough for him to exercise control over other actors and, by the deliberate use of
the inscription device, to curtail debate that might challenge his stable position.

To return to Law's concepts discussed earlier, this short meeting is all about
power to and *power over*. Chris is afforded *power to* by the use of the news grid and
decides in turn to use *power over* the other members of the meeting so as to
retain his position. The other members are unable and/or unwilling to challenge this decision, though interestingly the situation changes once the actors
leave the public arena.

Immediately following the meeting we return with the lunchtime producer
Steve to the production area where he occupies a desk two desk spaces away from
Chris, the main producer. The seat between them is unoccupied but is usually used
by the assistant editor or the output editor who discusses how the programme is
'shaping up' with the producer. Chris goes to get a coffee from the kitchen and
Steve discusses further story prospects. He tells me about a story that has not
yet appeared on the news grid, as it only came to light that morning. It concerns
a judge who is criticising the government's initiatives to curb antisocial behaviour,
by issuing 'ASBOs' (Antisocial Behaviour Orders). The story is to be covered by
the newsroom's new 'shoot/edit'.[4] Steve is concerned that this decision, made
by Chris before the prospects meeting, may not be the right one.

> I don't think he [the shoot/edit] is up to the job actually. The shoot/
> edit is supposedly not there to ask questions but just get pictures. But I
> am going to need this for a report for lunch as we don't have many
> prospects to go by so far. I need a report. I might even have to ask you
> to do it. [Laughs] Would you?
>
> (Steve, lunchtime producer, BBC Nottingham)

This short quote reveals the extent to which human actors exercise agency, utilise strategy, display subjectivity and, most significantly, conceive of all other human actors as belonging to a somewhat ill-defined but mutually understood hierarchy. Let's unpack it. Steve illustrates that contrary to what conclusions might have been drawn from the lack of interaction in the meeting, he is not satisfied that the prospects are adequate for his lunchtime programme. Furthermore he is not sure that Chris's decision to use the shoot/edit is correct, even though he never broaches this with Chris. Thirdly, he demonstrates that he doesn't think that the shoot/edit is 'up to the job' because he is not a reporter, thus indicating that he perceives reporters to be somehow more significant or at least, more effective, than nonreporters. Lastly, this leads him to ask me, as an observer, not a member of the newsroom, to construct the report for him. Steve knows he can ask this for a number of reasons. He knows I am able to perform the task as he has worked with me in the past and knows I have the relevant skills. He's also aware that this request will not interfere with the other significant actors within the network with whom he is most closely associated, in particular Chris. Yet he knows that I am also associated with him by my position as an observer and that having been afforded that privilege I may be persuaded to, in some sense, return a favour. His request is successful and I do subsequently construct the report.[5]

The next interaction involving a wider constellation of human actors reveals a more complex interplay of strategy and power and it is thus essential to chart each actor's socio-, chrono- and technogrammatic position so as to make sense of what is happening within the network at this specific point. The situation involves Steve's attempts to find material with which to fill his 11-minute lunchtime bulletin, which as he has already indicated, is proving to be a difficult task due to a lack of prospects. He approaches the sports desk, situated immediately behind the producer's desk to ask Rob, the sports reporter, whether or not he could provide any material for the lunchtime bulletin. The discussion is brief; Rob informs Steve that he is unable to assist him, as he hasn't got the time. He has to go to Leicester to do some filming for the evening programme. A few minutes later Rob approaches Chris and informs him that there is material for *his* programme from Scotland if he books a line to get it.

> I think BBC Scotland have an interview with Levine so you can have it –
> I've talked to their sports guy and it's all ready to go. So you'll have
> that and the filming from Leicester that I'm going to do now. That
> should give you about four minutes all up.
>
> (Rob, sport reporter, BBC Nottingham)

Rob leaves the newsroom and Chris approaches the media hub in order to book the line from Scotland for the material. He then returns to the producer's desk and informs Steve that the line is being booked at 11.30am, which will mean that Steve can use the material, thus ensuring that there will be a sports story in the lunchtime bulletin after all.

What has occurred here? On the face of it, simply that sports material, in the form of an interview with a football manager, has been shared by both producers to ensure that they both have the same opportunity to fill airtime for their respective bulletins. But using an ANT analysis, more interesting conclusions can be drawn, in particular with respect to human actor strategy, disparity and power, ironically the very characteristics that ANT is so readily criticised for not addressing, and in which it seems to demonstrate little overt interest.

All the actors involved in this scenario are of course defined by their network positions. Those positions are located upon separate socio-, techno- and chronogrammatic axes. Let us take each one in turn. Steve is defined by his position inside the newsroom as the lunchtime producer. As such he has no geographical mobility and can only gather news by means of verbal requests and communication with mobile actors who may leave the newsroom and return to it at anytime. He is also producing the shorter, lunchtime, bulletin considered to be less important by journalists than the evening programme. Therefore his sociogram is vulnerable. He is considered by other actors to be in an inferior position to the main evening producer. He is unable to go out and exercise autonomy over the retrieval of news, which also renders his technogrammatic position weak. He is solely dependent therefore upon the recognition of other actors and the use of associated technologies, such as the media hub over which he has no autonomous control, in order to construct the news for his specific time-slot. His chronogrammatic position is also considerably weaker than the other actors involved as his bulletin is due to be transmitted in three hours' time, leaving little time for journalists to film material and feed it back for him to use, exemplified by Rob saying he didn't have enough time to provide material. This was not an admission of the instability of Rob's own chronogrammatic position, but that Steve's own weaker position prohibited Rob from assisting.

If we turn to Rob, we find an actor with a much stronger sociogram and technogram. Rob has mobility, and is leaving the newsroom to gather the material he needs using his own camera, and he has considerably more time in which to achieve this. He needs to retain the stability of his sociogram, that is his role as the main sports reporter who offers material for the evening programme, hence his deliberately staged interchange with Chris. (He approaches Chris, not the other way around.) But once this has been achieved, he does not require any association with Steve in order to garner stability for his position.

Turning to Chris we find an actor whose associations are more complex than Rob's and whose actions are therefore less predictable. Chris's sociogram is relatively stable and strong. He is the producer of the main evening programme and though he is also relatively immobile, just as is Steve in that he is located in the newsroom and cannot gather material autonomously, he is still considered by other human actors to be a highly significant actor within the network as he presides over the construction of the main programme. His sociogrammatic strength in turn strengthens his technogrammatic position for although he may not understand how to use the media hub, he is able to demand that the operator of the hub order material at his behest. Therefore he decides to order that material at a specific time so that he can assist Steve.

Yet there is something more happening here, upon which as observers we may perhaps only speculate. Chris has no strategic interest in assisting Steve. This may be a moral decision, one that our ANT analysis is somewhat weak in providing for. Chris has a moral duty to get the job done well, even if Steve is performing the job, and this may well have motivated him. Thus we have an example of one human actor deciding to hand over power to another. There is autonomous strategy involved here based on a mutual recognition of the specific network location that Steve occupies. Chris knows what producing a lunchtime bulletin is like. He has done it himself, thus occupying the weaker position on the socio-, chrono- and technogrammatic axes, and his capacity for self-reflection leads him to decide to assist Steve.

But what is highly significant is that while this exemplifies the human actor traits, Latour seems to marginalise, or even ignore, these motives, strategies and actions are always intricately enfolded within the network's technological actors. Steve is afforded no power whatsoever without the technological capability of the hub to retrieve the material. The power that Chris hands to Steve may well originate from a specifically human and moral motive, or it could be essentially strategic in that Chris is hoping for future reciprocity should their positions be reversed, but whatever human motive is being exercised, it also equally comprises technological agency.

This example, of which there may be hundreds in the course of a single day, illustrates how by carefully identifying each actor's specific network position, and by using its own mechanisms and vocabulary with which to map that position, ANT can be used to illuminate the strategic actions of human actors, to emphasise their disparities from one another, and from nonhuman actors, as well as to recognise that notwithstanding these disparities human actors are continually enfolded into the technologies upon which they depend for the creation of alliances and the effective implementation of their future actions. Thus ANT may not ostensibly delineate a separate human subject, or articulate the divergences between actors, but its own methodology, in particular the ability to chart every human actor position along these three axes, does provide a more than adequate way to do so.

Hierarchy, invisibility and power – human actors outside the newsroom

Having observed the daily human interchanges that constantly occur among actors within the newsroom, we now need to explore the outside broadcast team of actors responsible for producing the live broadcast into the 1.30pm lunchtime bulletin on this particular day.

Boris and Tara, SNG1 and SNG2 respectively, are dispatched to the court as early as 10.00am that morning. Both Steve and Chris know they will want to include a live broadcast from the court in each of their own programmes as two separate local court cases are expected to finish that day. The reporter, James, is responsible for covering both court cases and will present from the court into each bulletin. The choice of story will be dictated for Steve, who occupies the weaker chronogrammatic position as the lunchtime producer, by whichever one ends first. Chris has more editorial choice as to which one to include as a live because his programme isn't transmitted until 6.30pm.

Without providing a detailed exploration of the network associations of human and nonhuman actors responsible for delivering the live broadcast, as we did in the previous chapter, the significance of this scenario is that each human actor's socio- and technogrammatic position is translated depending upon, either how they are perceived by other human actors within the network, or how the associations formed with other human actors in the network actually result in different configurations along these axes. Thus ANT is still necessary for any exploration of subject-specific motivation, as the following illustration makes clear.

The two truck operators remain outside the newsroom located on an external node of the network. As we saw in the previous chapter this immediately provides these human actors with the opportunity to reconfigure the positions of other human actors within the newsroom, and just as we have already witnessed a recognition of an established actor hierarchy within the newsroom, which we will return to in more detail later on, there exists a *separate* human actor hierarchy immediately noticeable among those actors working outside the newsroom. As we saw from this particular quote in Chapter 7, the positions achieved by actors on this specific hierarchy are attained by the actor's individual knowledge of the technical aspects of the work involved in the broadcast.

> Some of our journalists that come from a technical background, like Jeremy, well, he understands, but the ones that are purely journalists, and don't do technical stuff, and don't even like the technical, well, they're the worst.
>
> (Tara, SNG2, BBC Nottingham)

Not only is this hierarchy based upon a perceived recognition of human actors' differentiated technical expertise, it is also actualised by the associations and the interchanges the SNG operators have with actors in the newsroom. While it has been argued that Chris, as the main evening producer, is able to enjoy a strong sociogrammatic position within the newsroom, that stability is thrown into quick relief once external associations are made by those working on the truck. All the truck operators share a distrust of any producer's lack of technical expertise, but what seems to be more frustrating to these actors is their belief that the programme producers do not grasp what extra duties, and of what other networks they, the truck operators, may be constituted.

> What I normally do is to make a list of everyone who wants stuff, and I phone the technical managers in the gallery. Basically if you're doing my job, there's a lot of talking to people at the other end, like Network or *News 24*, and yes, I am happy to give you want you want, but it has to be at a certain time, because if it's not then I have to come off that transponder and start reconfiguring these boxes for our programme, and it's a different frequency and that takes time.
>
> (Boris, SNG1, BBC Nottingham)

Just as we saw in the previous chapter, on this particular day the SNG operators also know that they can use their stronger technogrammatic position to stabilise a strong position in relation to the programme producers. That power is specifically located by the network position of the truck, being external to the newsroom and thus invisible to the actors working in the newsroom, as well as by the specifically strong technogrammatic position of the operators. As was exemplified in the previous chapter the technogrammatic stability is often articulated most acutely in terms of the truck's propensity to go wrong. Just as Latour argues that 'resistance tests reality', the operators therefore depend for the strength of their own position on an alliance with the unpredictability and instability of the truck's own technogrammatic position, a position that relies upon human actor perception of it in order to maintain its validity.

> They [the producers] have to take my word for it. If I say there's a problem, it means there's a problem. It's a problem that I might not even be able to sort out, but I might know a man that does, and that's going to take some time to phone and explain the problem, and then get it explained to me and to try to sort it out if there's another way of configuring the truck and bypassing the box that has died.
>
> (Boris, SNG1, BBC Nottingham)

As a result of both the truck and its operators being part of a wider network involving network television, the communication channels that the SNG operators use with the regional newsroom to deliberately bypass the programme producers, and by establishing their own association with other human actors in the newsroom, the operators hand most power over to the camera diary assistant (CDA), which is itself perceived to be a rather insignificant role within the *newsroom's* separate hierarchy.

> We're reliant on camera diary all the time. We don't do anything without her say so, especially on a day like this. If Network and *News 24* want stuff, they have to book us through her. Then all the charge codes can be attached to it, because we don't come for free!
>
> (Boris, SNG1, BBC Nottingham)

Ironically this comment also indicates Boris's heightened strategic awareness. Unlike other human actors he cites cost as an important actant that contributes to his strong technogrammatic and thus sociogrammatic position. With regard to the operation of the truck he holds the purse strings and he uses this to bolster his own network position.

To summarise, in this scenario a *separate* human actor hierarchy exists to that which is articulated within the newsroom and it is constructed with significantly different criteria. Those criteria are constituted by an awareness of actors' separate and varying socio- and technogrammatic positions, dependent on whether or not they are proximate to the truck, as well as the SNG operators' individual abilities to respond to the rather unpredictable technological capabilities of the truck. Indeed, where this is concerned the hierarchy is refined still further, with those SNG operators who can respond more quickly or more effectively to such technical error gaining higher recognition from the others.

The transmission of the lunchtime outside broadcast

The lunchtime outside broadcast was observed back in the gallery from where the programme is transmitted. Once again, what is striking from this particular observation is the evidence of a constant translation of human actor positions, which are, as always, dictated by the associations they create and maintain with technological actors. Yet these translations are also characterised by the human actors' self-awareness of such alliances, and of the power that such awareness may afford.

The most striking actor translation occurs when Steve, the producer, enters the gallery in order to oversee the lunchtime programme transmission. He is ostensibly in overall control, and editorial decisions to change stories or drop items on air are to be made through him. Yet he rarely speaks and is seemingly unaware of a range of decisions that are being taken throughout the run-up to the transmission as well as when the programme is on air – decisions that are being made instead by the director – Mark. A small extract of what is known as gallery talk-back (which means the discussion that those actors in the gallery have with one another before and during the programme transmission) demonstrates Steve's transference of power to Mark, and through Mark to the presenter, Priya, and Kim who is responsible for timing the bulletin.

They are busy establishing contact with the reporter, James, to run through what they expect from him for the live element. The situation has been further complicated by the fact that a reporter from the rival news channel, ITV's *Central News East*, is also standing in the same location delivering a piece to camera, which is being recorded by a camera operator onto tape. This is unknown to those members in the gallery as they are not able to see this from the shot they are being presented with from the satellite truck.

Priya: [In studio] OK can you hear me?

Mark: [In gallery] You can speak at regular volume James.

Priya: Why you whispering?

Boris: [From the truck] There's someone on air next to us . . .

James: [Whispering] I can't talk to you because there's someone doing a PTC right next to me that you can't see.

Priya: Ah!

Mark: Can we ruin it for them if it's Central? [Laughter]

James: No! [More laughter]

Kim: Five minutes to the Opt you lot at the OB and you're five minutes into the programme so there's ten minutes to you.

Mark: You're third on the programme and there's an OOV that sets you up, OK James, you'll be in boxes so you'll be in vision while Priya puts the question to you. She will say 'Our reporter James Roberson has been following the case and joins us from outside the court, James what did the prosecution say about the state of the site?' That's your first question. Second question is 'What did we hear about the two men, and then what will happen this afternoon?' OK? And how long have we got for this please . . . [PAUSE] . . . you've got 1.15 and given that you've got three questions, that's a bit ambitious really [laughs] so keep the answers really short.

Kim: Four minutes to the Opt and then five minutes to OB.

[PAUSE]

Kim: Two minutes to the Opt.

Boris: No!

Kim: One minute to the Opt.

James: Why would she do a two-minute PTC? [Remarking on the Central TV reporter still recording a PTC next to him] It's only about a minute from our Opt.

Boris: Don't worry James, I can't hear her on your microphone.

James: But she can hear me on hers! [Laughter]

Boris: That's her problem!

Kim: Two minutes to the OB now ...

James: [Talking to the Central reporter – giving her directions to Enderby where the press conference for Rosie May is going to be]

Kim: James, 1.15 for your bit ...

Mark: We have a minute left on this report and then you.

Here power is transferred from the producer to the director who discusses the technical and editorial details with James and directs the transmission of the bulletin. The extract demonstrates that most of the discussion centres upon the technicalities of the broadcast, not the editorial content. It is precisely because the producer is aware that the director has a stronger technogrammatic position in the specific location of the gallery as he is more capable of understanding the technologies needed for programme transmission and for communicating with the satellite truck, that power is transferred to him. Once again an actor's sociogrammatic position is thus dependent on their technogrammatic stability and in this instance the director, Mark, therefore occupies a stronger network position. The added complication of sharing a location with a rival news station's reporter illustrates how the gallery actors do not share the same visual realm as those at the outside broadcast and there is thus an increased awareness of the *specificity* of each other's locations, and the implications of both that specificity and the invisibility of certain parts of the network.

The afternoon – constant reconfiguration of actors' socio- and technograms

During the afternoon the main programme producer, Chris, is preoccupied with the construction of the evening programme. There are significant translations that occur here all of which illustrate an actor's ability to reconfigure their own position, as well as to lay themselves open or simply become exposed to reconfiguration by other actors. A lack of space prevents a full analysis of all of these instances, but we can highlight two in order to demonstrate the acute self-awareness and adaptability of human actors, as well as their fluid, sociogrammatic vulnerability and the transference of power that can occur due to specific associations with other human actors. The main actant that will be analysed during these scenarios is what is communally referred to within the newsroom as 'nouse'.

> What is nouse? Well it's not common sense because it's really uncommon sense. It's not uneducated, because it could be educated. I think in news terms, it's really an instinctive knowledge of how to get right to the heart of a story, to recognise a story. It's so hard to define really – you just know if someone's got it.
>
> (John, ex-journalist, BBC Nottingham)

Defined by the Oxford English Dictionary as 'intuitive apprehension, intelligence, mind, intellect, practical intelligence, gumption', nouse is the key to recognising how within the news network, power can be recognised as both *potential* and as *force*. Nouse is innate, as the quote reveals, it's elliptical but 'you just know if someone has it'. Yet as we shall see it is also highly *performative*, used as a valuable currency between journalists to bolster individual positions or to destabilise other actors. Latour has strenuously argued that *inscriptions* are essential for the movement of actants within networks, just as we witnessed from the first example with the news grid. Yet nouse formally refutes this for it is its very *inability* to be inscribed that actually affords it its power within the network as the following interchanges demonstrate.[6]

Having spent the morning discussing story ideas with reporters, making calls to contacts and arranging for crews to meet at specific locations to film material, Chris has managed to construct a running order for the evening programme and knows roughly what his programme will contain. A brief discussion with him at around 2.00pm reveals that as stories have developed throughout the day, the programme has begun to look stronger, and he is particularly pleased with the developments of his lead story: the conviction of a young man for the murder of a ten-year-old girl at a Christmas party.

> Having heard what the judge said about his previous stuff and that he's considered to be a dangerous man, while we've got a very good backgrounder, which is filmed primarily with the victim's family – and they're actually talking about the previous incident that he wasn't prosecuted for – we would probably do well to do James from the court – so give us a bit of this and get a bit of reaction and to see the pictures of his family leaving the court, which we have. That will add more to the story ahead of the backgrounder – because sometimes you go into these backgrounders and the start is a little bit soft I find – it hasn't got that on-the-day edge to it. So to that end I am going to get James to go a short two-way – probably from outside the court and then we go into

the backgrounder and then I have a back ref, which is a statement from the Crown Prosecution Service saying that they didn't go ahead with the kidnap and dangerous-driving charges, even though he had admitted it – because it was not in the public interest – then in the backgrounder we've got the family outraged that nothing was done.

Q: So you've got a really strong lead?

Yes we've got a strong lead. I'm bringing up by the cod liver oil piece ... and the other case normally would be a package but given that it's another court case, outside the same court it's a bit too much and I can tell that story with an OOV – in 45 seconds rather than a minute-and-a-half of somebody twittering on, on the TV! [Laughs]

(Chris, programme producer, BBC Nottingham)

This extract illustrates the control Chris has over the editorial detail of the programme and as each editorial decision is fully justified in his own mind, there is a confidence in the actions he takes as a result. Chris's sociogrammatic position here is strong due mainly to his self-awareness that he is able to fulfil the function of his specific role. The stimulus that affords Chris such confidence at this stage is this collaborative professional ideology of 'news sense' or *nouse*. As I have discussed elsewhere (Hemmingway, 2004), nouse can be seen as the jewel in the crown of the newsroom, and those actors that use it assume enhanced valorisation from those that do not. It is the ability to define and then to own news. Crucially it is also the ability to manipulate other actors by offering them the opportunity to partake of that ownership, by overtly supporting the initial decision to define a story as *newsworthy*. The power that is passed between human actors within the production network is most often characterised by this cyclical transference of nouse.

This strongly echoes Latour's own observations of the *cycles of credit* shared by scientists in the Salk Laboratory. Latour uses the term *credit* in order to illustrate a dual action of recognition and reward.

If we portray scientists as motivated by a search for reward, only a small minority of the observed activity can be explained. If instead we suppose that scientists are engaged in a quest for credibility we are better able to make sense both of their different interests, and of the process by which one kind of credit is transformed into another ... Scientists are thus interested in one another not because they are forced by a special system of norms to acknowledge each others' achievements, but because each needs the other in order to increase his own production of credible information.

(Latour & Woolgar, 1979, p.202)

197

Defined in this way, Latour's analysis comes dangerously close to an exposition of power sharing and transference among human actors, though he never uses the term. The accumulation of the notion of *credit* as both *reward* and *credibility* is significant and is highly evident in the exchanges among journalists in the newsroom. Though Chris enjoys a stable position due to his increased notion of credibility at this stage in the day, this can be quickly translated by another actor and the position destabilised if nouse is offered but deliberately not taken up. This is illustrated by our second example outlined below. The difference between Latour's cycles of credit and nouse is that within the Salk Laboratory the gift-giving to which Latour and Woolgar refer is highly *visible*. The extraordinary strength that nouse affords individual human actors in the news network is characterised by its being *invisible* and usually wholly *uninscribed*.

At 3.00pm Chris holds a short meeting with the director, the graphic designer, the programme production assistant (who times the programme transmission) and the media hub operator. During this meeting Chris doesn't make any editorial decisions, or provide any journalistic judgments. Within this deliberately demarcated arena the discussion is entirely technical. Nouse is also specifically located and its currency would have little value in this arena. It is a newsroom commodity and shared primarily by journalists, not by more technical members of staff.

Chris is acutely aware that in this location his editorial decisions are not being challenged. These actors with whom he is now associated are only interested in how the programme will be technically constructed. Therefore to retain control, Chris needs to demonstrate technical adequacy, so as to stabilise his position having left the editorial arena of the newsroom and with it his own command of nouse. If he is able to translate the power he had over other actors as a result of his clear editorial judgements into control by means of an overt technical expertise, then his position will remain stable even though his association is now with a group of other actors, who are making radically different demands on him.

Chris: This is a woman who went sightseeing with her husband and part of a church fell on her!
Mark: That's a lovely story isn't it! [Laughs]
Chris: There's a two-year-old crushed under concrete so we've got a great programme! [Laughter] So we have Dom and Anne haven't we, then presumably Rob and Zara. At 6.00pm the inquest, at 6.15pm oil and fireworks – which don't mix! They're my promos. And at 6.30pm the court case with an upsound from her dad, inquest and Ellen as headlines. The inquest will be coming from Leeds at some stage. The lead story is the court case.
Mark: The intro is quite strong isn't it?

Chris: Yes. I'm going straight to my top story. I am not having the tease. I have taken that out – sorry – I have changed that since. It will be headlines, intro, because they'll say hello, and then going to the court case and we've got James at court with two short answers, first of which we'll be floating OOV over pictures of an upset family coming out and another upset family coming out but beating the public up! So contrasting reactions there from the family! [Laughs] It will be one OOV over the first answer – so we will ask James – what was the reaction of the family and he will say, blah, blah, blah and we will float pictures – he's scripting it – and we'll just do it as one OOV.

Graphics: Do you want boxes for this?

Mark: Yes I think so.

Chris: Yes, definitely.

Chris retains control throughout the meeting by his ability to reconfigure his position from one that was initially stabilised by the recognition of his credibility as a producer with sound editorial judgement or nouse, to a technologically adept actor who is able to construct the programme in technical rather than editorial terms. The use of humour and the speed with which the meeting is conducted both portray Chris's awareness of the strength of his position. Once again, this position is plotted along continually reconfigured socio- and techno-grammatic axes in each specific location in which Chris finds himself.

Returning to an exploration of Latour's *cycles of credit* and the way in which human actors not only define their own positions, but crucially those of others by the establishment of alliances, in our second example Chris's stable position is suddenly and momentarily translated by a brief association he now enters into with the assistant editor, Kevin. Kevin is already professionally defined as occupying a strong network position as he is an editor, thus senior to Chris. Although Chris has overall editorial control of the programme on this particular day, he is aware that his decisions need not be specifically ratified by Kevin, but they should be agreed upon. In this particular instance Chris has found a story that involves the trial of a so-called *loan shark* from Nottingham.[7] The court case starts tomorrow and Kevin is producing the programme that day. Chris calls him over to discuss the story. The fact Kevin comes over to him is also significant.

> This would make for you tomorrow, Kev. It's a good story. It's got a national edge to it, but the guy is from our patch.
>
> (Chris, producer, BBC Nottingham)

While this could be viewed as speculation, by focusing on the way in which nouse is used as a currency, I would argue that Chris's proclamation is an overt invitation for Kevin to take up his offer of nouse, and is thus deliberately shouted publicly across the newsroom for other actors to hear, so as to enhance Chris's own position as soon as the gift is accepted. Kevin only has to agree to publicly receive it and the cycle of credit will be complete. The credibility of Chris's position will be strengthened through the association that he has strategically engineered. But the response is not as he predicts. Kevin is not interested in the story, and what is significant is that he says so publicly, before wandering off to the planning desk where he becomes involved in a conversation with a planning journalist who has found what Kevin considers to be a more interesting prospect. With the public rejection, Chris is left floundering. Having not left his seat since after the 3.00pm meeting, he is now forced to get up and walk across the newsroom to where Kevin is standing, to deliberately enter into this separate discussion with the planning journalist.

In the following brief interchange Chris fervently agrees with Kevin's decision with regard to the planning journalist's new prospect and begins to discuss the details of it with him. The decision to enter into this association, though it is of no relevance to him in terms of his role as a producer is, I would argue, entirely strategic. He needs to avert attention away from Kevin's rejection of nouse, and restore his own position by publicly affirming Kevin's news judgement, which has now gained public precedence since his rebuttal of Chris. In this interchange the network positions of both actors are altered, though Kevin's less so than Chris's and with less detrimental effect. Chris, on the other hand, has been destabilised by an actor who already professionally outranks him in the hierarchy, and therefore whose affirmation he needs to glean. His sociogrammatic position may be strong while performing his own production duties, yet it becomes considerably weaker in association with actors who are external to that production process but whose network and professional position enables them to comment upon the effectiveness of that process.

The after-programme meeting

News production activity, just like scientific activity, is governed by norms, and the enforcement of these norms entails the existence of a special system of gift giving (Latour & Woolgar, 1979). This system, though a constant in the diurnal process of news making, is never made mention of by the participants. The *after-programme meeting* is one example of such gift giving and signals an important closure to the day's activities. On this particular day the programme is successfully transmitted and both Mark and Chris seem content with it, in particular with the fact that James has delivered his live broadcast from outside the court free from any 'technical mishaps'.[8]

The after-programme meeting is held in the newsroom immediately after the programme has been transmitted. All the available journalists, gallery staff,

200

presenters, producer and director as well as other newsroom support staff are in attendance. The meeting is usually led by Kevin, who, in his professional capacity as the assistant editor, is justified in giving his impressions of the content of the show. The tone is usually both humorous and collaborative as the following extract reveals.

Kevin: So, what did I learn tonight? Well actually what I want to focus on is Jeremy's piece. Now you all know my opinions of Ellen . . .

Rob [sports reporter]: Yeah, which is why we didn't tell you we were doing it!

Kevin: Oh I see! [Laughter all round] There were some classic script lines but the whole thing I thought was extremely entertaining. It was well put together. She came alive, for the first time. I have to say, she was interesting, and I think she is tedious in the extreme. . . .

Chris: They were bouncing up and down together weren't they! [Laughter]

Kevin: You know when you were bouncing up and down, where was Ellen at that point . . . [Laughter] . . . I thought her explaining all that gear was fascinating . . .

Jeremy: You mean where was she really? She was holding the camera!

Kevin: I was joking!

Chris: She was holding his camera!

Jeremy: She did all my camera work . . .

Kevin: Brilliant!

Rob: She was holding all sorts of his equipment! [Laughter]

The credit being offered and exercised here is one of mutual affirmation and collaboration between all human actors. Kevin is not analysing the content in depth. There are very few, if any, instances of serious exploration or debate over the interviews or pictures used in each news item. The purpose of the meeting is not to investigate the editorial worth of the programme. Rather the programme is itself being used to subtly enhance the credibility of individual actors, and the success of the programme is actually measured by the extent to which it facilitates the rapid conversion of credibility between actors within the cycle of credit. Kevin may have initially led the meeting, but the emphasis here is on multiple discourses. Yet unlike earlier stages of the day, where actors may well disagree with one another publicly or privately, here the interdiscursive arena is being used to emphasise the *mutuality* of opinion rather than to exercise individual power. The all-inclusive notion is that 'we have done well'! Once again nouse is the currency of exchange, but by all actors receiving and transferring it without debate or disagreement, the cycle of credibility is extended, even towards myself as I become no longer the observer, but a temporarily included actor, and humour is the predominant discourse.

Kevin: I liked that – I thought that was a really good piece as well – it was completely different from the lunchtime piece, and again, if Jeremy's piece hadn't won, you would have won!

Rob: Those lovely bits with the veins that you mixed in with the next shot . . .

Kevin: You know how we did that? We shrunk a PDP person and injected them . . . [Laughter]

Rob: Rosenblum says 'Take risks' so we killed somebody!

Kevin: Actually it was Jim so we didn't need to shrink him . . . [Laughter!] He's still in there, still in there, trying to get in someone's ear . . .

Chris: It was very well presented tonight – I really enjoyed the presentation . . . and thank you to Emma for turning out and helping us – she did at least three important jobs today!

James: She did actually . . . more than she ever did in her twelve years here! [Laughter]

Kevin: Good programme, thank you . . . It's Friday tomorrow so we'll take it nice and easy!

Conclusion

Analysing this series of interactions and associations made by human actors during the construction of the news programme in the course of a single day, we can draw a number of conclusions with regard to the status of human actors in the network, and to their relationship with nonhuman actors with whom they are entangled. The main premise of this chapter has been to explore the significant criticism of ANT as a reliable methodology to address the issues of human subjectivity, and to identify why it also seems impoverished when addressing issues of power, intention or motive.

This book has attempted to show that while there are grounds for such frustrations with ANT outlined at the beginning of this chapter, the very terminology and mechanics of ANT actually provide for a more than adequate method with which to explore the role of the human actor as distinct from the nonhuman, even though this may directly contradict Latour's own insistence on their de-differentiation. In this sense, ANT has it seems, outgrown its progenitor, and in its application to practice, is revealed as more substantial and encompassing than was perhaps previously considered.

It is thus imperative that we do not reject the basis of ANT as being an inadequate methodology for exploring human complexities, but that we adhere more strongly to the very methodology that ANT dictates. Returning once again to Latour's earliest premise that truth and reality are produced through networks of practical, social activity, it is clear from the events that occur in a newsroom, that reality is indeed constructed from the myriad of associative bonds all human and nonhuman actors establish and develop with one another. But to say this is not enough. It is necessary for us to explore these constellations of actor positions more carefully, so as to reveal the disparity not only between human and nonhuman actors, but also between human and human, and to fully grasp how the subtlety of each association, within each specific location, constructed of *specific* actor alliances, determines particular practices.

It is the notion of *specificity* to which we must so often return that is of crucial significance here. In each of the above examples of news work, the location and the actor's individual position within that location has been of the utmost importance. We have witnessed how even between human actors, those outside the newsroom share a distinct perception of those inside the newsroom, and adopt certain strategies of association and communication based upon that shared perception. Those inside the newsroom do likewise, but the perceptions of this constellation of actors are based on entirely separate criteria. It is only by striving to explore the specific locality of an actor's position and to recognise how that determines their perceptions, actions and ultimate stability, that the differences between human and nonhuman, and human and human actors begins to be revealed. By mapping each actor's socio-, techno- and chronogrammatic position, as we have done continually in each of the empirical chapters, we can see how the human cannot remain de-differentiated from the nonhuman actor for very long. This is primarily because human actors are self-aware and this self-awareness contributes to their ability to sustain their own network positions by complex and continual reconfiguration along our three axes.

This notion of specificity also extends to the position of the ethnographer herself. I remarked earlier in the chapter that my own position vis-à-vis each of the human actors observed is different depending upon my association with them, as well as the nature of their own discourse with one another. The chapter looks at different constellations of power and within each of these the observer is located differently. Let us briefly explore these.

In the first interchange between Steve, Chris and the sports reporter, the ethnographer needs to be situated close to the interchange and also to have some kind of innate understanding of the dynamic of the conversations, as well as to appreciate what is *not* being said. The recording of this interchange must therefore be in some senses fairly speculative, and its reliability is centred upon the observer's direct knowledge of and experiences of those involved. I may be asking the reader once again to take a small leap of faith here, but Steve's request that I actually participate in the news production process by recording a news item for the bulletin serves as a signal to the reader that the observer is trusted as competent by those she is observing. While that competence refers to her journalism skills, it may also enhance the trust that the reader has in her adequacy as a researcher.

In the second scenario, where the observer joins the satellite truck and records the conversations with the operators, the position of the ethnographer directly influences the outcome of the conversations. It is clear that Boris acts in a certain way because of the researcher's presence and that his intricate detailed explanation of the news processes with which the satellite truck is involved may also have heightened his own self-awareness.

In the third interchange between Chris and Kevin the observer needs to merely be in the room; the interchange is a public display of power and strategy, but even here the observer may need some kind of prior knowledge of the position of the two actors in order to draw conclusions, which themselves could still be considered rather speculative.

Thus, recognising the significance of specificity at all levels, even that of the researcher, and by using the very tools that ANT has provided, the human subject is not left to flounder undemarcated at the mercy of an insubstantial methodology, but can be illuminated and explored. And what is of crucial importance to the development of an understanding of news work is that the human subject can be clearly presented as an agent of particular and differing intentions, motives, strategies and powers. These are forever enmeshed and enfolded with the nonhuman actors on the network, and each association creates a particular translation of that network, so that the construction of news can be recognised as heterogeneous and contingent, equally determined by nonhuman actors as by human. But ANT researchers must have the courage to both argue and illustrate how the role of the conscious human subject is not inadmissible to ANT's central methodological premise that the enfolding of human and nonhuman actors is essential for our understanding of the determination of social practice.

CONCLUSION

The turn to performance is sometimes seen as constructivist, but it
has particular implications. It suggests that technologies, knowledges
and working may be understood as the effects of materially, socially
and conceptually hybrid performances. In these performances different elements assemble together and act in certain ways to produce
specific circumstances.

(Law & Singleton, 2000, p.774)

Throughout this book we have studied the micro, hybrid and contingent processes of news production so that we might answer a central question: how does
the everyday socio-technical structuring of media processes affect the nature of
media products in BBC regional television news? The question has continuously
challenged us to recognise that unless we pay equal attention to the role of
media technologies as we do to our human actors, our answer will be at worst
wholly inaccurate, or at best woefully incomplete. As Van-Loon argues, media
technologies are operative in the most banal and mundane practices of everyday
life; they affect us all and the link that we have with them has been further
enhanced by digitalisation, which has enabled mediation to become another
form of information processing where anything that happens anywhere can
potentially be brought instantaneously into the here-and-now of 'our' presence
(Van-Loon, 2007). Our own journey through the newsroom has shown us how
technologies do not simply facilitate the production of news, but that they
possess and exhibit a particular agency and that such technological agency is best
understood as a multiplicity of connected forces, or actor networks. By our
application of Actor Network Theory to media processes we have been able to
see these processes not as a series of individual but connected stages, but as a
continuous multiplicity of flows that are only ever partially or temporarily stabilised in emergent assemblages. Empirical work in media studies has primarily
concentrated on media industries, audiences or texts. Comparatively little work

has focused on actually understanding processes of mediation. It is quite remarkable that media analyses have not received the same kind of attention that, for example, science and technology has had, from where we have borrowed our ANT methodology. This is even more remarkable once we realise just how much media and technoscience have in common (Van-Loon, 2007).

> Science and Technology Studies [STS] has understood that heterogeneous engineers – agents whether human or not – are constituted in the arrangements of these materials. And it has understood that such processes of ordering, such processes of working on and giving shape to the overlaps, amount, in their precarious way, to what we call the social order. An intuitive feel for the ordering of heterogeneity, the construction and reconstruction of overlaps, the constitution of agency, that is the strength of STS; together with an insensitivity to 'natural' distributions.
>
> (Law, 2004, p.11)

In an attempt to explore this construction process ourselves, we have used ANT as a method for identifying and exploring what we have referred to as the *internal news episteme;* that is the practices of news construction within a specific newsroom during a particular, demarcated period of time. The argument has been that readings of media that seek to place under-researched glimpses of news practices in an unproblematic relationship with a deliberately externalised and stable society are enacted in a set of outmoded Euro-American blinkers.

In contrast to this, we have sought to explore the micropractices of news production and to argue that not only do these *affect* eventual news products, but that the artificial schism that is so often driven between the media process and the media product results in readings of news practice that fail to recognise the performance of practice, and how this performance is inextricably entangled with final news products. Performing news processes is one and the same as constructing news products. Instead of a division between the two, the adaptation of ANT enables us to recognise their coexistence and more importantly their interdependency.

By substituting the more traditional studies of media that have tended to hive-off media practice from the analysis of media products with the exploration of human and nonhuman actors within a contingent and fragile network, we are not seeking to simply impose a different orthodoxy on the reading of news production. We are seeking to move away from orthodoxy altogether. During our journey we have revealed what is hoped are illuminating insights into how humans and the technologies with which they are enfolded construct news, but as we accepted from the outset, we cannot paint a complete picture. We cannot provide a single explanation. The methodological and theoretical core of our explorations has been predicated upon the acceptance that in place of dichotomous orderings of news practice and news products, of humans and nonhumans, of journalism and society, or of reality and construction, there is a network that enfolds all of these things within it, from which there are no external or internal referents, and from which there is no extrapolation. It is a fluid network of haphazard associations, some of which may remain constant under our gaze, while others may fall apart. And by entering into this network, our own position becomes altered. We must shrug off the mantle of the detached observer, to become a simple actor within the network, and an actor within whatever text we construct to attempt to narrate that network. By adopting such a lowly position, by getting down in the dirt just like our humble stone-cutter, we are at liberty to explore this network in startling detail, but by the same token, we are unable to espouse orthodox and universal conclusions.

Specificity, in all of its forms, has been central to our explorations. It is all the more significant when we come to make our conclusions, for these very conclusions can only ever be specific, localised, partial and fragmented.

> After the sub-division of the universal we need other metaphors for imagining our worlds, and our responsibilities to those worlds. Localities. Specificities. Enactments. Multiplicities. Fractionalities. Goods. Resonances. Gatherings. Forms of craftings. Processes of weaving. Spirals. Vortices. Indefiniteness. Condensates. Dances. Imaginaries. Passions. Interferences. These are some of the metaphors for imagining method that I have sought to bring to life in this book. Metaphors for the stutter and the stop. Metaphors for quieter and more generous versions of method.
>
> (Law, 2004, p.156)

In this book a similar attempt has been made to provide an alternative vocabulary for reading news practice so that we can fully understand the complex role that media technologies play, and the even more complicated and unpredictable relationships they enter into with our human actors. As Latour adroitly recognises

> The main difficulty of integrating technology into social theory is the lack of a narrative resource. We know how to describe human relations, we know how to describe mechanisms, we often try to alternate between the context and content to talk about the influence of technology on society or vice-versa, but we are not yet expert at weaving together the two resources into an integrated whole. This is unfortunate

because whenever we discover a stable social relation, it is the introduction of some non-humans that accounts for this relative durability.

(Latour, 2005, p.111)

Our adoption of the vocabulary of ANT has certainly helped us to develop
this expertise. Yet it has also necessitated a significant epistemological leap from
the world of media production as an explicable and unproblematic arena from
which news comments upon society 'out-there' beyond the newsroom to a
hinterland of practice that is at the same time performative, sporadically self-
relexive, often invisible, and constituted by complex associations of human and
nonhumans. Boundaries between the world 'out there' and the internal world of
the newsroom are no longer sustainable as the tendrils of the network permeate
everywhere, and actors that may be absent from a particular node on the network are still translated by it and even traceable in their absence from the network action visible at that specific point. Furthermore, the position of the
researcher also becomes destabilised within the network, and close observations
soon give way to inclusive performances of all actors, including the researcher,
as we have witnessed in each of the empirical chapters.

Our conclusion will therefore provide a summary of the initial aims of the
book, clarifying the premise of our central argument, before reviewing our
methodological procedures. It will then summarise the main empirical findings
and relate these to our central argument, before positing suggestions for further
empirical studies. Finally we will provide a critique of the specific developments
of ANT as an effective tool for reading news work so that we can begin to ask a
wider range of methodologically relevant questions.

Finding a new language to describe a maelstrom of micro news processes

Latour and Woolgar take us some distance from everyday Euro-American
expectations about out-there-ness. Reality is neither independent nor
anterior to its apparatus of production. Neither is it definite and singular until that apparatus of production is in its place. Realities are
made. They are effects of the apparatuses of inscription. At the same
time, since there are such apparatuses already in place, we also live in
and experience the real world filled with real and more or less stable
objects.

(Law, 2004, p.32)

How then do we construct a new vocabulary for the examination of specific
media processes that have usually been bundled up in an epistemological

straightjacket subsumed by an overriding socio-political logic that privileges external prejudices and motivations? The answer lies in the adoption of a particular method of reading news that is able to subvert traditional epistemologies and question the ontological surety of an immutable, external and stable reality. Such a method will prise open the fixed dichotomies of nature and culture, reality and construction, human and nonhuman, and blow apart the methodological hegemony that has held such artificial distinctions in place thus far.

> Contrary to Euro-American common sense, Latour and Woolgar are telling us that it is not possible to separate out (a) the making of particular realities, (b) the making of particular statements about realities, and (c) the creation of instrumental, technical and human configurations, and practices, the inscription devices that produce these realities and statements. Without inscription devices, and the inscriptions and statements that these produce, there are no realities.
>
> (Law, 2004, p.30)

The main initial premise of ANT that has informed our study of news practice is what Law refers to here as 'the creation of instrumental, technical and human configurations'. Latour and Woolgar argue that their observations of scientific practices within the Salk Laboratory preclude them from sustaining the stable dichotomies outlined above. Their work reveals how scientists *construct* facts from a plethora of associated elements, which they refer to as *actors*, combining together in fluid and unpredictable ways within a network of specific scientific practice. These elements may be human and nonhuman, technological and textual, organic and artificial.[1] Their work further reveals that the methods by which scientists construct facts are deliberately honed so as to prevent the exposure of the network's heterogeneity, a methodological sleight of hand that may lead others to recognise and to accept a scientific finding as stable, singular and immutable.

> Even the smallest gestures constitute the social construction of facts. The micro processes whereby facts are socially constructed. As we have argued from the beginning, the sense in which we use the term social refers to phenomena other than the obvious influence of ideology or of macro institutional factors.
>
> (Latour & Woolgar, 1979, p.152)

Latour and Woolgar's proposal is that 'out there-ness' is accomplished or achieved rather than having a prior and determinate form of its own. Realities are *produced* along with the statements that report them. The argument is that they are not necessarily independent, anterior, definite and singular. If they appear to be so (as they usually do), then this itself is an effect that has been produced in practice, a consequence of method (Law, 2004).

The eradication of what we have called the 'mess of method' to which Law refers has made ANT crucially significant to the reading of news practice. A primary contention of this book is that it is the deliberate eradication of visible news construction in the transmission of the news event that has enabled the artificial schism of practice and product to be sustained. For example, an analysis of the technological hermeneutics shared between the two operators of the satellite truck in Chapter 7 illustrates how a deliberate masking of the mechanics of practice in the transmission of the final event is achieved by the operators' individual knowledge of the truck's technological capability. In direct contrast to this, when the visual opportunities of a live event are exhausted and the operators are then 'desperate for pictures', this action is reversed and the intestinal detail of the technical apparatus is deliberately exposed to the audience as a way to spark visual interest.[2] Such exposure is rare. For the majority of the time the audience witnesses what they perceive to be a singular event, which an ANT reading can reveal is an illusion made possible only by the very heterogeneity of the network itself.

This ability for the network to simultaneously reveal and conceal itself is first addressed in Chapter 3, where we see how the news network facilitates the exposure of actors' associations immediately present at a particular point, but that also contained within that presentation are the traces of those actors no longer present. We saw how this is further exemplified by the process through which the hub begins to digitise recorded pictures and by so doing folds into itself one presentation of an external reality only to facilitate a number of simultaneous and fluid 'other' realities by its ability to alter the material, and to re-present it at other locations on other computer screens across the newsroom, before the initial digitisation process has even been completed.[3]

While it is not our intention to dwell on the complex unravelling of hitherto defined external realities, it is significant to note that by adapting ANT to the reading of news work, it is finally possible to eradicate the artificial notion of internal and external worlds, and to recognise instead how a network of practice contains within it both of these, forever enfolded and intertwined. Such intertwining thus enables the crucial eradication of the notion of a separate process and a final product, coalescing both within this deliberate and complex 'mess of method' so that at one time the product may appear singular and external, but at another the network can facilitate its presentation as entangled within the entrails of its own processes.

Humans, technologies and the notion of specificity

The central tenet of ANT that has justified its adaptation for the reading of news practice is the recognition of the enfolding of human and nonhuman actors within the network. This has allowed us to explore in detail the central role that technologies play within news construction. Yet ANT will not permit an over-simplified account of the determining nature of technologies, insisting rather that technological actors are at one and the same time entangled within a net-work of human actors, and that it is the activity of the *network*, not any indivi-dual actor, that ensures translation.[4] As Law argues an ANT account will not sustain a monolithic technological analysis.

> A possibility – but one which I believe we should resist – is to look for simple answers in the technologies of representation: to embrace McLuhan's adage that the medium is the message. The reason for resisting this is quite simple. It is that it is technological determinism by semiotic means: the attempt to read off the character of subjectivity from the supposed features of a technology of representation.
>
> (Law, 1996, p.299)

A return to the subject of network translation also enables a further devel-opment of the significance of *specificity*, which has continued to inform our explorations throughout this book. Detailed network translation is not possible without the mapping of individual actors along the two axes Latour introduces in *Science and Action* to explain how an innovation may secure a place within a network, and may recruit more allies in order to strengthen its network posi-tion. We have used the sociogram and the technogram to provide a means by which actors may be defined by both their social position within the network, and their technical infrastructure, which itself contributes to the strength and stability of their network position. As we discussed in Chapter 3, any actor may be defined in the network by means of mapping its position along these two axes. We also introduced the chronogram, a third axis that refers to the tem-poral position that each actor occupies, for it is of specific significance to news practice where working to deadlines and within tight time constraints has a direct bearing on news construction. We have used these three axes throughout our journey to trace every actor's specific network position, so that translation of it, or of associated actors can then be properly examined. The methodologi-cal exactness provided by these axes ensures that while the network is vast, multifarious and impossible to observe as an entity, it can be examined in minute detail at each specific point. Furthermore, the use of these three axes also enables the observer to recognise the fluid performativity of each actor's network position, for the axes, while utterly specific, are forever shifting, as an actor moves within the network, or is translated by it.[5] It is the recognition of the performance of actors within networks that has enabled scholars to further develop ANT analyses to embrace what is often referred to as a *method assemblage*, a multiplicity of actor positions that are forever shifting, enacting a myriad of related actions at a specific time and location. These performances may never come to rest, but as Mol argues are 'multiple forms of reality itself' (Mol, 1999, p.80). And it is the continual performance of the network assemblage that further precludes the adoption of a singular externalised reality.

> An assemblage is an episteme with technologies added but that con-
> notes the ad hoc contingency of a collage in its capacity to embrace a
> wide variety of incompatible components. It also has the virtue of
> connoting active and evolving practices rather than a passive and static
> structure.
>
> (Watson-Verran & Turnbull, 1995, p.117)

The significance of specificity is also realised on the methodological level. We could be criticised for identifying too narrow a subject area for our purposes. Surely one cannot reach relevant conclusions regarding news production from the observation of a single regional BBC television newsroom? The response to this implicit criticism is twofold. As has been stressed, the purpose of our work is not to impose universal findings regarding media processes or to formulate hegemonic orthodoxies as has been a tradition in the past. We have continuously argued that the very adoption of ANT as a method for reading news work necessitates the jettisoning of singular, conclusive statements for the *description* of practice *as it is happening*. The use of the word description is deliberate and important as are both the specificity of the location and the time of this parti-cular study. We could have chosen a separate newsroom, and a different time to conduct our research. We would have then produced a different description of practice as we had observed and analysed it. We may have decided to compare two newsrooms, perhaps a BBC regional television newsroom and an indepen-dent national television newsroom. Our final text would have been entirely different to what we present here. But would our 'findings' be more valid? Would our 'conclusions' be more worthy of respect? Would we have 'explained' news practices more accurately? The answer is no. By using ANT, we move away from the provision of overarching explanations that somehow come after the accurate descriptions of observed practice, to provide instead a full, accurate description of specific practices, which explains itself or reveals itself in the textual account. Actor Network Theory cannot provide or sustain the adoption of singular conclusions that in some way represent a wider genre. It is more humble, but also more subtle. It simply allows us to tell a complicated story, a specific story, using accurate tools that remain faithful to the mechanics of practice at the minute level.

> The opposition between description and explanation is another of these false dichotomies that should be put to rest – especially when it is 'social explanations' that are wheeled out of their retirement home. Either the networks that make possible a state of affairs are fully deployed – and then adding an explanation will be superfluous – or we 'add an explanation' stating that some fact should be taken into account so that it is a description that should be extended one step farther. If a description remains in need of an explanation, it means that it is a bad description.
>
> (Latour, 2005, p.137)

Human intentionality and the development of Actor Network Theory

The study of human actors within this particular newsroom has necessitated both a critique and a slight departure from one of the main tenets of ANT, the symmetry upheld between human and nonhuman actors within a network. Previous studies of media that have failed to recognise the deliberate actions and self-reflections of journalists are rightly criticised by Cottle (2003) for under-estimating the role of human agency in the processes of news production, and it has been the purpose of our study to develop this by the observation of journalists, producers, managers and technical operators both within the newsroom and out in the editorial patch. This has led to a particular frustration with ANT as a method for its stubborn insistence in treating both humans and nonhumans as equal actors. It has been clear from the empirical evidence we provided in Chapter 8 that there must be a recognition that humans act differently within networks than do their technological partners. Indeed they are folded into one another, and this has been illustrated in all of the empirical chapters, but it is not accurate to argue that there is no difference between the actions, reflections and, crucially, the intentions of humans and the actions of technologies. Our critique of ANT focuses not so much on its inability to develop the human subject, as others have argued (Boyne, 2002; Couldry, 2006), but on its inability to adequately explore human intentions and strategies.[6]

It is not enough to argue that human actors maintain or develop their individual positions within networks simply by amassing allies to enable them to garner strength and stability. The lack of recognition that humans are complex, strategic thinkers, that their network positions must contain within them the harbouring of emotions, reflections, intentions, consciousnesses and passions

213

must surely limit ANT as a method for reading complex organisations such as newsrooms, or any other public arena where humans and technologies interact. It has been made clear from our study that human actors have the capacity to act on an 'interior motivation', that is not a direct effect of external force. It is of course possible to argue that computer programmes for example seem to suggest that nonhuman forms of network 'intelligence' can be 'spontaneous' or 'emergent' in some way, thus leading us to accept that technologies may also display certain forms of intentionality. Yet this line of argument opens up a much broader problem with ANT namely that its sole emphasis on the 'exteriority' of motivation disables it from adequately describing spontaneous emergences, creativity and what one may describe as 'intelligence' when it is more than simply processing information. Although new technologies may be starting to take on some of these capacities, they have *always* been central to the human condition. Thus Latour's own principle of non-reducibility should be also applied to the human 'will' making humans potentially rather distinctive types of actors. As we argued in Chapter 8, we need to develop ANT if it is to remain not only a justifiable but also an effective method for the analysis of socio-technical configurations.

Latour himself once described reality as that which resists trials; would it be possible we might ask that this 'interiority of will' of consciousness, of human intentionality is in fact showing itself as resisting manipulation by the very methodology that it finds itself imprisoned by and at odds with? It is interesting to note that in his recent book, *Reassembling the Social*, Latour (2005) returns to the notion of the human subject, as if to pre-empt those critics who accuse ANT of reductionism for its lack of exploration of this.

> Reductionism is not a sin one should abstain from or a virtue one should firmly stick to: it is a practical impossibility since the elements to which one 'higher level' is being reduced will be as complex as the 'lower level'. If only humans in the hands of critical sociologists could be treated *as well as* whales in zoology, genes in biochemistry, baboons in primatology, soils in pedology, tumors in cancerology, or gas in thermodynamics! Their complex metaphysics would at least be respected, their recalcitrance recognised, their objections deployed, their multiplicity accepted. Please treat humans as things, offer them at least the degree of realism you are ready to grant humble matters of concern, materialise them, and yes, reify them as much as possible!
>
> (Latour, 2005, pp.255–6)

It has been the contention of this book that Latour's insistence on the complete de-differentiation between humans and nonhumans is not tenable, and while his elegant quote may attempt to tackle this central criticism, it does not address the issue adequately. It merely continues to insist that the symmetry between nonhumans and humans can be in some way improved, which is far from compelling. Latour could be described as a fetishist in that he will not engage with ambivalence or perception. He simply asserts that the network provides the cause itself without grappling with issues such as motive or strategy. We have seen clearly that the network constructs news facts, but enfolded within it are motives and strategies and certain forms of power. The criticism may remain unanswered, but this does not mean that the validity of ANT as a method for reading human behaviour is destroyed. For as we saw in Chapter 8, a development of the mechanics of ANT can still provide a more than adequate means to read human behaviour, even in the face of Latour's personal insistence on the retention of the symmetry.

By painstakingly mapping each human actor's position along the same three axes described earlier, the empirical evidence reveals that human intention, motive and strategy is easily identified and accurately explored. Once more the significance of *specificity* of human actor positions assists us in observing particular viewpoints, perceptions, motives and intentions that may go unnoticed to even the most proximate of associated actors. These are forever enmeshed and enfolded within the nonhuman actors in the network, but as the evidence in Chapter 8 illustrates, such enfoldings do not necessarily have to be read as symmetries; but neither do they have to be ignored in order to sustain the credibility of an ANT account. An accurate ANT account, using its exact vocabulary and methodological mechanics, can reveal the complexity and the distinctness of human actors within a network, without straining the tenets of ANT in any way whatsoever.

ANT and the role of the ethnographer

Epistemology tells us something descriptively, more often prescriptively, about what we can know, and about how we should be gathering knowledge ... to be a relativist ... may lead us to an important form of intellectual caution: the sense that all knowledges are shaped, contingent, and in some other world, could be otherwise ... Ethnography lets us see the relative messiness of practice. It looks behind the official accounts of method (which are often clean and reassuring) to try to understand the often ragged ways in which knowledge is produced in research.

(Law, 2004, p.18)

Returning once again to the notion of performance, with which our explorations have been largely preoccupied, it is necessary to consider the implications that the adoption of a 'method assemblage' will have upon the veracity of the ethnographer and the final narrative, of which we are almost coming to the end. As we argued in both Chapter 2 and in Chapter 8, the position of the ethnographer must be as unstable as that of any other actor within the network. Yet this need not ring alarm bells through the corridors of the methodological chapel. As we have learned on our journey through the newsroom, and as we discussed earlier in this conclusion, the validity of a study does not rest upon the ability to 'fix' a stable meaning upon a page and then to attempt to explicate outwards from it in some way, whatever we may have been taught in the past. We are not offering a singular conclusion, or even a set of conclusions. We do not propose to provide a recognisable denouement from which the reader may come away satisfied that 'loose ends' have been well and truly tied. As the ethnographer of this particular narrative we have attempted instead to tell a story, to accurately, textually, represent an account of what we have seen and heard in all the recesses and dark corners of the newsroom through which we have travelled. This final text is but one aspect of the overall performance that we have witnessed, and it too becomes an actor in the network we have entered.

> Our argument is that the difference between telling a story and acting realities isn't so large. It's a continuum, not a great divide, which means that our stories aren't just innocent descriptions. They may make a difference, introduce changes, or, alternatively bring aid and comfort to the existing performances of technological reality – while it could be otherwise. Technologies could be enacted in other ways – imagined and enacted.
>
> (Law & Singleton, 2000, p.769)

But how do we ascertain the validity of such an account? Are we simply attempting to get ourselves off some methodological hook, or are we making a grander point? What is the purpose of an ANT account if the central quality is its fluidity, its performance, even its flagrant inability to adequately trace the network it attempts to explore? The answer lies in our continuing efforts to find value in the unstable, the indefinite and even the unknowable. We have accounts but we should refrain from affording these a universal validity that exceeds even our own capacity to understand them. They are simply glimpses of other worlds, and their value must only lie in the power of each individual glimpse.

> No matter how grandiose the perspective, no matter how scientific the outlook, no matter how tough the requirements, no matter how astute the advisor, the result of the inquiry – in 99% of the cases – will be a

report prepared under immense duress on a topic requested by some colleagues for reasons that will remain for the most part unexplained. And that is excellent because there is no better way. Methodological treatises might dream of another world: a book on ANT, written by ants for other ants, has no other aim than to help dig tiny galleries in this dusty and earthly one.

(Latour, 2005, pp.123–4)

This book has attempted to dig similar channels into the gallery of a specific newsroom in order to provide a way into a network, to wander through its rooms and along its corridors, to travel down its very tendrils, to provide both a voice and a narrative that rather than attempting to prove a universal theory of media, may just shed some light on the unnoticed minute practices of news work that are essential to the continuing performance inside the newsroom.

GLOSSARY

News production

Backgrounder   A short film or package where the viewer is presented with 'background' information to a story. This is most often used in court reporting where a court verdict or sentence may be reported and a 'backgrounder' is then provided to inform the viewer of the details and relevant context of the particular case.

Bi-media   This refers to the practice of reporting for both television and radio outlets at the same time. This usually involves a single journalist providing recorded or live material for both television and radio outlets.

Camera diary assistant (CDA)   A newsroom role that involves the organisation of the separate camera crews, video journalists and satellite trucks that operate from the newsroom. It will also involve the booking of transmission digital phone lines to retrieve material from other BBC newsrooms across the UK.

Central News East   This is the name of the rival independent regional news programme broadcast on the ITV network at 6.00pm every weekday evening. There are also similar shorter bulletins to the BBC regional bulletins broadcast on ITV in the morning and at lunchtime.

Citizen journalism   The term is used to describe recorded news footage or even still pictures that are provided by members of the public rather than trained journalists or camera operators.

Columbus   BBC Nottingham's digital play-out server that is responsible for the transmission of all the recorded material that makes up each news programme or bulletin.

Community producer   A newsroom role introduced during the BBC's local television pilot project that involves working with members of the general public making films and providing material for the local television programme.

Cut away   This refers to a type of camera shot. It is a single shot that is used as an editing tool so that the viewer is provided with a shot that literally cuts away from the subject of the film, so that the subject may move position without visually disorientating the viewer.

Digital technologies   The term refers to all of the technological machines, apparatuses or tools that are used in the production of digital news. These may include digital cameras, the media hub, the satellite truck, laptop editing systems, studio edit suites and the newsroom's digital recording and play-out servers, Omnibus and Columbus.

Director   A newsroom role that involves being responsible for the organisation of all the human and nonhuman actors that are involved in the transmission of the news programme or bulletin. The director has overall technical control in the gallery during every programme transmission. He or she is also responsible for all of the technical aspects of the programme.

East Midlands Today   This refers to the title of the BBC regional news programme that services the East Midlands area. It includes the cities of Nottingham, Derby, Leicester, Lincoln, Mansfield, Chesterfield, Kettering and Corby.

Electronic news production system (ENPS)   This refers to the BBC's electronic news production system that was developed by the Associated Press. It is the BBC's networked, desktop information service, enabling newsrooms across the country to communicate with one another, to view each other's material and to access news running orders.

Faith producer   A newsroom role introduced during the BBC's local television pilot project that involves working with members of the different religious communities in the local area to make films and news material for the local television project.

Gallery talkback   This refers to the recorded sound of all of the journalists, engineers, technicians, station assistant and the director who may be in the gallery at any time during the rehearsing and transmission of a news programme. The talkback is the recorded sound of their communication during this process.

Head of Regional and Local Programmes (HRLP)   The main managerial role that involves overseeing the operations of the BBC's entire radio and television output for a particular region. Both the Birmingham and Nottingham HRLP are interviewed and represented in this book.

Laptop editing system   This refers to a digital editing system that allows journalists to edit digitised news material on a small, portable computer that can be carried with them anywhere on location. The editing software that is used by BBC journalists is usually Avid.

Leica   A small, portable 35-millimetre film camera used by photographers during the 1940s, which could take up to 36 photographs before being reloaded.

Local TV   This refers to the BBC's nine-month pilot project where local television news was produced and transmitted throughout the West Midlands area. It could be viewed on demand via the BBC Internet *Where I Live* sites as well as in a linear format on digital satellite television.

Media effects analysis   This refers to a dominant paradigm within media and communications studies since the Second World War, which focuses on measurable, short-term behavioural 'effects' of media and concludes that the media plays a limited role in influencing public opinion such as voting behaviour and advertising. It also includes the analysis of certain more negative 'effects' on behaviour through exposure to portrayals of pornography and violence in the media.

Media hub   This refers to one of the main technological actors of the Nottingham and Birmingham newsrooms. The hub is an automated play-out server and is used to store all digitised video material for dissemination throughout the newsroom by means of an interconnected system of computers all of which house the digital editing system, known as Omnibus. The hub is also directly connected to the newsroom play-out system, Columbus, which is responsible for the transmission of all the news material.

Multiskilling   This is a newsroom term that refers to the working practice whereby a journalist is expected and able to perform more than one duty at a time. This may include newsgathering, filming and editing material for TV, radio and internet services. It may also refer to the ability of a journalist to be able to film and edit his/her own footage without the need of an editor or camera operator.

News episteme   This term refers to the internal daily routines, practices, tasks and responsibilities of both humans and technologies that together and in conjunction with one another constitute what we understand as news practice.

Newsgathering zone   This refers to an area of the Nottingham newsroom wherein all the roles that are involved with the gathering and retrieval of news operate. These include the forward planning department, known by those working in the newsroom as 'Futures', made up of one senior planning journalist, a second senior planning journalist and a third planning journalist. There are also four specialist television correspondents, and a resources subdepartment, which comprises all the technical resources available to the newsroom, from satellite trucks to camera crews, studio lights and mobile editing facilities. Newsgathering also includes the personal digital production operators (PDP), also known as video journalists.

News organiser   This was a newsroom role that had become a significant and undisputed position, even enjoying temporary black box status. The news organiser was responsible for overseeing the operations of the newsgathering department as well as communicating with the other radio stations in the regional cluster and all the national television newsgathering departments such as *BBC National News* and *News 24*. The role had been recently disbanded after the introduction of PDP or video journalism.

News product This term refers to the finished news items, packages, reports or live events that are transmitted during any news programme.

Nouse This is a rather ambiguous and ill-defined term that journalists in the BBC newsroom use to denote whether or not a person has a developed news sense. It refers to an instinctive knowledge of how to get to the heart of a news story, or how to recognise a story. Nouse is also the key to recognising how within the news network, power can be recognised as both potential and as force. Nouse is innate and somewhat elliptical. Yet it is also highly performative, used as a valuable currency between journalists to bolster individual positions or to destabilise other actors.

Omnibus A newsroom and industry term for BBC Nottingham's digital, integrated computer play-out system that is installed in all of the newsroom computers and is used for editing and transferring material from the media hub, the central server, to individual news stations within the newsroom and adjoining edit suites.

Operations editor This is a senior managerial role that involves organising and overseeing all BBC Nottingham resources and personnel departments including technical equipment, engineering and all output staff working in the newsroom. They report to the HRLP.

Outside broadcast (OB) This term refers to a television or radio live event transmitted via the satellite newsgathering vehicle (SNG) or a radio car into a radio or TV news bulletin or programme.

Organisational studies This refers to a dominant school of thought and mode of research within media and communications studies that places a greater emphasis on constructing detailed accounts of how particular newsrooms operate by concentrating on journalists' routines and work practices. These studies became popular during the early 1970s in both the USA and the UK and often involve ethnographic research methods of observation, interviewing and participation.

Out of vision (OOV) This is a television term used to describe a certain sequence of shots where the news presenter reads over edited footage but is not visible to the viewer. The presenter is literally out of vision, and all the viewer can see is the video sequence although they can hear the presenter's words.

Output editor This is a senior managerial role that involves overseeing and monitoring all BBC output of a particular newsroom. The editor does not carry out day-to-day production duties but oversees the production operations

and the content of all news bulletins and programmes. They report to the
HRLP.

Output producer   This is a senior journalist role that in the Nottingham
newsroom involves the newsgathering and production of the main evening
regional news programme, *East Midlands Today*, which is transmitted at
6.30pm. They report to the output editor and the HRLP.

Output zone   This refers to an area of the Nottingham newsroom wherein
all the roles involved with the filming, editing, production and transmission
of news operate. This will include the bulletin and programme producers,
the CDA, the media hub operators, the production journalists, and the
programme directors and station assistants.

Package (TV)   This term refers to a completed filmed and edited television
news report that is usually between one-and-a-half and two minutes in
duration. It will have a recorded and edited reporter script and a selection
of video sequences and interview clips that have been edited together to
narrate a particular news story.

Palmcorder   This refers to a small piece of equipment for recording video
footage. It is usually a compact mini digital video recorder that can sit
easily into the palm of the hand. It has a wide lens adaptor and battery
support kit.

Personal Digital Production (PDP)   This term refers to the earliest man-
ifestation within the BBC of what has now become more widely known as
video journalism. Personal Digital Production refers to the process whereby
a single person films and edits video material without having to be classified
as a reporter, camera operator or technician. The emphasis here is on
single-authored and autonomous retrieval of video footage.

Political economy   This refers to the popular and longstanding school of
thought within media and communications studies, which argues that media
functions by representing or reproducing the dominant political, economic
or cultural ideology of a given society. Significant proponents of the many
different variations of the political economy approach to reading media
include Stuart Hall, Noam Chomsky, The Glasgow Media Group, Philip
Schlesinger and Gaye Tuchman.

Satellite News Gathering Vehicle (SNG)   This is a term that refers to
BBC Nottingham's newsroom vehicle that is responsible for transmitting
recorded video footage live from a location back to the newsroom via a
satellite link.

Shoot/edit   This is a Nottingham newsroom term that refers to an individual
who films video footage and then using a laptop editing system, edits that
material in a small vehicle out on location before driving back to the
newsroom with the edited material.

Slice and dice   This is a Nottingham newsroom term that refers to the process by which after transmission the BBC regional news programme is re-edited and uploaded onto the BBC's internet *Where I Live* sites where it can be watched again on demand.

SNG1   This refers to the person who operates the SNG live broadcast vehicle. This role involves identifying and setting up the satellite link and liaising with all the other actors involved in the live event. These will include the immediate SNG2 person, selected television reporters and programme producers, the camera diary assistant (CDA), the hub operator and the programme director as well as less proximate satellite providers and individuals from other newsrooms who may also be involved in their own live broadcasting.

SNG2   Also known as the 'wet end' this refers to the individual who assists the SNG1 operator by laying out the relevant cables from the vehicle, setting up the live broadcast positions and filming the live event.

Upsound   This is a television term that refers to a short clip of speech that is edited onto the end of a sequence of pictures – usually an OOV – where the presenter will stop reading the script and instead the edited clip will be played. The director will 'bring up the sound of the clip' hence the name of the term.

Actor Network Theory

Actor Network Theory (ANT)   Actor Network Theory has its origins in materialist studies of the networks of interdependent social practices that constitute work in science and technology. Bruno Latour, Steve Woolgar and Michel Callon's analyses of a set of negotiations describe the progressive constitution of a network in which both human and nonhuman actors assume identities according to prevailing and specific strategies of interaction and association. Actor Network Theory has developed within the field of science and technology. Its central claim is that modern societies cannot be properly described without recognising them as having a fibrous, thread-like, wiry, stringy, ropy, capillary character that can never be captured by notions of levels, layers, categories, structures or systems. Actor Network Theory demands that instead of traditional and a priori notions of topology, ontology or politics, we pay attention to the actions of both human and nonhuman actors and the associations and linkages they make and break with one another. An actor network topology is thus described as logically grouped entities or elements associated and linked to each other via some relations. The relations, or links, have properties and characteristics through which the elements, as potential actors, can perform on the rest of the network as well as be performed by it.

Actor   An actor is a semiotic definition that refers to something that acts or to which activity is granted by others in the network. It implies no special motivation of human individual actors, or of humans in general. It may be a human, object, machine, tool, animal, spirit or god. It is therefore any elements that bends space around itself, makes other elements dependent upon itself. Actors try to convince other actors so as to create an alignment of the other actors' interests with their own interests.

Actant   An actant can literally be anything provided it is granted to be the source of action within a network. The word is also sometimes used as a neutral way to refer to both nonhuman and human actors, avoiding the strong human bias in the word 'actor'. An actant therefore refers to whatever acts or shifts action where action is defined by a list of performances through trails; from such performances are deduced a set of competences with which the actant is endowed (Akrich and Latour, 1992).

A priori   This term refers to any preconceptions of what may constitute knowledge. Actor Network Theory refutes a priori reasoning as it argues that such reasoning rejects or precludes an exploration of 'facts and machines in the making'. It assumes that we already know what we may find, before we begin our explorations.

Assemblage   Deleuze and Guattari initially use this rather confusing term to describe a method that connotes ad hoc contingencies and has the capacity to embrace a wide variety of incompatible components (Law, 2004). It is adopted by John Law to describe a method that is an episteme (that is a way of knowing) but involves technologies and is crucially active. It is a methodology that assembles or bundles together elements that are not fixed in shape and do not belong to any a priori list, but are often continually constructed in the very process of being entangled together. A method assemblage therefore has no general or consistent rules but actively grows as it crafts together elements and relations between those elements. Law uses this to try to imagine methods that no longer seek the definite or the stable and that have within them no a priori fixed positions, just as we have done throughout this book in our exploration of news processes.

Black box   An actor that has been able to establish strong enough associations with a number of allies or other actors to afford a strong, stable network position that resists translation. It is not simply the question of the number of allies, but that they act as a unified whole. When many elements are made to act as one, a black box is established.

Chronogram   (See Sociogram and Technogram.) This ANT term refers to the third axis along which any actor within a network may be mapped. The chronogram refers to an actor's temporal position, resistances and capabilities at a specific point in a network and is closely related to both its social position (sociogram) as well as its technical infrastructure (techno-gram). Only by charting all three at any specific point can an actor be satisfactorily mapped within a network. The chronogram is a new ANT term that has been developed during the research for this particular study of news production.

Cycles of credit   The term refers to the elaborate process Latour and Woolgar observed by which scientists in the Salk Laboratory transferred credit from one to another in a quest for both credibility and reward. This credit may be in the form of the exchange of scientific discoveries and results or the more general mutual acknowledgment of one another's sci-entific achievements.

Empirical   This term refers to any research carried out or evidence collected by means of observation or experiment rather than by the application of theory.

Enrolment   An ANT term that refers to the moment that another actor accepts the interests defined by the focal actor.

Epistemology   This is defined as the branch of philosophy that deals with and defines the varieties, grounds and validity of knowledge and knowledge claims.

Ethnography   Initially this was defined as the scientific description of races and peoples with their customs, habits and mutual differences. The term is also more loosely defined as a research method of analysing social situations by observing the actions and routines and behaviour of the people as well as conducting interviews and sometimes even participating in the situation being observed.

Immutable mobile   This is a specific ANT term that refers to a mobile and transportable actor in a network that can effect change within that network, usually by the translation of other actors, but that remains unchanged itself.

Inscription device   Within ANT inscriptions may include texts, images, databases, charts, graphs, spreadsheets of results, grids or documents that are central to knowledge work. Inscriptions make action at a distance pos-sible by stabilising work in such a way that it can travel across time and space and be combined with other work. Inscriptions are also central to the process of gaining credibility and enrolling other actors. They attempt to present work in such a way that its meaning and significance are irrefutable (see the prospects news grid, Chapter 8).

Intermediary   In ANT terms an intermediary is whatever transports meaning or force without undergoing any transformation. Therefore for all practical purposes an intermediary can be defined as a black box, but also as a black box counting for one, even if it is internally made of many complex parts. The term is often used pejoratively by Latour in his criticism of how social science brackets off such intermediaries, defining them as uncomplicated and thus not worthy of exploration. In contrast, an ANT account seeks to explore the actions and associations of all actors, so it will not bracket off that which it already assumes is uncomplicated or self-explanatory and will thus include many more mediators than intermediaries. (Latour, 2004, p.40)

Irreversibility   This ANT term refers to the degree to which it is subsequently impossible to return to a point where alternative possibilities exist. Therefore a black box has achieved irreversibility.

Mediators   (See intermediary above.) A mediator is anything that undergoes constant translation and change and whose input within a network cannot predict its output as its specificity must be taken into account in every exploration.

Multiplicity (multiple realities)   This term is used in ANT analyses to refer to the specific work of Annemarie Mol who suggests that reality is enacted or performed rather than simply observed in a stable or singular state. This implies that the traditional distinction between a subject and object is replaced by the concept of the actor and actor constellations as ontologically plural, endlessly performed and thus continually changing, often occupying different simultaneous realities at one time.

Network   In ANT terms a network comprises the components (actors) that include not only people and social groups, but also artefacts, devices, entities, objects and machines, and technologies.

Obligatory point of passage (OPP)   In ANT terms the obligatory point of passage refers to a situation that has to occur for all the actors to satisfy the interests that have been attributed to them by the focal actor. The focal actor defines the OPP through which the other actors must pass and by which the focal actor becomes indispensable (or achieves black box status).

Perspectivalism   This ANT term refers to the work of Mol who defines it as the first breakaway from the traditional monopolistic version of a single truth. It enabled philosophers and social scientists to entertain the concept of the existence of many different versions of truth or perception. But Mol makes the crucial distinction between perpectivalism, which multiplies the eyes of the beholders, and multiple realities, which reveals the viewed object as itself multiple, enacted through simultaneous performances.

Sociogram   This is an ANT term that refers to one of the three axes along which any actor may be mapped. Latour uses both the sociogram and technogram to explore how an innovation enrols other actors within a network to achieve successful translation and network stability. The sociogram refers to the alliances of actors the innovation is designed to enrol, whereas the technogram refers to what it is tied to so as to make that enrolment inescapable. A slight reworking and clarification of these terms within this book provides us with the means to map each actor according to its specific point within a network, to look at the social alliances it has established at this point which is defined by the sociogram, as well as its technical architecture and capabilities that are determined by their association with this specific social position.

Technogram This ANT term refers to the second axis along which any actor within a network may be mapped. The technogram refers to an actor's technical infrastructure, force, resistances and capabilities and is closely related to both its social position (sociogram) as well as its temporal position (chronogram). Only by charting all three at any specific point can an actor be satisfactory mapped within a network.

Translation This is an ANT term that refers to the process of creating and development of an actor network. This process involves numerous actors who attempt to enrol others into alliances or instead to withstand trials of force from other actors who may be attempting to enrol them into quite different alliances or constellations of actors. Numerous actors within a network are involved in a different process of translation, each with its own unique and unpredictable characteristics and outcomes.

NOTES

2 ACTOR NETWORK THEORY

1 Latour and Woolgar's methodology is reminiscent of Hughes's conceptualisation of technological development, recalling Hughes's insistence that 'Sociological, techno-scientific and economic analyses are permanently interwoven in a seamless web' (Hughes, 1983, p.271). Yet
   Latour's determination to construct networks of equal human and nonhuman actors represents a significant development of Hughes's Systems Theory, where technological development
   is considered to be part of a web, but within that web there still exist defined subjects and
   objects in the form of humans and machines.
2 The notion of translation is explored in more detail in relation to the development of video
   journalism in Chapters 4, 5 and 6.
3 A more detailed exploration of the mapping of technologies within the media-studies tradition
   appears later in this chapter.
4 A detailed discussion of the relationship between actor specificity and network translation
   appears in Chapter 3.
5 Further discussion concerning the methodological rationale of the selection of the BBC
   newsroom in Nottingham is also discussed later in the chapter.
6 The notion of translation is discussed in detail in the following chapter.
7 The term black box is explored in detail in Chapter 3 by means of an analysis of the media
   hub, one of the newsroom's most significant technological actors.
8 This is exemplified in Chapters 4, 5 and 6 with an analysis of the implementation of a new
   technology known as Personal Digital Production (PDP) in the news production network.
9 Actor Network Theory mainly focuses on the first two, and it is on these two that this book
   will also concentrate. It is only in later writings that Latour turns to questions of spiritual
   entities.
10 There are of course many established and important texts devoted to the study of media
   technologies, their influence and role within cultural or social processes, as well as their
   consumption or domestication by specific audiences (Williams, 1975; Winston, 1998; Silverstone & Hirsch, 1992). I have not spent time exploring these here as these works explore the
   issue of media technology with a predominantly historical focus, or look at the use and
   domestication of technology and more significantly do not explore the idea of technological
   agency with which this particular study is interested. Those authors that have engaged with
   the issue of technological agency (Cottle & Ashton, 1999) are discussed in the following
   chapter.
11 An example of this is found in Chapter 7 where certain satellite truck operators act without
   recourse to network conventions, thus causing confusion to other actors within the network.
   The network is thus complicated by its own operational unpredictability and this makes it
   more difficult to map.

12 A more detailed exploration of Couldry's insightful work on ANT, power and media processes will be explored in Chapter 8.

13 A detailed exposition of Boyne's analysis of Latour's presentation of the human subject can also be found in the opening section of Chapter 8.

14 The notion of the invisibility of practice also presents a possible further weakness of ANT as a method. Certainly in Latour and Woolgar's laboratory work, most if not all of the scientific practices were highly visible. The way in which invisible nodes of the network are still able to be analysed using ANT will be explored in detail in the following six empirical chapters.

3 ENTERING THE NETWORK

1 A glossary of specific ANT and newsroom terms can be found on p.218.

2 PDP signifies a relatively new addition to both the newsroom and to the newsgathering department. The innovation of PDP and its specific embedding and implementation within the network is the subject of Chapters 4, 5 and 6.

3 The role of the HRLP is discussed throughout the book as the individual HRLP changed during the period of research undertaken for the book and the impact this has on the network is analysed in more detail in Chapter 6.

4 For a more detailed exploration of the relationship between the output and newsgathering departments, see Hemmingway, 2004.

5 Situated within the local radio stations there are also separate PDP bureaux, based at Leicester, Derby and Lincoln, each staffed by two PDP operators.

6 The eradication of such a prominent actor as the news organiser position has had a significant effect on the stability of the network in specific places. This occurred as a result of a radical network translation following the embedding of PDP, which is discussed in detail in Chapters 4 and 5.

7 The changing role of the *News 24* team and the implications of the changes to this service and to the regional newsroom are discussed in Chapters 4 and 5.

8 The clip being referred to in the above quote is any 'piece' of video or audio that is loaded onto the Omnibus system and given a specific name.

9 The implications of the surrendering of autonomy have particular significance once PDP is introduced into the network, which is examined in the following chapter.

10 The impact of idiosyncratic, and often individual, human behaviour traits on the network is examined in detail in Chapter 8.

11 The quote also indicates the central significance of time within the network. The term *chronogram* is introduced and developed throughout the book as an accompanying term to ANT's existing *technogram* and *sociogram* that are introduced later on in this chapter.

12 An Aston refers to the title graphic that appears on screen to identify the person who is being interviewed.

13 In *Science in Action* Latour (1987) uses the terms *sociogram* and *technogram* to describe the success of an actor's initial enrolment within a network. I have adopted and slightly adapted these two terms for this book so that they refer more specifically to the continuing socialisation of an actor within a network as well as an actor's inherent technical infrastructure that assists it in achieving that socialisation.

14 The *chronogrammatic* axis is neglected by ANT. Latour tends to essentialise the temporal issue, rather than seeing it as both a conceptual and a determining factor in an actor's position within a network. The significance of the chronogram in the construction of news facts is examined in detail in the exploration of 'live' reporting in Chapter 7.

15 We will see how these frustrations are once again evident when we analyse the media hub's role in the newsgathering and transmission of local TV bulletins in Birmingham during the local TV pilot, which is discussed in Chapter 6.

16 Particular manipulations of the network and the series of challenges posed by specific human actors are explored in detail in Chapter 8.

4 VIDEO JOURNALISM (1)

1 Personal Digital Production is best understood as a form of video journalism where a single individual is trained to record and edit their own material without assistance from anyone else.

2 The main innovator is Michael Rosenblum but the analysis will also include PDP trainers situated at the BBC training school in Newcastle. The single authored characteristic of PDP is defined by the entire filming and editing process being carried out only by one person rather than a team of reporter and camera operator. This is explained in the following section.

3 All Rosenblum 2004 quotes are taken from transcripts of teaching sessions or from original interviews conducted during the period of March 2004 at the BBC PDP Training Centre in Newcastle.

4 It is significant to note that Rosenblum also eradicates the schism between process and product and refers to the practice of production as containing both practice and product simultaneously, undivided.

5 The BBC argues that these staff members will not be made redundant but will be trained so as to work as PDP operators, rather than as craft camera operators or videotape editors. In the Nottingham newsroom this was a strategy that was initially adopted, although after three years of PDP working practice, some staff have recently been made redundant.

6 'De-differentiation' is used here to denote the eradication of individual demarcated roles from which a person does not veer and the adoption instead of a belief that everyone is a filmmaker no matter what they might have been before.

7 The use of the inscription device can also be interpreted as a symbol of the entire methodological process of constructing any ANT narrative, suggesting that the inscribed account must itself grapple with the epistemological difficulties of defining a performative process, like news production, as a narrative text. Interestingly, the news grid remains unstable and in a short time disappears from the network altogether.

8 This is explored in more detail in Chapter 7, which examines the process of constructing live news events.

5 VIDEO JOURNALISM (2)

1 See Chapter 3 for a more detailed exposition of the individual newsroom departments and subdepartments.

2 Network in this instance is defined as BBC National News – the BBC's national coverage produced in the London television news centre at White City.

3 This is the second immutable mobile introduced to assist the implementation of PDP – again with the emphasis on actors inscribing and fixing details so as to engender a notion of stability.

7 THE SATELLITE TRUCK AND LIVE REPORTING

1 The 'outside broadcast' or 'OB', 'live news event' or 'the live' are all different terms that are used to describe a news process whereby the satellite truck – known as the Satellite News Gathering (SGN) vehicle – is driven to a location and from there a live news event is filmed, sent back to the studio via a satellite feed and transmitted live.

2 The concept of actors being invisible to one another during the construction of a live news event is significant in the exploration of news processes and is analysed in more detail later in the chapter. It is also a concept that is neglected by most ANT analyses and signals a significant limitation of using ANT as a tool for reading news work. This is also discussed later in the chapter.

3 The SNG1 operator, Ian, strengthens this position even further by reminding other actors that he built the SNG truck himself. He is thus the only individual who is able to understand its technical infrastructure and foibles in enough detail to minimise the potential for error. The

NOTES

other SNG operator, Boris, may also have been making an implicit reference to this in the quote on p.153 when he tries to re-emphasise the social skills needed by the operator as opposed to other SNG operators' purely technical expertise.

4 The audio pathway, though initially made possible by the successful lining up of the SNG with the satellite link is, however, also controlled by the technical manager in the gallery who can easily turn off the audio from the truck in the gallery thus silencing the SNG, should the producer or director wish to do so. This separate reality will be examined in the following chapter.

5 This last reference to the guest not being aware of the process is also vital to a recognition of the SNG's multiple realities and echoes the earlier analysis of the viewer's perception of the event as being devoid of production apparatus or interference, thus rending the production process invisible in transmission.

6 The invisibility of network points and the strength this affords to certain actors will be discussed in the later sections of this chapter as well as being explored in more detail in Chapter 8. It also exposes another limitation of ANT as a tool for reading news work as the network to which Latour refers is highly visible and he spends little or no time analysing the implications of actors' invisibility to one another.

8 HUMAN ACTORS, INTENTIONALITY AND ACTOR NETWORK THEORY

1 The attack and its aftermath, including Callon and Latour's response to Collins and Yearley is described in detail in Chapter 2. We return to it here merely to remind readers how the attack centred around ANT's reconfiguration of the human subject as a hybrid and unstable entity.

2 Textual inscriptions establishing actor translation by persuading others of the significance of individual findings were explored in Chapter 4 where managers attempted to stabilise the introduction of PDP by the use of the news grid.

3 This premise will be challenged in the later section of this chapter with an examination of a specific human characteristic known collectively as nouse.

4 The 'shoot/edit' is a shift that managers have introduced as a result of the development of PDP and involves a single camera operator who is responsible for covering smaller stories and editing them on location. It signifies yet another network translation due to the implementation of PDP.

5 The methodological issues regarding my participation in the day's construction of news, what this implies with regard to my role as an ethnographer, as well as how I have had to occupy various quite different positions in order to record the separate scenarios, is discussed in more detail later in this chapter.

6 Nouse does, however, still operate within what Latour refers to as 'cycles of credit' as is described below, thus it could be argued that nouse is in some senses inscribed by a handing over of perceived credibility from one actor to another, but it is not *textually* inscribed.

7 A loan shark is defined here as an individual who lends money to vulnerable people and charges extortionate interest rates. Collection of monies is usually accompanied by threats of violence.

8 Once again this illustrates the successful manipulation of production staff by the SNG engineers as it signals the heightened awareness among producers and directors that the SNG may go wrong at any moment.

CONCLUSION

1 The sentence reads as though Latour and Woolgar themselves divided these elements into dichotomous pairs. This is merely a stylistic convention inherent in the construction of the sentence and does not represent a methodological pairing of elements.

2 See Chapter 7 for a detailed examination of the construction of the live event.

3 See Chapter 5 for a detailed examination of the hub and the eradication of a stable, externa-lised reality.

4 The concept of translation is analysed in detail with the introduction of PDP to the news network in Chapters 3, 4 and 5.

5 For a detailed examination of the shifting nature of the three axes see Chapter 3.

6 For a detailed examination of the role of the human subject within ANT analyses see Chapter 8.

BIBLIOGRAPHY

Abercrombie, N., Hill, S. & Turner, B., (eds) (1980) *The Dominant Ideology Thesis*. Allen and Unwin, London.

Adam, B., Beck, U. & Van-Loon, J. (2000) *The Risk Society and Beyond – Critical Issues for Social Theory*. Sage, London.

Adorno, T. & Horkheimer, M. (1944) *Dialectic of Enlightenment*. Herder and Herder, New York.

Adorno, T. & Horkheimer, M. (1977) The culture industry (abridged). In Curran, J. *et al.* (eds) *Mass Communication and Society*. Edward Arnold, London.

Akrich, M. (1989; 1992) The de-scription of technical objects. In Bijker, W.E. and Law, J. (eds) *Shaping Technology/ Building Society*. MIT Press, Cambridge, Mass., pp.205–40.

Akrich, M. & Latour, B. (1992) A summary of a convenient vocabulary for the semiotics of human and nonhuman assemblies. In Bijker, M.E and Law, J. (eds) *Shaping Technology, Building Society: Studies in Socio-technical Change*. MIT Press, Cambridge, Mass.

Allan, S. (1999) *News Culture*. Open University Press, Buckingham; Philadelphia, Pa.

Altheide, D.L. (1976) *Creating Reality*. Sage, Beverly Hills, Calif., London.

Atton, C. (2003) What is 'alternative' journalism? *Journalism Studies*, Vol. 4, No. 3, 267–72.

Avilles, J.A.G., Bienvenido, L., Sanders, K. & Harrison, J. (2004) Journalists at Digital Television Newsrooms in Britain and Spain: workflow and multiskilling in a competitive environment. *Journalism Studies*, Vol. 5, No. 1, 93–102.

Bantz, C.R. (1985) News organisations: conflict as a crafted cultural norm, *Communication*, 8, 225–44.

Bar-Hillel, Y. (1954) Indexical expressions. *Mind,* Vol. 63, 359–79.

Barnes, B. (1982) *T.S. Kuhn and Social Sciences*. Macmillan, London.

BBC Broadcasting House (1996) *Extending Choice in the Digital Age*. BBC: Broadcasting House, London.

BBC Regional Broadcasting (1996) *Going Digital, the Challenge for BBC Regional Journalism*. BBC Regional Broadcasting, Broadcasting House, London.

Bijker, M.E. & Law, J. (eds) (1992) *Shaping Technology, Building Society: Studies in Socio-technical Change*. MIT Press, Cambridge, Mass.

Bijker, W.E., Hughes, T.P. & Pinch, T.J. (1987) *The Social Construction of Technological Systems: New Directions in the Sociology and History of Technology*. MIT Press, Cambridge, Mass. and London.

Blanchot, M. (1986) *The Writing of the Disaster*. University of Nebraska Press, Lincoln, Neb.

Bloor, D. (1973) Wittgenstein and Mannheim on the sociology of mathematics. In *Studies in the History and Philosophy of Science,* Vol. 4, pp.173–91.

Blumler, J. & Gurevitch, M. (1995) *The Crisis of Public Communication*. Routledge, London.

Blumler, J.G. (1969) Producers' attitudes towards television coverage of an election campaign: a case study. In Halmos, P. (ed.) *The Sociology of Mass Media Communicators*. University of Keele, Keele.

Boddy, W. (2004) *New Media and Popular Imagination: Launching Radio, Television, and Digital Media in the United States.* Oxford, Oxford University Press.

Born, G. (2004) *Uncertain Vision.* Secker and Warburg, London.

Bourdieu, P. (1991) The Peculiar History of Scientific Reason. *Sociological Forum*, Vol. 6, No. 1, 3–26.

Bourdieu, P. (1998) *On Television and Journalism.* Pluto Press, London.

Boyd-Barrett, O. & Newbold, C. (1995) *Approaches to Media, A Reader.* Arnold, London, New York, Sydney, Auckland.

Boyne, R. (2002) Subject, Society and Culture. In *Theory, Culture and Society.* Nottingham Trent University and Sage, London.

Breed, W. (1955) Social control in the newsroom: a functional analysis. *Social Forces*, Vol. 33, 326–35.

Brown, S.D. & Capdevila, R. (1999) Perpetuum mobile: substance, force and the sociology of translation. In Law, J. and Hassard, J. (eds) *Actor Network Theory and After.* Blackwell Publishing/ The Sociological Review, Oxford.

Bruck, P.A. (1981) The social production of texts: on the relation production/product in the news media. *McGill University, Graduate Program in Communications, Working Papers in Communications*, Montreal.

Brunsdon, C. & Morley, D. (1978) *Nationwide Television Studies.* Routledge, London.

Burns, T. (1969) Public service and private world. In Halmos, P. (ed.) *The Sociological Review Monograph*, Vol. 13, 53–73.

Callon, M. (1980) Struggles and negotiations to define what is problematic and what is not: the sociology of translation. In Knorr-Cetina, K. D., Krohn, R. and Whitley, R.D. (eds) *The Social Process of Scientific Investigation: Sociology of the Sciences Yearbook*, Vol 4. Reidel, Dordrecht and Boston, Mass., pp.197–219.

Callon, M. (1991) Techno-economic network and irreversibility. In Law, J. (ed.) *A sociology of Monsters. Essays on power, technology and domination.* Routledge, London, pp.132–64.

Callon, M. (ed.) (1998) *The Laws of the Market.* Blackwell, Oxford.

Callon, M. (1999) Actor Network theory – the market test. In Law, J. and Hassard, J. (eds) *Actor Network Theory and After.* Blackwell Publishing/The Sociological Review, Oxford, pp.181–95.

Callon, M. & Latour, B. (1981) Unscrewing the Big Leviathan: how actors macrostructure reality and how sociologists help them to do so. In Knorr-Cetina, K.D. and Cicourel, A.V (eds) *Advances in Social Theory and Methodology: Toward an integration of Micro- and Macro-Sociologies.* Routledge and Kegan Paul, Boston, Mass., pp.277–303.

Callon, M. & Latour, B. (1992) Don't throw the baby out with the Bath school! A reply to Collins and Yearley. In Pickering, A. (ed.) *Science as Practice and Culture.* The University of Chicago Press, Chicago, Ill., pp.343–68.

Carper, A. (1977) Marketing news. In P. Norris (ed.) *Politics and the Press.* Lynne Reinner, Boulder, Colo.

Clifford, J. & Marcus, G.E. (eds) (1986) *Writing Culture: The Poetics and Politics of Ethnography.* University of California Press, Berkeley, Calif.

Collins, R. (1975) *Conflict Sociology: Toward an Explanatory Science.* Academic Press, New York; London.

Collins, H.M. & Yearley, S. (1992) Epistemological chicken. In Pickering, A. (ed.) *Science as Practice and Culture.* The University of Chicago Press, Chicago, Ill., pp.301–26.

Cottle, S. & Ashton, M. (1999) From BBC newsroom to BBC news centre; on changing technology and journalistic practice. *Convergence, Journal of New Information and Communication Technologies*, Vol. 5, No. 3, pp.22–43.

Cottle, S. (1993) *TV News, Urban Conflict and the Inner City.* Leicester University Press, Leicester.

Cottle, S. (1995) The production of news formats: determinants of mediated public contestation. *Media, Culture and Society*, Vol. 17, No. 2, 275–91.

Cottle, S. (ed.) (2003) *Media Organisation and Production.* Sage Publications, London; Thousand Oaks, Calif. and New Delhi.

Couldry, N. (2003) *Contesting Media Power: Alternative Media in a Networked World.* Rowman & Littlefield, Lanham, Md.

Couldry, N. (2006) Transvaluing media studies: or, beyond the myth of the mediated culture. In Curran, J. and Morely, D. (eds) *Media and Cultural Theory.* Routledge, London, pp.177–94.

Couldry, N. (in press) Actor Network Theory and Media: Do they connect and on what terms? In Hepp, A. *et al.* (eds) *Cultures of Connectivity.* The Hampton Press, Mahwah, N.J.

Curran, J. (1978) The press as an agency of social control: an historical perspective. In Boyce, G., Curran, J. and Wingate, P. (eds) *Newspaper History.* Constable, London.

Curran, J. (2002) *Media Power.* Routledge, London.

Dahlgren, P. (1995) *Television and the Public Sphere.* Sage, London.

Dahlgren, P. (1999) *Imagining and Doing Democracy: Citizens, Civic Culture and The Media.* Pluto Press, London.

de Saxe, M. (1756) *Les Reveries, ou Memoires sur l'art de la guerre,* The Hague.

Deleuze, G. & Guattari, F. (1987) *A Thousand Plateaus: Capitalism and Schizophrenia.* Athlone, London.

Denzin, N.K. (2001) The reflexive interview and a performative social science. In *Qualitative Research*, Vol. 1, No. 1, 23–46. Sage, Thousand Oaks, Calif., London and New Delhi.

Denzin, N.K. & Lincoln, Y. (eds) (2003) *Collecting and Interpreting Qualitative Materials.* Sage, Thousand Oaks, Calif., London and New Delhi.

Durkheim, E. (1915) *The Elementary Forms of the Religious Life.* Allen and Unwin, London.

Ellul, J. (1964) *The Technological Society.* (Translated by John Wilkinson) Vintage Press, New York.

Epstein, E. (1973) *News from Nowhere.* Random House, New York.

Ericson, R.V., Baranek, P.M. & Chan, K.B.L. (1991) *Representing Order: Crime, Law and Justice in the News Media.* Open University Press, Milton Keynes.

Farnsworth, J. & Austrin, T. (2006) Fresh connections: illuminating media networks through ethnography and actor network theory in the case of mediated poker. Paper presented to the CRESC annual conference, Oxford 2006.

Fischmann, M. (1980) *Manufacturing the News.* University of Texas Press, Austin, Tex.

Fiske, J. & Hartley, J. (1978) *Reading Television.* 2nd edition. Routledge, London and New York.

Foucault, M. (1979; 1975) *Discipline and Punish: The Birth of the Prison.* Vintage, New York.

Gans, H. (1979) *Deciding What's News: a study of CBS evening news, NBC nightly news, Newsweek and Time.* Pantheon, New York.

Garfinkel, H. (1967) *Studies in Ethnomethodology.* Prentice Hall, Englewood Cliffs, N.J.

Garnham, N. (1979) Contribution to a political economy of mass communication. In *Media, Culture and Society*, Vol. 1, No. 2. Academic Press, London, pp.130–4.

Garnham, N. (1986) The Media and the Public Sphere. In Golding, P., Murdoch, G. and Schlesinger, P. (eds) *Communicating Politics.* Leicester University Press, Leicester.

Geertz, C. (1988) *Works and Lives: The Anthropologist as Author.* Stanford University Press, Stanford, Calif.

Gerbner, G. (1961) The individual in a mass culture. In *The National Elementary Principal,* Vol. 961, pp.49–54.

Gerbner, G. (1967) The press and the dialogue in education: a case study of a national educational convention and its depiction in America's daily newspapers. *Journalism Monograph,* Vol. 5.

Gerbner, G. (1969) Toward cultural indicators: the analysis of mass mediated public message systems. In Allen, W.H. (ed.) *AV Communication Review,* Vol. 17, No. 2. Department of Audiovisual Instruction, Washington, DC, pp.137–48.

Giddens, A. (1976) *New Rules of Sociological Method: a Positive Critique of Interpretive Sociologies.* Hutchinson, London.

Giddens, A. (1984). *The Constitution of Society: Outline of the Theory of Structuration.* University of California Press, Berkeley, Calif.

Glasgow University Media Group (1976a) *Bad News.* Routledge and Kegan Paul, London.

Glasgow University Media Group (1976b) *More Bad News.* Routledge and Kegan Paul, London.

Gouldner, A.W. (1971) *The Coming Crisis in Western Sociology.* Avon, New York.

Habermas, J. (1989; 1962) *Structural Transformation of the Public Sphere.* Polity Press, Cambridge.

Hall, S. (1977) Culture, the media and the ideological effect. In Curran, J., Gurevitch, M. and Woollacott, J. (eds) *Mass Communication and Society.* Arnold, London.

Hall, S. (1980) Encoding/decoding. In Hall, S., Hobson, D., Lowe, A. and Willis, P. (eds) *Culture, Media, Language.* Hutchinson, London.

Hall, S., Critcher, C., Jefferson, T., Clarke, J. and Roberts, B. (1978) *Policing the Crisis: Mugging, the State and Law and Order.* Macmillan, London.

Hallin, D.C. & Mancini, P. (1984) *Comparing Media Systems: Three Models of Media and Politics.* Cambridge University Press, Cambridge.

Hammersley, M. & Atkinson, P. (1983). *Ethnography: Principles in Practice.* Tavistock Publications, London.

Haraway, D. (1992) The promises of monsters: a regenerative politics for Inaproapriate/d Others. In Grossberg, L. *et al.* (eds) *Cultural studies.* Routledge, New York, pp.295–337.

Hardt, H. (1990) Newsworkers, technology and journalism history. *Critical Studies in Mass Communication,* Vol. 7, pp.346–65.

Harrison, J. (2000) *Terrestrial TV News in Britain: The Culture of Production.* Manchester University Press, Manchester.

Harrison, J. (2006) *News.* Routledge, London.

Harrison, M. (1985) *Television News: Whose Bias?* Hermitage, Berkshire.

Hemmingway, E. (2004) The silent heart of news. *Space and Culture,* Vol. 7, Issue 4, 409–27.

Hemmingway, E. (2005) PDP, The news production network and the transformation of news. *Convergence,* Vol. 11, No. 3, 8–28.

Henze, B. (2004) Emergent genres in young disciplines: the case of ethnological science. *Technical Communication Quarterly,* Vol. 13, Issue 4.

Herman, E.S. & Chomsky, N. (1988) *Manufacturing Consent: The Political Economy of Mass Media.* Pantheon, New York.

Herzog, H. (1944) What do we really know about daytime radio listeners? In Lazarsfeld, P.F (ed.) *Radio Research.* Duell, Sloan and Pearce, New York.

Huffaker, B., Mercer, B., Phenix, G. & Wise, W. (2004) *When the News Went Live.* Taylor Trade Publishing, Lanham, Md.

Hughes, T.P. (1971) *Elmer Sperry: Inventor and Engineer.* John Hopkins University Press, Baltimore, Md.

Hughes, T.P (1983) *Networks of Power: Electrification in Western Society, 1880–1930.* John Hopkins University Press, Baltimore, Md.

Kalocsai, C. (2000) The multi-sited research imaginary: notes on transnationalism and the ethnographic practice. Paper to Comparative Research Workshop, Yale University. December 4, 2000. [http://72.14.203.104/search?q=cache:0elZUKQp1m0J:www.yale.edu/ccr/kalocsai.doc+multi-sited+ethnography&hl=en&ct=clnk&cd=2] Accessed 10 August 2006.

Kaniss, P. (1991) *Making Local News.* University of Chicago Press, Chicago.

Katz, E. & Lazarsfeld, P.F. (1955) *Personal Influences: The Part Played by People in the Flow of Mass Communication.* The Free Press, Glencoe.

236

Katz E., Blumler, J.G. & Gurevitch, M. (1974) Utilisation of Mass Communication by the individual. In Blumler, J.G. and Katz, E. (eds) *The Uses of Mass Communications: Current Perspectives on Gratifications Research.* Sage, Beverly Hills, Calif., pp.21–9.

Kellner, D. (1995) *Media Culture.* Routledge, London.

Knorr-Cetina, K.D. (1981) Social and Scientific Method or What do we make of the distinction between the Natural and Social Sciences? *Philosophy of Social Sciences,* Vol. 2, Part 3, 335–59.

Kuhn, T. (1962) *The Structure of Scientific Revolutions.* University of Chicago Press, Chicago, Ill.

Kung-Shankleman, L. (2000) *Inside the BBC and CNN. Managing Media Organisations.* Routledge, London.

Latour, B. (1986) The powers of association. In Law, J. (ed.) *Power, Action and Belief: a New Sociology of Knowledge?* Routledge and Kegan Paul, New York, pp.264–80.

Latour, B. (1987) *Science in Action.* Harvard University Press. Cambridge, Mass.

Latour, B. (1988a) *The Pasteurisation of France.* Harvard University Press, Cambridge, Mass.

Latour, B. (1988b) The politics of explanation: an alternative. In Woolgar, S. (ed.) *Representation in Scientific Practice.* MIT Press, Cambridge, Mass., pp.19–68.

Latour, B. (1988c) A relativist account of Einstein's relativity. *Social Studies of Science,* Vol. 18, 3–44.

Latour, B. (1990) Drawing things together. In Lynch, M. and Woolgar, S. (eds) *Representation in Scientific Practice.* MIT Press, Cambridge, Mass.

Latour, B. (1991) Technology is society made durable. In Law, J. (ed.) *A Sociology of Monsters? Essays on Power, Technology and Domination.* Sociological Review Monograph. Routledge, London, pp.103–31.

Latour, B. (1992) Where are the missing masses? The sociology of a few mundane artefacts. In Bijker, M.E. and Law, J. (eds) *Shaping Technology, Building Society: Studies in Socio-technical Change.* MIT Press, Cambridge, Mass.

Latour, B. (1993) *We Have Never Been Modern.* Harvester Wheatsheaf, Brighton.

Latour, B. (1997a) On recalling ANT. In 'ANT and After' Workshop. Keele University, Centre for Social Theory and Technology.

Latour, B. (1999) *Pandora's Hope. Essays on the Reality of Science Studies.* Harvard University Press, Cambridge, Mass., London.

Latour, B. (2002) Morality and technology. *Theory, Culture and Society,* Vol. 19, No. 5/6, 247–60.

Latour, B. (2005) *Reassembling the Social: An Introduction to Actor Network Theory.* Oxford University Press, Oxford.

Latour, B. & Woolgar, S. (1979) *Laboratory Life – the Social Construction of Scientific Facts.* Sage, Beverley Hills, Calif. and London.

Law, J. (1975) Is epistemology redundant? a sociological view. In *Philosophical Social Science.* University of Keele, pp.317–37.

Law, J. (1986) On power and its tactics: a view from the sociology of science. *The Sciological Review,* Vol. 34, 1–38.

Law, J. (1991) Introduction: monsters, machines and sociotechnical relations. In Law J. (ed.) *A Sociology of Monsters? Essays on Power, Technology and Domination,* Vol. 38. London, Routledge, pp.1–23.

Law, J. (1994) *Organising Modernity.* Blackwell, Oxford.

Law, J. (1996) Organizing accountabilities: ontology and the mode of accounting. In Munro, R. and Mouritsen, J. (eds) *Accountability: Power, Ethos and the Technologies of Managing.* International Thompson Business Press, London.

Law, J. (1997) Traduction/trahison: notes on ANT. In *TMV Working Paper, No. 106.* University of Oslo, Oslo, pp.1–26.

Law, J. (2004) *After Method, Mess in Social Science Research.* Routledge, London.

Law, J. & Hassard, J. (eds) (1999) *Actor Network Theory and After.* Blackwell Publishing/The Sociological Review, Oxford.

BIBLIOGRAPHY

Law, J. & Singleton, V. (2000) Performing technology's stories. *Technology and Culture*, Vol. 41, 765–75.

Layton, E. (1977) Conditions of technological development. In Spiegel-Rosing, I. and de-Solla Price, D. (eds) *Science, Technology and Society: A Cross-Disciplinary Perspective*. Sage, London; Beverly Hills.

Mackenzie, D. & Wajcman, J., (eds) (1985) *The Social Shaping of Technology*. Open University Press, Milton Keynes and Philadelphia, Pa.

Mackinnon, E.A., (ed.) (1972) *Problem of Scientific Realism*. Appleton-Century-Crofts, New York.

Mannheim, K. (1936) *Ideology and Utopia: an Introduction to the Sociology of Knowledge*. (Translated from the German by Louis Wirth and Edward Shils.) Routledge and Kegan Paul, London.

Marcus, G. (1998) Introduction: Anthropology on the move. In *Ethnography Through Thick and Thin*. Princeton University Press, Princeton, N.J., pp.3–31.

Marcus, G. (2000) What is at stake in the idea and practice of multi-sited ethnography? (Talk presented as part of a colloquium series on transnationalism, area studies, and ethnographic methods at Yale University on October 31, 2000.)

Marvin, C. (1988) *When Old Technologies Were New: Thinking about Electric Communication in the Late Nineteenth Century*. Oxford University Press, New York.

Mattelart, A. (1994) *Mapping World Communication*. University of Minnesota Press, Minneapolis, Minn.

McLuhan, M. & Fiore, Q. (1967) *The Medium is the Message*. Penguin, Harmondsworth.

McQuail, D. (1994) *Mass Communication Theory: An Introduction*. Sage, London.

Merton, R.K (1975) *Social Theory and Social Structure*. Free Press, New York.

Mol, A. (1999) Ontological Politics: A Word and Some Questions. In Law, J. and Hassard, J. (eds) *Actor Network Theory and After*. Blackwell Publishing/The Sociological Review, Oxford, pp.74–89.

Mol, A. (2002) *The Body Multiple: Ontology in Medical Practice*, Duke University Press, Durham, N.C.; London.

Mosco, V. (1996) *The Political Economy of Communication*. Sage, London.

Mulkay, M.J. (1979a) Science and the sociology of knowledge. In *Controversies in Sociology*, No. 8. George Allen and Unwin, London.

Mulkay, M.J. (1979b) Knowledge and utility: implications for the sociology of knowledge. *Social Studies of Science*, Vol. 9, 63–80.

Murdoch, G. & Golding, P. (1979) Ideology and the mass media: the question of determination. In Barrett, M. *et al.* (eds) *Ideology and Cultural Production*. Croom-Helm, London.

Neyland, D (2006) Dismissed content and discontent. An analysis of the strategic aspects of actor-network theory. *Science, Technology & Human Values*, Vol. 31, No. 1, 29–51.

Nietzsche, F. (1968) *The Will to Power* (Translated by Walter Kaufman and R.J Hollingdale.) Vintage, New York.

O'Neill, J. (1992) Journalism in the Marketplace. In Belsey, A. and Chadwick, C. (eds) *Ethical Issues in Journalism and the Media*. Routledge, London.

Ogburn, W.F. & Thomas, D. (1972) Are inventions inevitable? A note on the social evolution. *Political Science Quarterly*, Vol. 37, 83–98.

Rosenblum, M. (2002) *The Complete Guide to the Digital Video Revolution*. Rosenblum Associates Incorporated, New York.

Scheffler, I. (1967) *Science and Subjectivity*. Bobbs-Merrill, Indianapolis, Ind.

Schiller, D. (1981) *Objectivity and the News*. University of Philadelphia Press, Philadelphia, Pa.

Schiller, H.I. (1971) The international commercialization of broadcasting. In *Mass Communications and American Empire*. Beacon Press, Boston, Mass., pp.94–103.

Schlesinger, P. (1978) *Putting 'Reality' Together: BBC News*. Constable, London.

Schudson, M. (1991) The sociology of news production revisited. In Curran, J. and Gurevitch, M. (eds) *Mass Media and Society*. Edward Arnold, London.

Schudson, M. (2000) The sociology of news production revisited (again). In Curran, J. and Gurevitch, M. (eds) *Mass Media and Society.* Edward Arnold, London.

Serres, M. (1982) Turner translates Carnot. In Harari, J.V. and Bell, D.F. (eds) *Hermes: Literature, Science, Philosophy.* John Hopkins, Baltimore.

Silverstone, R. & Hirsch, E. (eds) (1992) *Consuming Technologies: Media and Information in Domestic Spaces.* Routledge, London.

Sokal, A. & Bricmont, J. (1977) *Intellectual Impostures: Postmodern Philosophers' Abuse of Science.* Profile Books Ltd, London.

Soloski, J. (1989) News reporting and professionalism: some constraints on the reporting of news. *Media, Culture and Society,* Vol. 11, 207–28.

Spinks, L. (2003) *Friedrich Nietzsche.* Routledge, London; New York.

Stevenson, N. (2002) *Understanding Media Cultures – Social Theory and Mass Communication,* 3nd edition. Sage, London; Thousand Oaks, Calif. and New Delhi.

Tuchman, G. (1978) *Making News. A Study in the Social Construction of News.* Free Press, New York.

Tunstall, J. (1971) *Journalists at Work.* Constable, London.

Ursall, G. (2001) Creating value and valuing creation in contemporary UK television: or 'dumbing down' the workforce. *Journalism Studies,* Vol .4, No. 4, 31–46.

Van-Loon, J. (2002) *Risk and Technological Culture. Towards a Sociology of Virulence.* Routledge, London.

Van-Loon, J. (2007) *Media Technology.* Open University Press, Milton Keynes.

Van-Loon, J. & Hemmingway, E. (2005) Organisations, identities and technologies in innovation management: the rise and fall of bi-media in the BBC East Midlands. *Interventions Research,* Vol. 1, No. 2, 125–47.

Walker, D. (2002) Low visibility on the inside track. *Journalism: Theory, Practice and Criticism,* Vol. 3, No. 1, 101–10.

Ward, S.C. (1994) In the shadow of the deconstructed metanarratives: Baudrillard, Latour and the end of realist epistemology. *History of the Human Sciences,* Vol. 7, No. 4, 73–94.

Watson-Verran, H. & Turnbull, D. (1995) Science and other indigenous knowledge systems. In Jasanoff, S., Markle, G.E., Petersen, J.C. and Pinch, T. (eds) *Handbook of Science and Technology Studies.* Sage, Thousand Oaks, Calif., pp.115–39.

Wheeler, M. (1997) *Politics and the Mass Media.* Blackwell, Oxford.

Whitley, R.D. (1972) Black boxism and the sociology of science: a discussion of the major developments in the field. In Halmos, P. (ed.) *The Sociology of Science (Sociological Review Monograph* 18). University of Keele, pp.61–91.

Williams, R. (1975) *Television: Technology and Cultural Form.* Schocken Books, New York.

Williams, R. (1985) *Toward 2000.* Penguin, London.

Williams, R. (1989) Isn't the News terrible? In *What I Came to Say.* Hutchinson, London.

Winner, L. (1977) *Autonomous Technology: Technics-out-of-control as a Theme of Political Thought.* MIT Press, Cambridge, Mass.

Winston, B. (1998) *Media Technology and Society: A History: From the Telegraph to the Internet,* Routledge, London.

Woolgar, S. (1988) *Science the Very Idea.* Tavistock, London.

Woolgar, S. (1991) The turn to technology in social studies of science. *Science, Technology and Human Values,* Vol. 16, No. 1, 20–50.

INDEX

240

edit suites/workstations 49, 53, 54, 56, 56–57, 92
Electronic News Production System (ENPS) 51–52, 57, 60, 70–71, 86, 186
engineering staff: satellite truck 149–50, 150, 152, 157
English, Jim 4, 5
epistemology: and ethnography 35, 215; Latour's concerns 16–18, 69, 178; straitjacket confining media analyses 15, 208–9
ethnographic approach 14, 28–29, 181, 215–17; Couldry's ANT analysis 44; Latour and Woolgar 16; specificity 20, 203–4
evening news programme 195, 196–97

facilities assistants 56
faith producers 121, 123, 126–28, 130–31
Farnsworth, John 43–45
film camera coverage: example of Nottigham regional news item 7; Huffaker and colleagues vi
filming practices: impact of PDP on journalists 85, 98, 102–3; post-PDP reversion to more traditional methods 105–6; reconfiguration by PDP 79, 83
Flaubert, Gustave 8
Freeview television 118

gallery 49; staff liaising with SNG1 operator 150, 160, 162, 165, 185; transmission of outside broadcast 193–95
Gaza Strip 77
Green, Steve (Chief Constable of Nottinghamshire Police): setting up for interview with 155–56, 160–62
Griffy, Andy 117, 119, 120–21; on likely impact of local television project 120–21

Hall, Stuart 25–26
Hankal, Bob 4, 5
Hardt, H. 48–49
Hastings 120
headline sequences 54, 95
Head of Regional and Local Programmes (HRLP) 40; BBC East Midlands 42, 106, 107, 109; BBC West Midlands 117, 132
Hemmingway, Emma 11; as observer and actor in news production process 188, 203
Hereford and Worcester 115, 121
Her Majesty's Inspectorate of Constabularies (HMIC) 155

Holdsworth, David 117
Huffaker, Bob: vi–vii; account of coverage of JFK assassination 2–6, 142; on live broadcasts today 143, 168
Hughes, T.P. 19
Hull: local television experiment 117, 118
human actors: ANT's under-representation of 177; differences with nonhuman actors 173, 180, 184, 203; differences with other human actors 203; in local television project 123, 131, 138–39; motivation and intentions 177, 180, 182–85, 204, 213–15; in news production process of one day 185–90, 202; self-awareness and 'nouse' 195–97, 203; specificity of positions and perceptions 203–4, 215; in television news network 29, 34–35, 58, 105, 137; translation process of PDP trainees 85–86
human agency: in daily newsroom practice 188; media studies' failure to recognise 36, 213; tension with technological agency 55, 95, 177–78
human/nonhuman actor associations: ANT 16, 18, 31–32, 176, 209, 211, 2158; in news production process 119, 132, 175, 176, 206–7, 215; technological assemblage of live broadcast 170, 171, 172, 176

independent films: community journalism 119
inner city areas: local television project 126–27, 139
inscription devices 89–90, 185–86, 187, 208, 209
intermediaries: Latour on difference with mediators 74–75; translation 138
internet poker: ANT analysis 43–45
internet service see BBC Where I Live sites
ITV (Independent Television): launch of local television 120–21; see also Central News East

journalists: contribution to production of news 175; disagreements over for local news project 122; divide with SNG engineering staff 152, 191–92; impact of PDP on 85, 97–98, 104, 105; nouse shared by 198; reflexivity 36; in regional newsroom 40, 41; restructuring with new technologies 86–87; training local people in digital technology 119; see also video journalists

Kegworth, Leicestershire: outside broadcast 168–71

136; PDP translation 106; translations in
local television project 125–26
specialist television correspondents 40
specificity: ideas of Kuhn and Latour 18–19,
28; importance to author's research 19,
28, 203–4, 207, 211–13, 215
sports reporter (Rob) 188–89, 190, 201,
202
Staffordshire 115, 121
stories: discussion on lead in evening news
progrmme 196–97; editorial choice for
live broadcast 191; effect of PDP practice
on finding 83, 85, 96; Nottingham HRLP's
new focus on 109–10; 'nouse' in
recognising 196–97; regional television
147; Rosenblum's ethos for PDP work
106–7, 109, 111
subjectivity: ANT's refusal to recognise
31–32, 176–77, 178–79; use of ANT to
chart 180, 204

teamwork: as basis for staff restructuring
for PDP 88, 89; overarching belief in
111; PDP's signaling of eradication of
83–84, 88
technical resources 40
technical staff: liaising with SNG1 operator
150, 162, 185; satellite truck 149–50,
153, 157–58
technogrammatic axis 59, 60, 63, 66, 180,
181, 184; actors in live news events 146,
153, 157, 159–60, 162, 165, 171, 172;
actors in news production process of one
day 188–90, 191–93, 195; Birmingham
hub in local television project 134–35,
136; PDP translation 106; translations in
local television project 125–26
technological actors/machines: Actor
Network Theory 16; associations with
human actors x, 8–10, 12, 45, 116, 166,
175, 211; media hub 55; satellite truck
148, 153
technological agency: actor networks 138,
205; affecting news production processes
55, 95, 139, 155, 190; Williams's
arguments against 47–49
technological determinism: moving away
from ideas of 46, 72, 211; philosophy of
PDP production 79, 81, 82
technologies: assemblage in live broadcasts
164, 170; elimination of traditional
production practices 78–79; general

public's capabilities 125; glimpse of actual
process during live broadcast 167–68, 210;
ideas of Kuhn and Hughes 19; Latour's
ideas 49, 55, 65; news reporters'
relationship with 2, 3, 7, 8; regional
newsroom 45; socialisation 48–49, 66;
translation process 115, 116, 131;
Winston's study 46–47; see also digital
technologies
Television Centre, London 42, 59
time: different notions and demands in media
hub 80, 94, 95–96; PDP operators' frame
102–3, 105; in Rosenblum's conception of
news production 80–81; see also
chronogrammatic axis
transmission profile 54
Turnbull, D. 212
Turner, J.M.W.: The Iron Foundry (painting)
73–74

Ursall, G. 79–80, 83

Van-Loon, J. 13, 48, 118, 205
video journalism 20, 71, 124; lack of finished
state 144; satellite bureaux 29
video journalists 40, 107; in BBC
experimental local project 112, 123,
133–34; since introduction of PDP 70
videotape: transferral of film coverage to 7
videotape editors: added role taken on by
SNG1 171; in Nottingham newsroom 40;
replaced by laptop editing stations for PDP
79; time taken to edit material 80
viewers: concerns with reconfiguration of
news agenda 104, 109; of live news
event 147, 153, 163, 165, 166; watching
destruction of World Trade Center
146–47

war coverage: Capa 1
Ward, Steven 17
Watson-Verran, H. 212
weather: traditional use for outside broadcasts
166–67
weather presenter 40, 164, 167
West, Jeff 6
West Midlands: BBC local television project
28, 70, 115, 117, 124
Williams, Raymond 47–48
Winston, Brian 46–47
Wise, Wes: account of coverage of JFK
assassination 2–6